To Audrey —
"A true kindred [spirit]

All my best — — —

Larry

# Performance-Oriented Management

## A PRACTICAL GUIDE FOR GOVERNMENT AGENCIES

# Performance-Oriented Management

## A PRACTICAL GUIDE FOR GOVERNMENT AGENCIES

Larry M. Pederson

░
**MANAGEMENT**CONCEPTS
Vienna, Virginia

### ⫘ MANAGEMENTCONCEPTS

8230 Leesburg Pike, Suite 800
Vienna, Virginia 22182
Phone: (703) 790-9595
Fax: (703) 790-1371
Web: www.managementconcepts.com

Printed in the United States of America

**Library of Congress Cataloging-in-Publication Data**

Pederson, Larry M., 1944–
    Performance-oriented management: a practical guide for government agencies/Larry M. Pederson.
      p. cm.
    Includes bibliographical references and index.
    ISBN 1-56726-132-9
    1. Administrative agencies—United States—Management. 2. Performance.
    I. Title.

JK 421 .P357 2002
352.3'0973—dc21

2002067828

# ABOUT THE AUTHOR

**Larry Pederson** has extensive experience helping organizations improve their performance. Early in his career, he established and directed the Army's first residential treatment center for drug- and alcohol-dependent Vietnam returnees. Subsequently, at Fort Eustis, Virginia, he directed the Alcohol and Drug Prevention and Control Program. He had oversight of the preventive, educational, and clinical aspects of alcohol and drug abuse for the community.

In 1990, Larry transferred to Fort Monroe, Virginia, and Headquarters, Training and Doctrine Command, where he had oversight of alcohol and drug programs throughout the command. It was during this time that Larry became involved with the Army's morale, welfare, and recreation programs, particularly in the area of program plans and analysis, and became interested in the Malcolm Baldrige criteria and organizational performance. He became an examiner for the Army Communities of Excellence and the President's Quality Award.

In 1996, Larry led a strategic planning cell for base operations support that led to the development of the organizational strategic performance plan. Using his knowledge of the Baldrige criteria, he developed organizational performance instruction for Army installations and facilitated numerous strategic planning offsites. Larry's work in the development of the installation management doctrine, performance standards, and associated metrics is all designed to assist organizations in reducing bureaucratic stovepiping and transitioning to a performance framework and orientation. Larry advocates the need for organizations to do more than simply strategic planning. He sees the opportunity to combine organizational strategy with continuous improvement to form a "performance orientation" spearheaded by the organizational map—the strategic plan.

He received a BA, MS, and EDS (Specialist Diploma) from the University of North Dakota in Grand Forks.

# TABLE OF CONTENTS

**List of Figures**

# PREFACE

The United States government, with its sprawling bureaucracy and numerous organizations, has never been viewed as a model of efficiency and effectiveness. Surveys (conducted by the government!) indicate that only 27 percent of the general population would look to the government to accomplish something effectively and with quality results. The bureaucracy can be stifling and even overwhelming at times.

The private sector, however, is not protected by this bureaucratic shield. It has had to get the customer in the game because of the need to make a profit and respond to the never-ending pressure to continuously improve the quality of goods and services—just to survive. This pressure has become even more intense in the past 10 to 12 years. The rapidly changing environment on a global level has led to changes never before thought possible, with technology leading the way in many cases.

This pressure hasn't presented itself in such a dramatic fashion in the government, so the sense of urgency hasn't always been felt. Therefore, the gap between the government and private business has gradually widened and become increasingly visible as the need to compete and perform in the private sector has escalated.

This situation gave rise to the Government Performance and Results Act (GPRA) of 1993 and the Vice President-led National Performance Review. GPRA requires that every government organization transition to a more performance-oriented method of management, with a primary focus on results. As part of that requirement, a strategic plan with an identified mission, vision, values, goals, and measurable objectives, and specifically outlined action plans are to be developed.

Under GPRA, the first assessment of the results of that performance plan was due to be reported in April 2000. Unfortunately, this did not occur government-wide. Without sufficient information and education on how this was to be accomplished, and without a framework for transition, a large majority of government agencies and activities waited until the last minute or did nothing. The year 2000 rolled around with only some organizations on board with a performance orientation that emphasized continuous improvement and quality results. The intent and approach of GPRA were never unilaterally deployed, and no follow-through took place.

Some government organizations, however, did begin to transition to a performance orientation on their own, using the tools available at the time and applying GPRA's guidelines. They used the Malcolm Baldrige National Quality Award criteria as the framework for change and performance assessment, benchmarked private industry to improve rapidly, and transitioned from a bureaucratic way of operating to a performance orientation. These government organizations, while in the minority, are rapidly moving forward as they recognize the need to improve continuously and to achieve results.

There is a tremendous need for the government as a whole to incorporate the performance and results mindset into its culture. That is the purpose of this book. The huge, vast, diverse organization of the federal government has not employed a common framework and subsequent guidelines for transition to a performance orientation. This book outlines an inclusive methodology for accomplishing that transition for any government organization immersed in bureaucracy and interested in change and improving its performance. It offers a general guideline for transitioning to a new way of doing business—a new way of operating and thinking—and embarking on a journey of continuous improvement.

## WHO MAKES THE CASE FOR CHANGE?

The bottom line is that the customer is demanding change. The customer in a government organization, or for that matter in any public service agency, is the taxpayer. Revenues realized from taxes enable the service to exist, and those who pay have a right to use that service. In the past, taxpayers were relatively satisfied with simply knowing where their tax dollars were going—how the money was being spent. That is no longer the case. The public has ready access to information and can make real-time comparisons among the various goods and services it is receiving. Today's taxpayers want to know how well those services are performing. Are those entrusted with the revenue providing the best service possible? In other words, how is your performance, and can you provide documentation?

This is about more than just accountability: It's about the taxpayer—the customer—having available choices based on real information. This contributes greatly to the competitive factor and gives the taxpayer an opportunity to have a voice in the management of that service. The customers will choose the service that most closely meets their requirements, thus creating a competitive situation and in effect issuing a challenge to be better.

Change is occurring at an ever-increasing pace throughout the government and the private sector. The boundaries that used to separate private business and government business are becoming less clear and less well-defined. The private sector traditionally has been in a more competitive environment, but as the private and public sector boundaries become less clear, the requirement to keep pace affects everyone. One thing is becoming increasingly obvious: Change is occurring more rapidly all the time, and the drivers of that change are not going away; instead, they are becoming more numerous and more intense.

Another obvious fact that is becoming more real all the time is that change is occurring in government. Leaders must address this change for success to occur. In November 2001, the President's budget chief, Mitch Daniels, Jr., addressed the National Press Club and quipped: "There are a number of people in Washington who appear to have attended the Debby Boone School of Public Policy, where the school song is 'It Can't Be Wrong If It Feels So Right.'" Daniels continued by noting that it's not enough for a program to feel right and have a nice title; if the performance isn't there, we ought to be looking for a better place to make an investment. Daniels said the budget will now take into account the evidence of whether a program can prove its effectiveness. Those programs that can offer proof of contributing value and being effective will be strengthened, and those that cannot will be drawn from.

It's crucial to note that Daniels did not say if a program *was* effective, but if it could *prove* its effectiveness. Proof is a key word and the theme of this book. Government organizations must transition from "feel good" programs and methods of operation to objective, performance-oriented management. Proof is a key ingredient for success and is driven by the customer—in this case, the taxpayer. Simply put, the government is being held accountable.

Success can be defined in many different ways and can fall anywhere along a continuum; accordingly, it's incumbent on leadership to come to grips with the reality that change is occurring and to decide what to do about it. At one end of the continuum is the reactive mode: Change is going to happen, so let's see what it involves, and we'll deal with it when it comes. In the past, under a traditional, bureaucratic system, that may have worked, but the world is far too competitive and globally linked today to sit around and wait for change to happen. What may happen is that change may be defined as elimination for those organizations.

A popular phrase that's been coined lately and used in quality jargon is "embracing change." While that may sound progressive and proactive, what does it really mean? The term connotes acceptance, but the whole concept lacks action. Embracing change may be as dangerous as reacting to it, because in reacting to change, one has a predefined position—the old way of doing things. Embracing change implies uprooting the old, steadfast ways of the organization and embracing whatever change brings. While leadership could identify opportunities that would emerge from that strategy, it could also be an invitation for chaos. Organizations operating in this scenario could easily fall prey to whatever is popular at the moment.

Leadership throughout the government must lead, and that includes leading change. To get ahead of the power curve and avoid the maelstrom, government leaders need to make change happen. In *Leading Change*, John P. Kotter repeatedly emphasizes the need for leadership to make change happen. That is where government leaders need to be on the continuum: making change happen.

For leaders to make change happen, there must be full recognition that change must occur throughout the organization and with everyone in the organization. Organizational behavior must be altered. Otherwise, it's only a change on paper, and the workforce will remain undeterred and unwilling to go through what will seem to them to be a lot of trouble and effort for no value. This is why the whole organization must be involved in the change process. It is leadership's responsibility to make that happen.

*Larry Pederson*
*June 2002*

# Chapter 1

# PLANNING TO PLAN

No one enjoys being a victim, whether it's circumstantial, being mishandled as a customer, or as part of an organization that must operate in reaction to a budget that's handed down on an annual basis. In these types of organizations, the budget drives the decision-making. Such is the case for the vast majority of government organizations. The budget is allocated, and the response is to take what's given in order to operate for the next year.

If performance and results are a concern, however, the plan and strategy should drive the budget. Performance should indeed be a concern because government is the ultimate service provider for the country's general population, i.e., the taxpayers. Planning should reach beyond the next year or two and cause the budgetary process to focus on the future as well. That is, resources (funds and staff) should be allocated to meet the standards and objectives laid out in the plan as opposed to depending on an operating budget that focuses on just the upcoming year.

Strategic planning for the future is about controlling destiny as much as possible as opposed to being a victim of scarce resources. Yet, the case with many government organizations is that we become content with the status quo and allow those in charge of the resources to do our planning for us. This situation will continue until the organization disappears or a major change occurs. Most of us, given the choice, would prefer change.

Making change happen, and doing so with optimum results, requires considerable thought and planning. Simply wishing for change or directing it to happen will result in failure. The organization's most important asset, its people, are the key to a successful transition. Positioning the organization for maximum involvement and participation of the workforce is the beginning of a transition process that will lead to a performance management system with an eye on the future.

## IT'S LEADERSHIP'S RESPONSIBILITY

Being stuck in a status quo organization begs the question, "What is the purpose of executive leadership?" Leadership that is content with the status quo certainly is not controlling the destiny of the organization and may be doing nothing more than deciding and prioritizing which projects should get funded given available resources. Organizations with this type of executive leadership are generally at a standstill. They fall far short of being dynamic and certainly are not focused on the future.

An ever-present danger in this reactive type of environment is a disgruntled, disillusioned, and even demotivated workforce. The organization becomes a team that's lost its will to win and is content with merely existing. This "status quo" mindset is not about a management method used to successfully design the future, but more about how to get through the year without any major disasters. Leadership's role in this type of scenario has been diminished so that what exists is a real contradiction of what leadership should be all about.

What leadership should be about is envisioning the future state of the organization and then mobilizing it to undertake the journey to that destination. It is leadership's responsibility to create that vision—a desired end state that will increase the organization's chance of moving into the future.

What has to occur? The mindset has to change at the top. Leadership must realize that change is necessary and imminent. This applies not only to government leaders of specific organizations, but also to government leaders across the spectrum. Ultimately, senior executive leadership must drive the change. It won't happen on its own.

The first step is for senior leadership to become mobilized. If they're content with the way things are, then it's likely that change will not occur. Being content with the status quo is a disaster waiting to happen. The most profound examples of this today are the CIA and the FBI. Most government organizations with that mindset these days are targets for elimination, or at least massive restructuring and reorganization. Those possibilities tend to cause considerable uneasiness, if not downright fear, throughout the workforce, opening the door for chaos. Assuming this is not desirable, what must senior leadership do to initiate change?

## WHERE TO BEGIN

The need to do business differently is becoming more of a reality in government agencies, and it affects everyone. For any government organization, the transition to a performance-based, results-oriented type of management system begins with those in charge acknowledging their current state, i.e., the status quo, and recognizing the need for change. Ever-changing resource environments and the fast-paced advances driven by technology are the two main drivers for change. Leadership must begin viewing this situation as a crisis and must sound the alarm. Once the acknowledgement is made and everyone at the top understands that change is necessary, the transition process can begin.

The first step for senior executive government leadership is to become educated on the entire subject of strategic planning and performance management. There is much more to this subject than meets the eye. Leadership's natural tendency is to feel like this is their organization, no one knows it better than they do, and they will run it as they see fit. However, a willingness to leave that paradigm and learn a "new way" from the beginning is essential if the transition process is to be successful.

This "new way" means looking at the organization from a systematic point of view. The organization must transition from one of "low" maturity to one of high-level system development (see Figure 1-1, System Maturity Characteristics). If you were running your own business, wouldn't you want a system that was mature and focuses on performance (see Figure 1-2, If You Were Running Your Own Business)? Or would you be satisfied with what's on the left side of the chart? If you wanted to stay in business, the choice is obvious.

While it is possible that senior leadership has the lion's share of knowledge about the organization, this knowledge

---

**Figure 1-1.** System Maturity Characteristics

| *LOW* | | *HIGH* |
|-------|---|--------|
| Scattered examples of good approaches | → | Systematic, appropriate, and effective aproaches |
| Reactive (fix it fast) | → | Improvement-oriented and prevention-based |
| Highly regulatory (rules-based) | → | Unnecessary rules eliminated (performance-based) |
| Major gaps in deployment | → | Deployed everywhere appropriate |
| Each approach in isolation | → | Approaches all work together |
| Random good results | → | Excellent results sustained in key mission areas |
| No benchmark comparisons | → | Comparisons with benchmarks and leaders |

**Figure 1-2**

# If You Were Running Your Own Business,
## Which Characteristics Would You Want?

| | |
|---|---|
| ☐ Destiny controls you | ☑ You control your destiny |
| ☐ Static organization | ☑ Learning organization |
| ☐ Leadership has no direction | ☑ Leadership sets direction, focus |
| ☐ Customer's needs are ignored | ☑ Customers needs are valued |
| ☐ Workforce is neglected | ☑ Workforce is developed |
| ☐ Management by gut-feel | ☑ Management by fact |
| ☐ Unimproved products/services | ☑ Continuous improvement |
| ☐ Results unimportant | ☑ Results focus |
| ☐ Unresponsive contractors | ☑ Responsive contractors |
| ☐ Waning opportunities | ☑ New opportunities |
| ☐ Financial degradation | ☑ Financial growth |

usually pertains to the current state. The goal, however, is to prepare the organization for a journey into the future. While the leadership may have some sort of idea about what they want the organization to become, the vision remains just that—someone's idea that's never attained. To move the organization into the future, leadership must have both the "how to" knowledge and a system in place to do so. Change and planning require work. Nothing will occur on its own.

## THE BALDRIGE CRITERIA AS A FRAMEWORK

Leadership must first decide on a set of valid, well-tested assessment criteria to use as a framework before developing a plan and deploying a system that will provide a vehicle for the journey. This is critical. This framework must also provide for the selection of the right metrics for measurement accuracy.

Every set of assessment criteria has its own terminology, and everyone in the organization needs to be speaking the same language. The most comprehensive criteria focused on performance excellence that have universal applicability are the Malcolm Baldrige National Quality Award criteria. These criteria encompass all aspects of an organization, from core values and concepts that an organization must be built on, to results—what every performance-based organization should be primarily interested in. The criteria may be applied to government and non-government organizations alike. They are truly universal and can be used by anyone interested in quality and performance. How these criteria can be specifically used for planning and performance will be thoroughly addressed in later chapters.

## SENDING THE MESSAGE

Once leadership makes the decision to move forward, develops an in-depth understanding of the criteria, and determines how strategic planning is a critical part of the overall system, they will have (intellectually, at least) the start on a performance management system and they can go about positioning the organization to facilitate change. How can this be accomplished most effectively? How can leadership send the message that they truly mean business and that this is not just another add-on initiative or program?

Senior executive leadership must first get the direct reports on board and get them to accept—and even be champions for—change. While this may sound like a simple matter, keep in mind that directors are senior people who have been in the establishment for a considerable length of time. Many are approaching the twilight of their careers. Changing from the status quo to high-level performance may be causing disruption to a "comfortable" situation. Just making an announcement in a director's meeting is not enough. Bringing the directors into the process should begin on a more personal level. This occurs by the senior executive bringing in each director for a personal one-on-one session.

There are several reasons for this strategy. The directors make things happen. Or the opposite can also be true: They can prevent change and be "toads in the road." They are in charge of the human resources that make the organization function. Their support is crucial. Having a one-on-one session personalizes the request for support as well as reinforces the confidence in each director that they're vital to the organization and are needed to conduct the transition process.

While there are bound to be differences of opinion, another big plus for getting the directors on board is getting each director's perspective. Their input will yield valuable ideas to aid the transition process. It's important to note that these sessions should not be designed to determine *whether* change is going to occur (that decision has already been made), but to inform them that transition is about to begin and their help is needed.

"Walking the talk" begins here. Leadership must do much more than just announce that changes are forthcoming. Action must accompany the words. Lip service will not work. The announcement and subsequent changes must occur simultaneously. And what are these changes?

As a signal that leadership means business, a separate department or group must be formed, and it must be fully resourced with dollars and full-time, qualified people. Many organizations that do not have performance as a major priority will either assign the whole strategic planning development process to existing elements of the organization as "other duties as assigned" or view the effort as too resource-intensive and contract out the whole endeavor.

The problem with the "other duties as assigned" scenario is that the mindset that results is "I'll get to it when I have time." The whole initiative is then viewed as another task or simply another program that's being added to an already full plate. Getting enough time never happens. Change never becomes the priority, and the effort is doomed to failure before it begins.

Contracting out the planning process is another approach that is commonly employed. Contracting out the effort may produce a fancy plan, but usually does not involve key people in the organization. This scenario results in lack of ownership by the workforce; the plan is viewed as the consultant's and not theirs. Contracting out the effort involves a considerable expenditure of funds, yet permanent change is less likely to occur. Consultants can be used at various intervals to facilitate offsites and other organizational initiatives, but putting them in charge of the entire organizational transition process may lead to disappointment and a failed effort.

Forming a core group of three or four people to spearhead the effort is usually the best way to begin. Of course, this depends on the size of the organization, but a planning cell of this size can have tremendous impact on organizations of up to 1,000 employees or even larger. The establishment of the planning cell should be well-publicized. The signal that change is on the way should be rendered dramatically and often.

Leadership should clearly announce their intentions as the cell is formed. Each member of the newly formed cell should be introduced in a public forum, such as a town hall meeting. In addition, each member of the core group should offer a brief description of what he or she is going to do, at least in the beginning. This is important because the core group will not be working in isolation, but rather will be involved throughout the organization. Full disclosure from the beginning will help with buy-in as the transition process unfolds.

## CREATING A LEARNING CULTURE

The entire organization will be going through change, much of it in uncharted waters. This will (and should) affect every person in the workforce. Since all are affected, it only makes sense that everyone be involved from the very beginning. This is a key ingredient in preparing a seed bed to grow ideas—an investment in human capital. The workforce must be prepared to absorb, understand, and respond to the changes that are about to occur.

A learning organization begins by eliminating barriers to learning, aligning individual learning strategies with organizational strategies, and ensuring that individual learning plans are integrated with the goals and objectives of the organization. (The process for developing a learning culture will be fully addressed in Chapter 8, Human Resources.) Deciding to develop a learning culture later in the transition process will be confusing, slow down the process, and run the risk of being counterproductive. The workforce must understand from the very beginning the need and subsequent desire to change and create a culture based on learning and knowledge.

A positive way to get the workforce involved and send a message that change is on the horizon is to offer Stephen Covey training for the entire workforce. The core group can initiate this effort. Covey teaches that the people in the organization are the most important raw material. This is personalized training that signals a change from a reactive way of operating to a proactive means of supporting creative thinking. This training can move everyone from feeling like a survivor to making positive, creative contributions and impacting the organization's future. Covey's *7 Habits of Highly Effective People* stresses fundamental change, innovation, aspiration, and playing to win; these are key ingredients in preparing for the journey to the vision of the future. Covey also stresses destroying walls and building bridges, which begins the process of engaging people, energizing learners, and allowing leaders to unleash ownership. Remember, this is everyone's journey.

The next item in the core group's charter is to begin educating the workforce on the new, proposed ways of doing business. Education is key. If the entire workforce has little or no understanding of what's expected, the whole transition process is doomed to failure. The workforce is the engine needed to make it happen. This must be everyone's plan, everyone's initiative, and while leadership is responsible for getting the ball rolling, the entire workforce must be involved if change is to be successful.

What sorts of things need to be taught? First of all, planning should not be a secret. It should not be done behind closed doors by just a few. Everyone's involvement, at varying levels, is crucial. Getting everyone to understand not only the process, but where and how they play a role in the process, will yield big benefits at every step. The whole process should be explained through a series of briefings and town meetings, and supported through the organization's e-mail system. The goal is not to make everyone an expert, but to eliminate the mystery surrounding what is about to take place.

The question "Why are we doing this?" must be answered from the very beginning. The follow-on question "What's in it for me?" must also be addressed. And, of course, what everyone wants to know: "How will this change my life?" These questions do not need to be answered in excruciating detail at this time, because many of the concerns will be addressed as the process unfolds, but everyone's curiosity must receive primary consideration and these basic questions must be addressed.

Fundamentally, the reason most organizations begin the transition to performance management, is, at a minimum, to survive, and optimally, to become a world-class organization focused on providing quality products and services. Every employee should understand that what's in it for them first and foremost is increased job security. If the status quo is allowed to continue, the organization becomes a target for the restructuring artists and puts resource management in control.

A less direct but positive fringe benefit arises from being part of an organization that's making a difference and is on a continuous journey of improvement. Job satisfaction should increase immensely. The change will affect work lives dramatically. There will be far less concern about who's supervising whom and who's looking over whose shoulder. The workforce will transition to working in teams, which will be involved with managing or working in processes with an eye toward continuously improving not only the process but the entire organization. Everyone will have a clear picture of how they're contributing to the organization's mission and journey to the vision.

The education of the workforce should also include proposed timelines of events for at least the upcoming year, what their involvement will be, and what will be expected of them every step of the way. Not only does this reduce fear of the unknown, but it will help foster ideas that may improve what is already planned. It's also important that the workforce understand what leadership is doing during this process. Remember, no secrets, and no mysteries.

# Chapter 2

# ASSESS YOURSELF

Organizations that are in a performance-oriented system can be viewed as being on a journey, with a starting point and a destination. The opposite scenario is a status quo organization. The problem with the status quo is that the environment, especially as it pertains to resources, has often dictated the course of that journey. The "environment" is usually characterized by a lack of resources, a highly bureaucratic and regulated system, a focus on tasks and reactionary management, a high degree of supervision, a lack of teamwork, and a lack of emphasis on process. Unfortunately, this describes the majority of government organizations.

Organizations are composed of many parts, and traditionally in a status quo environment, performance is viewed as only the sum of those parts. This places the organization at the mercy of whatever the environment dictates. Leadership is not in control of that journey to the extent they should be, and the parts are impacted in various ways and to varying degrees. The result is that leadership becomes immersed in the operational aspect of the organization, with little attention directed toward the strategic aspect. Once these realities are recognized and accepted, the next step is to determine the journey's starting point.

If leadership has adequately prepared for the transition to performance management, they will recognize the need for a starting point, or a baseline. How that baseline is determined is crucial in terms of how the journey is to take place. Leadership will have also recognized that the organization should be viewed as a total performance system, not simply a conglomeration of parts stuck together. The key to performance in the future is how well the system works as a unit to provide results. This requires interaction among various components of an organization; the better the synchronization, the better the performance.

The lens through which an organization is best viewed as a performance system—and the one that government organizations should use for assessment and as a framework for change—is the Malcolm Baldrige National Quality Award criteria (see Figure 2-1, A Performance Management System). These criteria emphasize a total system approach and deployment; moreover, they provide a universal language for

**Figure 2-1.** A Performance Management System

government organizations as well as the private sector. Leadership should have familiarized themselves with these criteria so that they start viewing their organization with a systematic mindset, and thus are equipped to lead the transition effort.

## CRITERIA FOR ASSESSMENT

The private sector and for-profit companies were the first to use the Malcolm Baldrige National Quality Award criteria to assess their performance. However, application of the criteria is not limited to the type of organization. The Baldrige National Quality Award was created by Public Law 100-107 in 1987 as a means for U.S. companies to be competitive in international markets, especially in the areas of technology and the automotive industry. This law led to the creation of a new public-private partnership.

The award is named for Malcolm Baldrige, who served as Secretary of Commerce from 1981 until his death in 1987. The Baldrige National Quality Program is managed by the National Institute of Standards and Technology (NIST), a non-regulatory federal agency within the Commerce Department's Technology Administration. NIST's primary mission is to strengthen the U.S. economy and improve the quality of life by working with industry to develop and apply technology, measurements, and standards.

Other government organizations have developed their own approaches to applying the Baldrige criteria. The Department of Defense has launched numerous quality initiatives with assessment and performance as the mainstay. In 1989 the Air Force began transitioning to quality and performance management, and in 1995 the Army began using the Baldrige criteria, calling it the Army Performance Improvement Criteria (APIC), for the Army Communities of Excellence (ACOE) competition.

While major organizations have established performance and quality awards using the criteria and anyone may apply for competition, the vast majority of companies and organizations do not apply for an award. They simply use the criteria as a framework and tool to improve their performance. Using the criteria in this manner introduces the organization to performance management as a total system and launches a quality journey that pays big dividends. The decision to compete for an award can always be made later, when the performance system is working well and producing results.

The Baldrige criteria are adjusted and improved every year to meet the changing environment in both the public and private sectors. The environment is strongly influenced by advances in technology and socioeconomic and political considerations. Also, and perhaps more importantly, innovation, improved processes, and different perspectives are addressed and incorporated into the criteria.

## CORE VALUES AND CONCEPTS

Most important, however, are the core values and concepts on which the Baldrige criteria are built. These values and concepts lay the foundation, ensuring that the criteria fulfill their purpose of delivering ever-increasing value to their customers and improvement of overall organizational effectiveness and capability. It's crucial for organizations to incorporate these core values and concepts into their everyday business operations and make them a part of the organizational culture. They're very difficult to take issue with and surely describe in an optimal manner what an organization should be striving for.

The organizational assessment should begin with an understanding of these core values and concepts, if a true and thorough performance management system is to be developed. It would be highly valuable and interesting, for example, while listing the basic philosophy and tenets of the Baldrige criteria, if we also linked the antithesis to these core values as a means to begin looking at an organization from the perspective of quality and value. Where would your organization likely fall along the continuum of each core value?

## No Direction vs. Visionary Leadership

Senior leadership must set the direction for the organization. That direction, or road map, should describe a final destination or vision that the entire organization can identify with and rally behind. The vision should carry with it strategies that guide the activities of the organization. A further guide for the workforce points to clear and visible values that provide "road signs" that inform everyone about the behaviors and expectations on the performance journey.

It's not enough, however, to simply map the course and set expectations. Senior leaders should inspire and motivate the entire workforce, plus serve as role models by reinforcing values and fostering initiative throughout the organization.

## Customers Not a Priority vs. Customers' Needs Have High Value

Customers drive the quality of the products and services provided by the organization. This goes far beyond merely responding to complaints or addressing only what's wrong. The organization must identify everything it does that contributes value to the customer and leads to satisfaction and loyalty. This also involves anticipating future customer desires and needs.

Valuing customer needs must be a part of organizational strategy. It demands developing and retaining a loyal relationship with customers as well as being sensitive to their changing needs. This requires organizational responsiveness and flexibility. Government organizations have customers—make no mistake about it. Getting the government culture to see and accept that becomes an issue very quickly. That's why it is crucial to begin the transition process by looking through the lens of universal criteria such as the Baldrige criteria for a systematic view.

## Static Organization vs. Learning Organization

Visionary leaders understand that to achieve the vision of the organization, an environment must be created that is conducive to continuous improvement and adaptive to change. Learning must be part of the organizational culture—that is, be a regular part of daily work, be practiced at all levels, be shared, and result in root cause problem-solving. The benefits are many, but the most immediate payoffs are more satisfied employees, organizational and cross-functional learning, an environment for increased innovation, and—the bottom line—improved performance leading to better results. These ingredients for a learning organization should continue to be fostered and infused into the daily operation. A learning organization is crucial in the development and establishment of a culture that is performance-oriented.

## Human Resource As an Expense vs. Valuing Employees

Committed, visionary leadership values and appreciates the importance of a satisfied employee. They realize that the human factor is what makes the organization function and will determine the level of performance that the organization will eventually achieve. A performance-oriented organization recognizes an ever-increasing need for more flexibility and work practices that are tailored to employees with diverse needs both in the workplace and in their personal lives. This recognition directly influences the type of culture that will develop.

Organizations must consider all aspects of the workforce requirements, and leadership must demonstrate their commitment. This includes instituting innovative incentive and awards programs and creating an environment that encourages risk-taking. This philosophy extends to organizational partners such as unions for labor and management and suppliers, contractors, educational organizations, and other government agencies.

### Highly Structured vs. Agile

Technology has given the customer numerous options and will continue to do so in the future. This environment demands that the organization be able to change rapidly and be flexible to meet customer requirements. An agile organization must have a trained and ready workforce prepared to meet customer needs. Process time may be lessened considerably and quality enhanced by competitors. As knowledge grows, so do quality and productivity, as long as the knowledge is applied.

In today's world, customers realize that they can go elsewhere at a moment's notice. Highly structured, bureaucratic organizations with a lot of central control simply cannot and will not be able to respond accordingly. These types of organizations have too many layers requiring approval and will thus miss the opportunity to respond to customer needs.

### React to Taskings vs. Focus on the Future

The strategic planning development process should anticipate future developments and the effects that these developments will have on the organization. For example, considerations should include technological developments, customer expectations, new partnering opportunities, and evolving regulatory requirements. This future orientation requires training and developing employees and suppliers, seeking opportunities for innovation, and providing ever-increasing value to the customer. All goal-setting and strategies to achieve those goals should be developed with a focus on the future. Compare this to simply reacting to tasks being administered on a regular basis in a highly bureaucratic environment.

### Top-Driven vs. Managing for Innovation

Everyone in the organization is capable of coming up with good ideas to enhance performance. In fact, in high-performance organizations, most good ideas come from all levels of staff. However, the majority of government organizations are top-driven and are not structured in a manner conducive to the generation and communication of good ideas. Organizations should be structured in a way that encourages the workforce—and provides incentives—to promote positive change. The work culture should be a learning environment instead of routine responses to top-driven taskings, which eventually results in a robotized workforce.

### Management by Gut Feel vs. Management by Fact

Organizational performance must be measured if improvement is going to occur. Granted, it's much easier to make decisions based on "what feels right," what's popular, or what's politically correct, but those types of decisions are usually not tied to any of the organization's strategic goals and objectives. Further, attention must be paid to measurement of the right things.

Balancing what's vital to the organization and measuring performance in those critical areas are the starting points of continuous improvement. This approach also helps align organizational activities with organizational goals. Once quantifiable results are attained, analysis can then take place to improve processes and thus improve performance. Without facts, there is no basis for analysis, and the opportunities for improvement are minimized.

### Operate Independently vs. Public Responsibility and Citizenship

Every organization, whether in the government or private sector, is part of a surrounding community and subsequently has a responsibility to the public and a charter to be a good citizen. In fact, government organizations supported by the taxpayer may well (and should) have a higher level of responsibility to the public. Strategic planning should anticipate and prevent adverse impacts to the community from organizational operations. The planning process should seek to prevent problems and abate public concerns when and where appropriate. Leadership must support the practice of good citizenship throughout the organization by improving education, health care, conservation of natural resources, etc. The organization could also take the lead in influencing other organizations to partner for these purposes.

### Results Not Important vs. Results Focus

Results should be the main purpose the organization exists and should define accomplishment of the mission. The organization's strategic planning efforts should design the performance expectations and measurement system while focusing on key results, i.e., those that are directly related to mission. Results should demonstrate how the organization is creating value for all the key customers and stakeholders. By using a composite of indicators that fully represents what the organization does, a basis can be formed for improving results, thus driving improved performance. If results don't really matter, the mission has no meaning and the accomplishment of goals isn't important.

### Functional Alignment vs. Systems Perspective

Most government organizations are functionally aligned or "stovepiped" as opposed to operating as a total system. A systems perspective is critical if government organizations are ever going to make transition happen. A systems perspective means understanding and managing the whole organization to achieve performance improvement.

The "system" is composed of the organization's core values and concepts along with the approach, deployment, and results outlined in the seven Baldrige categories. Performance can and should be defined as how well these components work together to produce results. This is in contrast to traditional organizations, which are functionally aligned and where performance is viewed as adding up the sum of these individual functions or stovepipes. There is a vast difference in how these organizations operate.

An analogy can be made to an automobile, where all parts of the automobile are specifically designed for the performance of that particular unit. Traditional, functional thinking would lead one to assemble the best parts available with no idea whether they work together and call that performance. Such a scenario involves no planning, no designing, and no monitoring for performance, i.e., no system.

Developing a system where all the parts are in synchronization provides the basis for performance and continuous improvement. There are huge implications for measurement within a system perspective. Under functional alignment, the organization cannot go beyond determining status, but must be content with "counting" vs. "measuring." Counting only reflects the current score; it does not adequately describe the game, not to mention the strategy for the game or, for that matter, the strategy for the current season and the years to come.

Based on the foundation of these core values and concepts, and holding up your organization in comparison, what sort of picture is emerging? Where on the continuum does your organization fall? If you can say you are mostly on the ledger's right side, then you have a great start on a performance management system and a quality journey. On the other hand, if your organization falls mainly on the left side of the ledger, the need to begin the journey to strive for excellence should start to become obvious. What lies ahead is determining a starting point so the journey can begin.

## THE SENIOR LEADER'S PERFORMANCE SURVEY

While familiarization with the Baldrige criteria is a must, it may be somewhat overwhelming to expect an organization's directors and managers to employ the criteria in their entirety during the first assessment. Therefore, there may be some advantages to using a condensed version of the criteria to begin the assessment process. The criteria can be foreign to conventional thought and cause leadership to throw up their hands in frustration before ever getting started. By using a condensed version, i.e., a leader's survey, these problems can be avoided.

A leader's survey offers many advantages. First of all, the main purpose and focus of each category can be highlighted. This will give the members of the organization time to reflect on the full meaning of what the criteria require, and also provide an opportunity to apply the main purpose of the category to the organization. Moreover, a leader's survey keeps a focus on "the big picture" and helps the top level of the agency stay out of the details. While the details are certainly important, they should be part of and focused on re-

finement of a quality system already in place. Being attentive to the main purpose of each item of the criteria is more
about the establishment of a quality system. Becoming immersed in too much detail in the beginning can be confusing and discouraging, as the effort may seem too difficult.

As the criteria change somewhat each year, the condensed
version should undergo adjustment accordingly. This is not
a major effort, but care must be exercised to retain the accuracy of each category and item in the leader's performance
survey. A sample leader's performance review is provided as
Appendix A.

### Administration and Scoring

Some planning has to go into administering the first performance review. Certainly the size of the organization is a
factor. If the workforce consists of several thousand people,
administering the assessment to everyone will not be practi-
cal. In very large organizations, the effort may be limited to
the executive level and a representative cross-section of the
rest of the workforce. In smaller organizations, say 100 to
200 people, the directors, division chiefs, and managers can
get involved, along with much of the workforce. The main
purpose is to obtain adequate and representative feedback
from a cross-section of the organization. The better the representation, the more accurate a picture will emerge of the
organization's baseline.

It's important to be clear from the beginning about the
purpose of the assessment and its use to begin the transition
to a performance management system. This will help everyone view the effort as a performance initiative. Also, the process should not be allowed to drag on. A firm date for
completion should be established from the beginning.

While allowances must be made for special circumstances, such as vacations, allowing the assessment process to go beyond ten days may cause the initiative to lose momentum.

Individuals may score their own assessments by simply following the instructions. As each assessment is scored, they should be gathered by work group or division so that the assessment results may be combined and a picture of each organizational segment, and, subsequently, the whole organization begins to unfold.

## Using the Results Well

It is crucial that the assessment results be used to optimize the opportunity to transition to a performance and continuous improvement system. Using the assessment simply to determine "where you are" with no plan to move forward from that point is a waste of time and resources. Understanding the criteria and their hierarchical nature can help focus on the basic and essential areas first. Identifying and fixing a major foundation problem can serve to correct many down-line areas for improvement.

The next step is to conduct a reality check to determine if the assessment results really reflect what is occurring in the organization. Does the assessment score seem about right with what's really happening? Conducting a reality check will help avoid expending real resources on fictional problems. Following a reality check, conduct a gap analysis to help understand where the organization differs from similar organizations, especially those that are the best at what they do. This reality check can also be used in comparison to established organizational standards, if they exist. The assessment will help define the gap between where the organization currently is and where it aspires to be. This will provide direction on where to focus the most effort.

The assessment results should be incorporated into the planning cycle for continuous improvement and learning. Potential projects should be identified by specific area so that the organization can group, balance, and sequence the improvement effort. This also helps preserve the integrity of what the organization is doing well while targeting weaknesses.

Care must be taken to prioritize improvement projects as part of the strategic planning process. High-level, broad-based projects should be identified and focused on first, and details should be avoided. A high-leverage improvement project may serve to eliminate numerous smaller tasks that have been consuming valuable time. The number of high-leverage projects should be kept manageable, however. While everyone may be eager to "fix" things quickly, the organization runs the risk of being overwhelmed both from the standpoint of too much work and not enough resources to complete every project identified. Selecting a vital few projects is the best way to go. The final step in this process is to resource the projects with dollars and people and to ensure integration into the organization's overall direction and strategy. (See Figure 2-2, How to Use Assessment Results Well).

One of the most recent and perhaps best examples (certainly having major impact) is the Secretary of the Army's 2001 decision to undergo a major restructuring that is resulting in a huge corporate realignment. A wealth of information concluded that the way the Army was organized was somewhat ineffective and certainly inefficient. The assessment information showed that the Army was involved in numerous activities that were getting in the way of the mission and that mission personnel were too involved in base operations, which are largely business-oriented. Secretary White decided to have the Army focus on its core mission—war fighter—and make major decisions on how to structure the Army from that basis or starting point.

**Figure 2-2.** How to Use Assessment Results Well

**❶ Understand the structure of the criteria and scoring system**

–Knowing the hierarchical nature of the criteria can help focus efforts on the most fundamental and essential areas first.

–Fixing a foundation problem can often serve to improve a variety of down-line areas for improvement.

**❷ Do a "reality check"**

–Does the assessment score reflect what is really happening in your business?

–Helps avoid the risk of expending resources on fictional problems.

**❸ Conduct a gap analysis:**

Understanding where you differ most from "the best" can help you decide where to focus the most improvement effort.

**❹ Identify potential projects by area**

–Organizing by area helps group, balance, and sequence improvement effort.

–Also helps preserve integrity of strengths while improving weaknesses.

**❺ Prioritize and select 5–10 high-leverage improvement projects**

–How does all this fit with your overall direction and strategy?

–How much can you really afford to expend on improvement efforts?

---

The result was a major restructuring of the Army as a whole. Secretary White decided to regionalize Army installations and remove them from the direct chain of command of the war fighter altogether. This decision essentially returned the war fighter to the core mission and got the war fighter out of the business operations of running an installation. Secretary White's philosophy has as its premise that the war fighter knows little about base operations and that he or she should stick to what's familiar—direct mission performance. This is certainly an attempt at becoming more efficient. Further, the resources stay in their designated areas; mission can no longer use base operation resources when they've exhausted theirs. Meanwhile, the base operations can focus totally on implementing best business practices without the direct influence of Command. Missions differ, but base operations are quite generic, so the opportunity for standardization and performance improvement on a corporate scale is great.

This bold, innovative move established a structure that can now adopt more of a performance orientation. Previously, bureaucracy was in charge, and performance was stifled. This bold decision was the result of visionary leadership implementing a high-leverage initiative that focuses on the future and allows for innovative management. Certainly the details have yet to be worked out, but the restructuring and realigning of the corporate Army is a first step—one that had to occur so that base operations could have more opportunity for continuous improvement.

A much broader, larger restructuring occurred when President Bush recommended that the Department of Homeland Security incorporate numerous related agencies. This was viewed by some as the creation of additional bureaucracy, but closer inspection reveals an alignment of agencies with like missions in an attempt to address a new and much more critical issue: defense and protection of our homeland. This is an example of using current environmental assessments to restructure for effectiveness on a grand scale.

# Chapter 3

# PREPARE FOR AN INITIAL OFFSITE

Once the initial assessment is completed and the results are identified, a facilitator should be selected to work with senior leadership to ensure readiness to begin the planning process. The facilitator should be trained in the Baldrige criteria, have experience facilitating similar types of meetings, and have at least a basic understanding of the organization. This is a major endeavor, and it will initiate the organizational transition. The initial offsite is where the planning process officially begins; thus, it represents a major change in direction for the entire organization; things will never be the same.

It is now time to formalize everyone's commitment, especially leadership's, so that trust, teamwork, and commitment can be established. Without a high level of trust, teamwork, and commitment, the planning process is likely to fail. Senior leadership and directors need to consider some key questions:

- Are we ready to begin the strategic planning process?

- Are we willing to commit the time and resources necessary for effective, productive strategic planning?

- Is the organization ready to commit to strategic planning for performance as a way of doing business?

- Are we ready to commit to transitioning the organization?

- Who are the organization's principal stakeholders, and should they be involved?

The facilitator and leadership must now clarify roles, establish an infrastructure for planning (including guidelines and timing for strategic planning), develop an approach to integrating strategic planning with other resource-intensive activities, and initiate activities to familiarize participants with the approach. This activity provides a basic foundation for going forward and embarking on the preparation process, which involves:

- Assessment of readiness

- Agreement on what approach to strategic planning will be used

- Agreement on resources to be used

- Senior executive agreement to prioritization, funding, and sequencing of strategic initiatives before committing them to general publication

- Program for increasing the organization's capabilities for strategic planning.

Directors and senior leaders should involve subordinate-level leaders from the beginning and during the different steps of the strategic planning process to promote ownership, obtain timely feedback, improve the effectiveness and accuracy of strategic planning products, and integrate strategic planning with other planning and financial management.

## THE OFFSITE LOGISTICS

Once the groundwork is established and senior leadership is fully committed, it is time to start putting into practice the results of the initial assessment and begin the transition to a performance management system. The most effective method for beginning the transition and getting started is to conduct an offsite. Offsites just don't happen. There are many factors to consider to increase the chances of success.

The first offsite should be scheduled for three days and announced at least two months in advance. Attendance should be mandatory, and the guidelines should be clearly spelled out.

Leadership must be fully committed and drive the process. This is not the type of initiative that can simply be tasked out to a committee and everyone's full cooperation be expected. Senior leadership must monitor the plans for the offsite every step of the way and lead the effort. The administrative details can be assigned to a task force, but everyone in the organization must know that leadership is squarely behind the entire process.

In planning an offsite, it's helpful to have a checklist of items and activities so nothing will be overlooked. It is essential to choose a site that's a good distance from the office and somewhat isolated. Participants should be free from distraction and away from daily office business (including a ban on the use of cell phones). Interruptions should be allowed for emergencies only. The facilities should be comfortable and easily accessible but private enough so that distractions are held to a minimum. Lodging and food should be on the premises or at least close enough to be convenient for everyone. The meeting room should be spacious enough to accommodate all participants comfortably and allow for room to stand up and move around if desired. Placing the meeting table in a U shape with a presentation area at one end so everyone can face one another adds to group dynamics and allows everyone to view presentations easily. Break-out rooms should be available, as there will be a need to form subgroups to work on specific tasks. Make writing materials and easels readily available, as this is a working session.

Attendance should be limited to no more than 30 people and should include senior-level leadership and all directors, if possible. At minimum, the major decision-makers for the organization should be in attendance. This is all about determining the organization's future and the transition to a new way of doing business. Those in attendance should be ready to plan, should have a level of commitment to follow through with the process, and should be willing to devote the time required.

It's preferable to hire a professional facilitator for an offsite. It is important for the person guiding the process to be as objective as possible. There may be skilled facilitators in the organization, but it's impossible to eliminate all bias if they've been working for the organization. Another factor is the perception that senior leaders may have of someone within the organization. If the facilitator is outranked by some or all of the attendees, it becomes difficult to determine what should be prioritized for discussion as well as to achieve consensus. The process becomes compromised.

An outside facilitator reduces the possibility of these obstacles emerging. Plus, an outside facilitator has less investment in the organization and the personalities involved. An outside facilitator will contract for services with a specific outcome and performance level defined.

To optimize success, the facilitator should gather as much preliminary information as possible and conduct at least one organizational visit well in advance of the offsite. This fact-finding visit allows the facilitator to have a face-to-face inter-action with the organization's leadership with the goal of determining in some detail their expectations for the offsite and the organization's future. The pre-offsite visit should also include interviews with a representative sample (all, if possible) of the directors to gain as thorough an organiza-tional perspective as possible. Information should also be gathered about the organization's level of knowledge con-cerning customers, performance, planning, current state, and vision of the future. This will give the facilitator an indi-cation of where and how to begin the offsite and set the agenda. More importantly, it will give the facilitator valu-able information for developing the offsite materials so that the participants will have a hands-on guide explaining the process to be followed, what is expected from them, and the desired outcome.

The successful facilitator will put together an offsite pack-age that not only focuses the attendees but educates them as well. Participants who are relatively at the same level of knowledge will be able to work together more readily and achieve better results. Assessment results addressed in Chap-ter 2 should be high on the agenda.

## THE RIGHT STUFF

Attention to logistical detail and doing the right thing are important. Actually, the planning team should view offsite attendees as customers with requirements waiting to be sat-isfied. The experience should be planned to exceed their expectations.

The offsite is not about a group of people running off somewhere to discuss what's going on in their organization. While this is certainly going to happen at some level, the offsite should be viewed as the first major event in an evolv-ing process. As far as the organization is concerned, this is a big deal. The accommodations must be comfortable, meals must be well-planned and thought-out, and special dietary requirements considered. Breaks should be appropriately spaced and located in a way that optimizes conversation and mingling. The surrounding environment should be conducive to some outside activities, weather permitting, such as walking or some leisure recreational activity. The supporting staff should have each hour planned and accounted for and know specifically what is needed for each segment of the day.

The right stuff goes far beyond the amenities. Audiovisual and technological support should be checked out in advance so that everything is operational. Designate recorders to take detailed notes for the development of a complete report. The planning tem should be drafting the plan as the offsite progresses. This event should yield a tangible product.

## THE AGENDA

The first offsite should be dynamic, but remember that this may be a first-time experience for many. Design the agenda to allow plenty of time for discussion. The learning curve may be steep for some. The offsite is gathering individuals from numerous disciplines, most of them used to working within their own activities. They must now start working together toward the same goal. Barriers must be removed, paradigms broken, and differing perspectives taken into account.

The emphasis is now on teamwork. Planned social gatherings during the offsite will be helpful in fostering that teamwork. An evening at the end of the offsite where spouses can participate, such as a dinner, can assist in enhancing communication and promoting teamwork. Every effort should be made to ensure that this is a positive experience. The more pain and struggle that are associated with the transition to a performance management organization, the more resistance will be encountered.

The agenda can help smooth the way and be a tool to help remove barriers. The read-ahead package should contain a copy of the agenda. It should give a general outline of what to expect during the offsite and desired outcomes. Care must be taken that the agenda is thoroughly integrated with the strategic planning process model.

## FORMULATING A PROCESS MODEL

The strategic planning process can result in chaos if it is not clearly outlined and described. Using a process model that graphically depicts each step of the process can be of tremendous assistance. (See Figure 3-1, Strategic Planning Process Model.) The model can be distributed to all the prospective attendees a week or two ahead of time, along with the agenda. Mapping the process for everyone can provide focus and keep everyone engaged. This should be part of the read-ahead so that everyone has some idea what to expect.

**Figure 3-1.** Strategic Planning Process Model

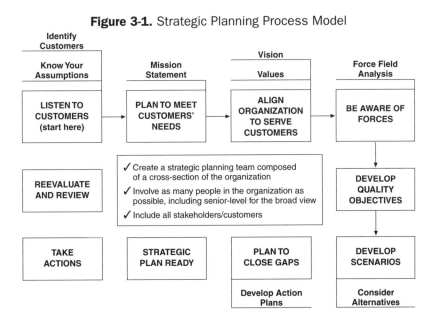

The model can and should be outlined to meet the requirements of the Government Performance and Results Act (GPRA). GPRA establishes the requirement for federal agencies to develop strategic plans, action plans, and performance measures. Specifically, the strategic plan must contain:

- A comprehensive proposed mission statement covering the agency's major functions and operations

- General goals and objectives, including those related to outcome, for the agency's major functions and operations

- A description of how the goals and objectives are to be achieved, including a description of the operational processes, skills, and technology, and the human, capital, information, and other resources required to meet the goal and objectives

- A description of how the performance goals delineated in the performance plan are related to and consistent with the general goals and objectives delineated in the strategic plan

- An identification of the key factors external to the agency and beyond its control that could significantly affect achievement of the general goals and objectives

- A description of the program evaluation or assessment used in establishing or revising general goals and objectives, with a schedule for future program evaluations.

Once everyone has an idea of the structure of the planning process, and what's required as a starting point, then the actual offsite event can begin with everyone sharing the same mindset. Of utmost importance is that everyone understand that the plan must be measurable if it is to have value. Remember, this is not about simply recording a score, but about planning the future and measuring progress toward its success.

## OFFSITE CHECKLIST

### *Facility*
- Ensure that the facility is away from the office but not so far that it would be a major disruption.

- Provide billeting accommodations at the same facility as the offsite.

- Make reservations well in advance so there will be sufficient time to work details/special considerations.

- Ensure that the facility has a large room for general meetings and break-out rooms for work groups.

- Ensure that facility staff completely understand the requirements.

- Configure tables in a U-shape so attendees can be visible to one another and the facilitator can move around.

- Place projection screen at the end of the U so that it's visible to everyone.

- Provide for plenty of walk-around space behind the tables.

### *Facility/Meals*
- Plan for three meals per day and vary the menu.

- Allow for working lunches if desired.

- Plan for morning and afternoon breaks.

- Determine any special dietary considerations for the attendees.

- Know the costs well in advance.

- Ensure that the dining area and the meeting area are separate but convenient.

- Schedule an icebreaker for the first night.

### Agenda
- Start developing the agenda as soon as a date is determined.

- Start and finish at the same time each day.

- Allow plenty of time for discussion.

- Schedule senior leader first, to outline direction and expectations.

- Specify dress code on the agenda.

- Send out agenda at least two weeks in advance.

### Invitation
- Send out initial invitation from senior leader.

- Ensure that secretaries get copy of specifics/logistics.

- Clearly spell out requirements for accommodations (e.g., reservation information, cutoff dates).

**Technology/AV/Administrative Support**
- Computer/projector (with back-up equipment)

- Large screen

- Extension cords

- Flags/flagstand (if applicable)

- Easels/markers/tape

- Scribe/notetaker

- Name tents

- Conference packets

    –Books with updated agenda and slides

    –Writing materials

    –Name tags

- Telephone access

- E-mail capabilities in rooms.

## WHAT'S GOING TO HAPPEN AT THE OFFSITE?

It's a good idea to repeat the process of developing a performance system several times and in various forums. One step must occur before another can be built on it. For example, defining the organization's boundaries and determining who the customers and stakeholders are must occur prior to developing the organization's mission and vision. This is about correctly framing the organization, which is really the first step in focusing and aligning for performance. In other words, conducting the offsite is really about "planning to plan."

# Chapter 4

# THE FIRST OFFSITE

The first order of business for the offsite participants is to define their organization's mission clearly. While the private sector is driven by financial considerations, the mission is the focal point for the public sector. Determining and clarifying an organization's mission can be an enlightening process.

## IDENTIFYING AND CLARIFYING THE MISSION

Many organizations in the federal government have defined their mission, especially in the Department of Defense. Often, however, the mission statement is either outdated (i.e., it doesn't specifically apply to what the organization does any longer) or it is too wordy and fails to focus on the heart of what the organization does. The planning team should provide examples of good mission statements and a couple of drafts for the organization so everyone won't get bogged down.

The bureaucratic tendency is to develop mission statements that are all-inclusionary and too detailed. This often occurs to ensure that the budgetary process includes everything possible, thus maximizing allocation of resources. It becomes extremely difficult for the workforce to buy into the mission and believe in it, let alone remember what it is. Further, the mission statement not only serves the workforce, but also the public the organization serves, so the clearer and more easily grasped mission statement will probably be more effective.

Analyzing the mission produces the public mission statement, which clearly states why the organization exists, whom it serves, and what it can legitimately demand of its people. The mission needs to be discussed and operationally defined clearly so that each member of the planning team understands the mission completely.

The mission statement should be distributed for feedback prior to publication. In general, a mission statement expresses the primary reason for existence and answers the following four questions:

- Why does the organization exist?

- Who are its customers?

- What do the customers need and expect?

- How are the customers' needs met?

The mission statement should be broad enough to capture these questions, but narrow enough to be easily remembered by the average worker. A good reality check is to ask the question: "Will members of the organization buy into the mission statement because they believe it is realistic and achievable?" It should be succinct and easily memorized by everyone. (See Figure 4-1, Creating a Mission Statement.)

A good mission statement, either directly or by implication, includes the customers and some component of performance and quality. The questions an organization can ask itself to get started, put another way, are: "What do we do, whom do we do it for, how well should we do it?" Answering the what-do-we-do question helps the organization get started on good mission statement.

**Figure 4-1.** Creating a Mission Statement

| What | Why | How |
|---|---|---|
| A concise statement that expresses the core purposes of the organization | Provides a focus for the organization<br><br>Serves as a guiding principle for the strategic plan | Charter a team that represents all levels and perspectives within the organization |

An effective organization will develop a mission statement that embodies its purpose, focuses on meeting the needs of customers, and embraces quality as a core factor.

✓ A mission statement is a public declaration for all customers and stakeholders that gives direction on what the organization exists to do.

✓ Create a mission statement that will guide the organization's efforts to delight its customers!

✓ Should be concise and easily understood.

✓ Guidelines for an effective mission statement:
   1. State what the organization does
   2. State how quality relates to this purpose
   3. Define the relationship to customers

The following steps can be used to produce an effective mission statement or evaluate an existing one:

- Perform an environmental scan—What are the existing forces affecting the organization?

- Define the organization's primary external customers, suppliers, and their requirements

- Define key result areas (KRAs)—What do we want to achieve?

- Define key processes—What key things do we do, operationally, that are critical for our success?

The first offsite must be about setting the stage to get to the mission statement. Once this is accomplished, the framework is set.

## Perform an Environmental Scan

Environmental monitoring is generally necessary to provide data to the organization in its daily work and is especially necessary for the planning team at every sequential step. There is a need to know what is occurring within both the organization and the external environment. Each of the sequential phases requires that the organization take some action steps; the planning team must at least provide feedback to the organization about what decisions have been made.

During the initial planning phase, the planning team should gain a thorough understanding of what the environmental scanning process entails and how it should operate in the organization. The environmental monitoring process should be continual, so that the appropriate information about what is happening or is about to happen in the various environments is always available.

Using the environmental scan information as input into the plan will enhance the relevance and add to the performance orientation of the plan. This type of applied strategic planning provides an opportune time for using these data. Learning not only to collect relevant information but to organize, interpret, and use this information is critical to strategic success. For this reason, each key manager—and perhaps even groups of employees—should be given permanent assignments of vital areas to be monitored, particularly those areas where key results are expected. They also must be given a clear and simple way in which to channel useful information back to the organization's leadership.

It is important that this monitoring, interpreting, and application of data become a constant way of life in an organization. The importance of developing environmental intelligence—and the willingness and ability to act on it promptly and with enthusiasm—cannot be overemphasized.

Finally, it should be remembered that data gathering is a mere exercise unless analysis follows the assimilation and gathering of data, and action follows the analysis. An organization's environmental monitoring is a function of driving forces and may eventually help reveal the organization's foremost driving force.

Environmental monitoring will help separate the critical from the trivial, as well as become an ongoing validation that the hard work is on the right track. It focuses on the issues that both the agency and its customers will need to address in the future; in some cases, this is an early warning of changes needed. The scan can be used to generate one or more scenarios that make the future more realistic for everyone. If the agency chooses, it can use the common trends in its scenarios to create a most probable scenario.

It's up to the organization to define customer requirements and future gaps. The agency can then begin to analyze how these gaps will impact the key results areas and develop strategies to close those gaps. Some of the aspects in the internal environment that might be reviewed include:

- Facilities

- Leadership turnover

- Clear definition of roles/responsibilities

- Quality of life

- Personnel turnover

- Training

- Resources.

**Define Primary Customers, Suppliers, and Their Requirements**

Primary customers are those for whom the organization provides goods or services. Primary customers can be external or internal to the organization. The primary customers are the reason for the organization's existence and receive the organization's output in the form of materials, services, or information. Each primary customer has specific requirements that must be identified by the planning team.

Primary suppliers are those who provide materials, service, or information input into the organization. They, too, can be internal or external, and their requirements must also be identified.

The offsite participants should have adequate knowledge of the organizational system to identify the requirements; nonetheless, the requirements must be validated by the customers themselves before finalizing the mission. In identifying your primary customers and suppliers, keep the numbers small—do not use a shopping list mentality. The focus should be on the primary customers and suppliers that involve the majority of the organization's time, energy, and business.

**Define Key Result Areas**

The next major step for the offsite participants is to identify the KRAs, or critical success factors, for the organization. A KRA is a major category of customer requirements that is critical for the organization's success.

KRAs are those strategic or key outcomes that the organization must do, and do well, to meet customer requirements and fulfill its mission. Simply put, if you don't accomplish the KRAs, you will cease to exist. KRAs should be studied relative to the organizational values/culture. Each KRA is then linked to a key/critical process. This linkage helps the organization focus on worthwhile improvements. After identifying the KRAs, the participants should study the interrelationships, if any, and understand their relative importance to each other in setting priorities.

KRAs must be derived from the mission because those result areas will indicate how well the organization is performing its mission. The KRAs and their linked key/critical processes will be the basis for assessing any gap between what is needed now (current requirements) and what the organization expects the customers to need in the future (future requirements). If there are gaps, the organization will need to determine what critical issues create or represent the gaps.

Both KRAs and their internal key processes should be validated and prioritized with your customers and coordinated with your suppliers. Some of this can be accomplished during offsite pre-work, but optimally, representative customers and suppliers should participate in the planning offsite. This dialogue should provide excellent feedback and be valuable for improving all of the organization's processes.

**Define Key Processes**

The organization must have some method for fulfilling the KRAs and thereby supporting the mission and satisfying major customer requirements. These methods are the key processes. The identification of key processes allows the organization to focus its resources on what is important to the customer. Key processes normally cross several functional boundaries and therefore require a team effort to fulfill.

The organizational leadership should define organizational key processes at the macro level. Once defined, major, macro-level processes provide the framework for formulating the support processes. This may do much to eliminate needless work and help the organization become more efficient. (Process identification and management will be thoroughly covered in Chapter 9.)

## GUIDELINES FOR MISSION ANALYSIS

Determining or clarifying an organization's mission must be done with the primary customers and their requirements in mind. The offsite participants can identify key customer needs (especially changing needs) in the following ways:

- Use current knowledge to brainstorm current customer needs. There is a danger of missing dynamic or subtle needs. This is why environmental scanning is so important.

- Invite customer representatives to be part of the strategic planning process.

Much of this work can be accomplished by the strategic planning team prior to the offsite. Much of this information can be furnished as read-ahead information or as part of the offsite packet. Conduct a series of focus groups with customers at each of the appropriate levels of servicing—especially those who actually use the product or service to do their work on a daily basis.

In conducting customer dialogues, look for the classic customer need data. These data include the following:

- **Customer requirements**: What do you need to be successful in doing your job, regardless of who does it or should provide it?

- **Processes**: What do you do with what we currently provide you? How do you handle it? What do you add to what you get?

- **Gaps**: What is the difference between what you need and the results you are getting? What is the difference between what we think you need and what you think you need? What is the difference in how you measure quality?

- **A dynamic environment**: How is your world changing your processes, suppliers, mission, resources, philosophy of operations, sense of purpose, alignment with your customers, and personnel characteristics?

- **Measurement**: What measures do you and your customers agree will adequately measure or assess quality requirements?

It is crucial that the organization's primary customers always be kept in focus and remain the number one priority. Those primary customers are the ones mentioned or implied in the mission—the ones for whom the organization exists. An analogy may be made with throwing a rock in a pond. The first ripple or two are the primary considerations, and the subsequent ripples lessen in importance. Caution should be exercised to be attentive to the primary "ripples."

## ENVISIONING THE FUTURE

Producing the vision statement is what makes strategic planning "strategic." Without a vision of the future, the organization is only planning for sustainment. To plan for progress and the future, the decision-makers must determine the direction the organization will take, visualize its future state, and describe what it looks like. The vision statement will complement the mission statement, and in some cases may even cause the unit to revisit the mission statement. (See Figure 4-2, Creating a Vision Statement.)

Developing a vision statement must take place *after* identifying and clarifying the mission. This is very important, be-

**Figure 4-2.** Creating a Vision Statement

| What | Why | How |
|---|---|---|
| A statement of what the organization is to become | Gets people to agree in principle on what is important for the organization to do | Strategic planning team discusses what they want the organization to become over time |

A vision statement builds on the mission statement by creating an image of what the organization must become to achieve its mission.

✓ One of the best ways to involve a group in preparing a vision statement is to ask them to imagine that it is ten years in the future.

✓ Envision that the organization has been highly successful in accomplishing its mission.

✓ Identify the attributes, factors, or conditions that have made the organization successful.

cause the organization must know very well what it is all about before it can define a desired future state. It's also extremely important to develop the vision immediately following defining and clarifying the mission. Doing so will clearly describe the distance and direction for the goals and objectives to build the future.

Performance planning begins with the end in mind and builds back to the present—what the organization does today. The vision is the image of the desired future state (seven to ten years) developed and agreed upon by senior leadership. It will be used to inspire, clarify, prioritize, and recruit support for the organization's strategic improvement initiatives—many of which will demand that people do different things. We may call it a vision statement, a focus or horizon statement, or any other term that conveys the commitment to change for the sake of the customer and its direction.

A good vision causes the organization to work toward it each day. The vision should be customer-focused, clear, concise, far-reaching, inspiring, and worth doing. A vision is a picture or an image of the future. It is more than a slogan—a vision is what you want to become. While the mission describes the business you're in, the vision determines your direction and helps you focus on what's important. Vision doesn't happen overnight. It's a slow, steady process that requires sustained work. A common mistake is to develop the vision prior to clarifying and analyzing the mission. (See Figure 4-3, Relationship between Mission Statement and Vision Statement.)

## VALUES ASSESSMENT

A value is an enduring belief that a specific mode of conduct or end-state of existence is personally or socially preferable to an opposite or converse mode of conduct or end-state

**Figure 4-3.** Relationship between Mission Statement and Vision Statement

*Mission Statement*
(Emphasis on quality)

*Vision*
(What we want to become)

*Strategic Plan*

**Describes the path we will take to achieve the mission and the vision.**

**Vision**
**What we believe about ourselves that guides us in selecting the path we pursue.**
- *Driving out fear*
- *Participative leadership*
- *Use of data*
- *Continuous improvement*
- *Commitment to learning*

of existence. A value system is an enduring group of beliefs concerning preferable modes of conduct or end-states of existence along a continuum of relative importance. Organizational values are those beliefs or behaviors that drive actions that are desired and understood internally and recognized externally. What are the behaviors that the organization should follow and exhibit as it embarks on the journey to the vision?

Assessing values marks the starting boundary of the planning process. The values assessment is important because it:

- Begins the culture reflection process

- Provides first information about direction needed

- Reveals some "real rules" about making change

- Can begin to build commitment

- Can identify "gaps" in organizational initiatives

- Can identify values that may block improvements

- Can provide early indicators of issues in time to act

- Can help the organization identify the posture needed for changes.

In short, the process of assessing values produces the public values (and behaviors) statement that will be supported, rewarded, and needed to accomplish the improvements and achieve the goals of the organization. It will also provide clear descriptions of value-based behaviors to counsel managers and supervisors on current behaviors or work approaches that would conflict with the organization's strategic direction.

The products and accomplishments of assessing values are:

- An official and supported value statement for the organization

- A published set of leadership behaviors needed to support the specific strategic initiatives selected

- If extended to other organizations' members, an identification of differences in values vertically and horizontally in the organization

- Knowledge of the "de facto" values at work in the organization and how they apply

- Knowledge about how to link de facto values with your specific organization.

Stated values may or may not match real values (as exhibited by behavior). Three interrelated elements determine the organization's value system.

### Personal Values

Personal values of individuals can help or hinder change. Indicators of personal values that may provide obstacles include:

- "If it ain't broke, don't fix it!"

- "If it's not invented here, it's not good!"

- "Risk-taking and job security are incompatible."

Regarding personal values, it is important to remember "differences" in the values of individual offsite participants.

They need to be identified, clarified, and (where possible) resolved. If these values are not fully examined, the team may reach little or no agreement about how the organization's future will fit with the expectations of the members of the management group.

### Organizational Values

The "chain of command" concept traditionally assumes that those in command because of age, experience, and authority are the key decision-makers. The values that exist within an organization, both personal and organizational—expressed and unexpressed—define the organizational culture. Each organization can have additional values that apply to its specific mission. These values will mark the boundaries of the planning process and serve as the baseline for future decisions.

The purpose of the planning team conducting a values assessment is not to change anyone's personal values but to understand clearly the values, their interrelationships, and the organizational philosophy and culture formed by them. If you choose to establish organizational values, you must define them; they will become a behavioral norm for the organization. Once the offsite participants have developed a draft set of values (with definitions), they need to be deployed to all members of the organization (once they return to the worksite) for feedback. Do the expressed values mirror the values routinely exhibited in the organization? The values that help form the organization's culture will form the foundation of the operating philosophy.

The organization's operating philosophy relative to values and quality is expressed in documentation (e.g., regulations, operating instructions) that address quality results, quality performance, and quality processes. Some documentation might be changed or generated to increase awareness of quality. Some quality documents might not have a common focus, and benchmarks for operations might not be available.

### Signs of Success

The following conditions indicate whether the values assessment was successful:

- There is a strong sense of ownership of the de facto values as well as the official values statement.

- People are more aware of the behaviors that convey the values that are in conflict with the higher values espoused.

There may be several arbitrary points at which to conclude the first offsite; these may be difficult to determine ahead of time. The process should be allowed to dictate progress. Completing the values portion may provide a natural break.

## GETTING FEEDBACK

It is extremely important to get feedback about the first offsite from the participants. This helps them to be more a part of the organization and will produce many good ideas that will help improve the next offsite.

A short, concise survey of no more than 10 questions can be developed that gives everyone an opportunity to respond. A key point is to ensure that the most significant suggestions are incorporated into the next event. The process for offsite planning must be on a performance improvement cycle of its own. It's also important to announce the next offsite prior to departure. This will ensure a clear calendar and help everyone understand that the whole effort is moving forward. A predetermined date and site should be established. The next offsite should occur within six months, preferably in three months, so as not to lose any momentum or enthusiasm.

At the same time, it's important not to rush the process. Remember, everyone must be brought into the transition for it to be successful. Therefore, it's not crucial that all the major steps be accomplished prior to conclusion. It's more important to gain buy-in and do it correctly.

## PROVIDING FEEDBACK

It is crucial to keep the lines of communication open throughout the entire initial strategic planning process and beyond. The planning team should develop and distribute an after-action report within seven to ten days following the offsite. The after-action report should summarize what transpired, plus provide a clear picture of where the organization is in terms of the strategic planning process.

A comparison should also be made between where the organization was prior to the process and the present state. Everyone should have clear visibility of the direction the organization is moving in via the strategic planning process. This serves the purpose of practically educating everyone in the process of strategic planning as well as assuring them that progress is being made.

## LETTING IT SINK IN

A relative balance must be achieved between giving everyone enough time to think and reflect on what just occurred and getting prepared to move forward in planning the next offsite. It would be beneficial to conduct a brief review session using the material provided in the after-action report. This gives everyone ample opportunity for discussion and to provide ideas and suggestions. Most importantly, however, everyone can feel more ownership of the plan.

Everyone should be given ample opportunity to return to their jobs and take care of their business before rushing off to another offsite. Remember this is a transition process that takes time. Too radical and revolutionary a change in the beginning may detract from the overall success of the effort.

## SAMPLE MISSION STATEMENTS

### Health and Human Services
To enhance the health and well-being of Americans by providing for effective health and human services and by fostering strong, sustained advances in the sciences underlying medicine, public health, and social services.

### CP-11
To provide professional resource managers who support the full spectrum of Army operations and deliver pertinent, timely, and reliable information and advice to decision makers.

### MARTA
To provide our customers with the highest level of safe, clean, reliable, and cost-effective transportation. We are committed to maintaining the highest standard of safety and security and offering our patrons the highest quality service possible.

### GSA
We provide policy leadership and expert solutions in services, space, and products, at the best value, to enable Federal employees to accomplish their missions.

### Army Broadcasting Service

- Provide effective targeted information that satisfies the needs of the customers.

- Deliver high quality entertainment services to the largest authorized audience possible.

- Support Continental United States broadcasting operations.

### Army Installation Management

Provide policy guidance and program management on all matters relating to overall management and resourcing of Army Installations Worldwide. Ensure the availability of efficient, effective base services and facilities.

### Coast Guard Reserve

To provide an organized, quick response, military force in ratings and skills required to supplement the active Coast Guard during surges and during routine operations.

### FAA Airports

To provide leadership in planning and developing a safe and efficient national airport system to satisfy the needs of aviation interests of the Unites States, with due consideration for economics, environmental compatibility, local proprietary rights, and safeguarding the public investment.

### Department of Transportation

Serve the United States by ensuring a fast, safe, efficient, accessible and convenient transportation system that meets our vital national interests and enhances the quality of life of the American people, today and into the future.

### Space and Missile Defense Technical Center
Provide Space and Missile Defense Capabilities for the war fighter and the nation.


## SAMPLE VISION STATEMENTS

### Department of Transportation
A visionary and vigilant Department of Transportation leading the way to transportation excellence in the 21st century.

### Florida Highway Administration
Create the best transportation system in the world.

### Army Broadcasting Service
To be the indispensable media of choice.

### Army Corps of Engineers
The world's premier engineering organization. Trained and ready to provide support anytime, anyplace. A full spectrum Engineer-Force of high quality, dedicated soldiers and civilians:

- A vital part of the Army

- The Engineer Team of Choice—responding to our nation's needs in peace and war

- A values-based organization—Respective, Responsive, and Reliable.

### Colorado Army National Guard
Home of the best led, trained, and equipped soldiers. A Force dedicated to caring for the soldiers and their families, Holding the High Ground.

### Space and Missile Defense Command

A diverse team of dynamic soldiers and civilians providing essential space and missile defense capabilities to protect U.S. interests and ensure the World's Best Army, as part of a joint team, activities, Full Spectrum Dominance.

## VALUES

### U.S. Army

The Army developed a values statement that applied to the entire organization. Using the acronym LDRSHIP, values were assigned to each letter: Loyalty, Duty, Respect, Selfless Service, Honor, Integrity, and Personal Courage. Organizations within the Army were allowed the flexibility to tailor their values statement to their own specific organization while retaining the corporate values. For example:

### Space and Missile Defense Technical Center

• Customer and employee satisfaction

• Dedication to our nation's war fighters

• Integrity, honor, and trust in all our actions

• Loyalty to our organization, our leaders, and our fellow workers

• Stewardship of time, resources, and facilities

### Colorado Army National Guard

• Visionary leadership

• Value employees

• Customer driven

- Focus on the future

- Management by fact/valuing results

- Systems perspective

- Managing by innovation

- Valuing organizational and personal learning

- Public responsibility and leadership

- Agility

These values are taken from the Malcolm Baldrige National Quality Award core values and concepts. Apparently, the Colorado Guard felt it was important to list these additional values in defending and serving their state and local community.

### U.S. Army Corps of Engineers—Huntington District

Some organizations choose to translate corporate values into guiding principles, which essentially define a desired organizational culture:

- Empower people to execute missions efficiently, effectively, and safely

- Encourage open and honest communication

- Stress individual and organizational accountability and timeliness

- Meet customer's needs

- Strive for excellence

- Encourage learning

- Foster teamwork and celebrate team accomplishments

- Encourage and reward innovations and improvements

- Support coaching and mentoring as leadership methods

- Attract and retain a diversified, high-quality workforce

- Embrace the corps' values of professionalism, integrity, quality, and esprit de corps.

### Fort Leavenworth

While embracing the Army (LDRSHIP) values, Ft. Leavenworth uses a different approach in stating its values. The values are segmented into three areas: professionalism, service, and integrity—and then what's included in each category is defined. Professionalism—competence, commitment, responsibility, and accountability. Service—doing things for others, customer focus, and dedication to excellence. Integrity—fairness, truth, and candor.

### Fort Huachuca

Others have decided to simply make a statement regarding their values. Fort Huachuca considers itself "A value-based organization that embraces the Army values and is committed to good stewardship of the natural and government resources committed to our care. We value partnerships and the contributions of our employees. We strive for quality in all that we do."

## CUSTOMERS IN THE GOVERNMENT

Identifying customers in government organizations is always an interesting challenge. Many agencies struggle at length to define their main customers, but three general rules should make the task easier.

First, as a government organization, it's important to realize that the taxpayer has a right to the goods and services your organization provides. What is provided may not be directly applicable, but the taxpaying public has a right nonetheless. (One doesn't think much about the National Guard until a crisis demands its presence).

Second, look closely at the organization's mission. What does the organization do? What is the purpose of its existence? That purpose should provide the basis for determining who the primary customer is.

Third, for whom is the majority of the energy being exerted? Who receives what the mission states? Envision a rock being thrown into a large pond. The pond is representative of the taxpaying public, but the first few ripples are the customers who are affected and benefit from your existence as an organization. Defining those first primary "ripples" or customers is crucial to the organization's planning and performance.

It's impossible to know what customers require unless the organization identifies who they are, particularly by group or segment. Many organizations have segmented their customers by internal and external and have gone on to prioritize them.

### Colorado Army National Guard

This organization recognized the importance of serving all those internal to the Guard—soldiers and families, employees, former members, and other organizations. The external customer segment groups include federal agencies, state agencies, and local community organizations and citizens. By segmenting the customers in this way, the organization can more easily align customers with mission and planning priorities.

### Fort Monroe, Virginia

Many tenants reside on military installations and are viewed as customers with requirements, both on an individual and an organizational level. Fort Monroe segmented its customers into external (those tenants), internal (all those who provide support for those tenants), and potential (those organizations and individuals who are receiving services elsewhere but could benefit from what Fort Monroe offers).

### General Accounting Office

On a much larger scale, the U.S. government has a responsibility to its major customer group, the taxpayers and citizens. The requirement, or demand, placed upon government decision-makers and managers is to improve service, making the government more economical, efficient, and effective; in other words, better performance. This is a good example of how a customer group on a grand scale can identify its requirements and make demands for those requirements to be met.

While the entrance point for making those needs known is the General Accounting Office, this reform cascades down into every government agency. As information technology advances and the pressures of economic globalization increase, products and services become more readily available—thus the need to improve performance continually.

## ENVIRONMENTAL SCANS

Situations can change very rapidly, creating the need to conduct a scan to determine how the organization must prepare itself to respond to these changes. Scans should be in the form of brainstorming sessions that encourage out-of-the-box thinking and everyone's participation. An environmental scan should always be followed by a strengths, weaknesses, opportunities, and threats (SWOT) analysis so that the organization can respond to current and anticipated needs.

### Family Readiness Plan for Reserve and National Guard

Department of Defense planning considered both environmental scanning and organizational capabilities at its strategic planning conference. (See Appendix B, Guard and Reserve Family Readiness.)

## ORGANIZATIONAL PROFILE

An organizational profile is a snapshot of the organization and should be thoroughly and formally established prior to undertaking any restructuring, transitioning, or assessment. The profile should describe how the organization operates and identify any influence that may affect the operation both currently and in the future. The organizational profile can be broken into two parts: (1) a description of the organization, which includes the organizational environment and the organizational relationships, and (2) a description of the immediate challenges, the competitive environment, and the strategic challenges. Finally, the organizational profile should include a brief description of how the performance improvement system that is in place addresses all the considerations outlined in the profile.

The organizational profile should form the baseline or set the tone for what the organization does and is all about. Performance is more about setting an example than following one. While learning from others can accelerate an organization's performance and position, being unique and finding a niche is crucial in today's rapidly changing world. The organizational profile should outline the environment and the key relationships with customers, suppliers, and other partners.

The profile should include the organization's mission, vision, values, and purpose for existence. What are the main products or services, and to whom are they provided? What does the customer require of your organization in providing these goods and services?

Knowing what your organization does and for whom sets the stage for describing the rest of the environment. What is the composition of the workforce? Does the workforce consist of the right educational and skill levels to meet the customer requirements adequately? Does the workforce have special requirements that may affect how well the mission is to be performed? The organizational environment should also include a listing of the major technologies, equipment, and facilities. Also, the regulatory environment must also be strongly considered, as the government is nearly always in the business of developing policies and enforcing regulations.

Until recently, little thought has been given to key customer groups and market segments in government organizations. The attitude has been largely that the customer has been determined for us, and we have little choice in the matter. Closer scrutiny, however, has provided a different point of view. Government organizations do indeed have customers, and their requirements are as many and varied as in the private sector. Determining who the agency is in business for has become of utmost importance because the private and public sector are in competition as well.

That leads to describing the agency's competitive position for the sector it serves when formulating the profile. More importantly, what are the critical factors that determine the organization's success? When establishing the organizational profile, it is important to consider any changes that may be looming in the future that might affect those critical success factors.

Some of these changes can be translated into strategic challenges that should be addressed in the environmental scan. Identifying them will play a major role when it comes time to develop measurable objectives for the strategic plan. The profile lays the groundwork for the planning process. It also lays the groundwork for the development of a systematic way to improve performance. The profile applies definition and purpose to the organization and essentially is the first step in the development of a performance improvement system. The profile identifies the key processes and the system that's in place to make them better.

# Chapter 5

# COMMIT TO CHANGE

Citizen demands for more economical, efficient, and effective government are not limited to the United States. These demands are being made in major democracies around the world as the pressures for economic globalization increase, driven by advances in information technology and rapid communications. These demands have created a unified, strategic direction that has management reform and performance at the helm.

## THE MANDATE

The U.S. federal government has responded to the demands for higher performance over the last decade. Congress put a statutory framework in place to promote, create, and sustain high-performing federal organizations. To implement the framework, Congress sought to shift the focus of government accountability from the activities to the results that the activities generate. The framework includes the Chief Financial Officers Act of 1990 and related financial management legislation, the Clinger-Cohen Act of 1996 and the Paperwork Reduction Act of 1995, both relating to information technology reform, and the Results Act. Why change? The taxpayers have spoken, and the federal government has passed laws requiring it.

Specifically, the CFO Act, as amended by the Government Management Reform Act of 1994 and the Federal Financial Management Improvement Act of 1996, sets expectations for agencies to develop and deploy modern financial systems to routinely produce accurate, reliable, and timely program cost information and to develop results-oriented reports on the government's financial condition. The information technology reform legislation is based on the best practices used by leading public and private organizations to manage information resources more effectively. These best practices help ensure that information technology dollars are directed toward prudent investments that achieve cost savings, increase productivity, and improve the timeliness and quality of service and delivery. Under these laws, agencies are required to link their technology plans, and management must use the information resources more directly in developing their programs' mission and goals.

The last piece of the statutory framework was the Results Act, which was enacted in part to improve federal program effectiveness and public accountability by promoting a new focus on results, service quality, and customer satisfaction. The Results Act is intended to improve the efficiency and effectiveness of federal programs by establishing a system to set goals for program performance and to measure results. The Results Act requires executive government agencies to prepare multi-year strategic plans, annual performance plans, and annual performance reports.

The President's budget chief, Mitch Daniels, Jr., makes a specific case for the federal government being rated and rewarded for program performance. Beginning in 2003, the federal budget process will highlight performance budgeting, which simply means rewarding those programs that can prove their value objectively by enhancing their budget and drawing from those "feel good" programs that have little or no information supporting results. Daniels also mentioned the budget will include a "management scorecard" that rates major agencies on how well they are meeting the President's goals.

Finally, the Results Act prompted the Federal Human Resource Development Council to publish "Getting Results Through Learning" handbook. The task force that developed the handbook included members from the Department of Defense, Department of the Navy, Department of Transportation, Office of Personnel Management, and Department of Agriculture. The handbook addresses cultural change and the development of a learning environment to facilitate that change. The handbook is applicable to any organization and can be obtained from the U.S. Department of Agriculture.

## COMMUNICATING THE NEED

Simply conducting an offsite is not going to cause an organization to change. Granted, offsites are key to helping leadership recognize the need for transition and develop a focus on the future, but the vast majority of the workforce doesn't attend the offsite. Depending on the size of the organization, the workforce at large may view the offsite with mild curiosity or, depending on the organizational climate, feel suspicious or even threatened.

The issue that immediately faces leadership at this point is how well do they know the workforce? For a strategy to be developed and transformation to occur, the workforce must be behind the effort and have a part to play in the change. Otherwise, the transformation will fail. Knowing the overall organizational mindset will provide some clear indicators of how to proceed.

If leadership began this effort with a true sense of commitment (see Chapter 1, Sending the Message), then a sense of urgency to change should already have been established.

This sense of urgency must consist of more than "because the boss wants to do it" or "everyone else is doing it." The reasons for change must truly be compelling—for example, we must change in order to survive, or, on the positive side, pointing out the many opportunities that are available if business were conducted differently. A sense of urgency may be something as simple as being unable to meet the customer's needs under the current, traditional, bureaucratic way of functioning.

## LEADERS MUST LEAD THE EFFORT

The participants in the first offsite should be the movers and shakers of the organization. While it is important to have a core strategy group spearheading and planning the effort, the actual decision-makers should wield the power and persuasiveness to make change happen. The workforce knows precisely who makes things happen and who is trusted at the higher levels, regardless of the particular position they occupy. This group of senior leaders must form a coalition and work as a team to facilitate and guide change.

This process must be well thought-out. Change simply for change's sake seldom works; also, simply talking about it certainly communicates intent, but words are not enough. A mental picture must be created—an image of the future desired state of the organization. This is where creating and communicating a vision become crucial. This should have taken place at the first offsite. The organizational vision should have been created by those involved in facilitating change, and complete understanding and agreement should have been reached regarding that vision.

The vision can accomplish a lot of things if it's constructed and used properly. A vision that's too wordy or fails to inspire will cause confusion and may demotivate the workforce from the very beginning. A good vision statement is short (5–10 words) and clearly defines a desired state or destination. The image that is conjured by the vision should cause people to want to move from where they currently are to that better place. The picture painted by the vision should define a pathway to the future—not step by step (that's what the strategic plan is for), but a general direction and a guided pathway. A good vision will also provide a general feeling of where the organization is going, even if only implied, thus giving the workforce the direction to follow and the pathway to get there.

## MARKETING THE VISION

This is no time to be taking things for granted, however. The vision must be communicated however and whenever appropriate. Making the assumption that it's going to cascade throughout the organization is not sufficient. For the vision to become a part of the organizational culture, or "institutionalized," leadership must make the vision its "mantra" or "battle cry."

Many organizations treat the vision too lightly. Sometimes it's developed simply because the process calls for it, and the true value and power of a well-communicated vision are never fully understood or employed.

As the vision begins to be communicated, there should be a growing sense of recognition throughout the workforce that the vision is indeed achievable—i.e., there is a line of sight from where the organization is currently to where the organization is going. This line of sight does not have to be explicit, but the mental image of a desired state—what the organization aspires to be—should map out a direction and a pathway. If a certain level of vision clarity is not present at this point, then there will proportionately be difficulty in its deployment.

## FORMING THE CULTURE

Once the vision is established, the work of training, educating, and strategizing to get the organization moving begins. This is where the foundation of commitment is built and where the new performance culture has its beginnings. As the senior leaders communicate and discuss the vision with members of the organization, a subtle but very important phenomenon is occurring—one that is crucial for leadership and the transition process itself. Trust is being established, and faith is being formed that the organization can indeed achieve the vision. This belief and faith in the future can best be played out if employees have the opportunity to participate in the organization's destiny and become advocates for the process and the journey.

Having a stake in the organization's future and knowing what part to play lends itself to empowerment. Involvement meets apprehension, fear, and anxiety head on. On the contrary, if employees are made to stand on the sidelines, or find themselves in a highly controlled environment, involvement will not occur, and there will be few, if any, advocates. In this scenario, the only group pushing for change will be some of the senior leaders. They can drive change, but the cost may be excessive, and the change will only be temporary. Most will "go along for the ride" because they were told to. Is that truly change, or is it simply forcing a new environment? What is likely to happen is that a "we-they" mentality will develop, and a major obstacle will stand in the way of the vision: the organization itself.

If we try to put ourselves in the employees' shoes, we can begin to feel the doubt and apprehension. The "here we go again" attitude looms as a real possibility. This is where the leading coalition must walk the talk. If they are truly committed to change, they must prove it. How is that accomplished?

It goes beyond the elaborate organizational charts and outlined strategy and processes; it means supporting ideas and initiatives that enable the organization to get to its vision. Innovation must be rewarded. Out-of-the-box thinking is encouraged. So, what signals is leadership sending to the workforce? Are measures being taken and publicized that would prove that leadership means business?

Chapter 2 presented some core values and concepts on a continuum that can provide an excellent starting point. The core values and concepts that depict a performance organization (i.e., the right side of the continuum) can be a lens through which the organization can begin viewing itself. Most of the workforce will immediately recognize where they are along that continuum. Leadership's opportunity is to acknowledge that recognition and to communicate to the workforce its commitment to moving out of where they are to more of a performance-based organization.

However, simply saying that something is going to happen is not good enough; there must be action. That action can begin to be deployed by marketing the vision throughout the organization. Another action that can readily be taken is to clearly identify the customers for everyone and ensure that the importance of meeting the customers' needs is clearly articulated. Paying all this attention and developing a relationship with the customer may be a new experience for many, so at least there will be a heightened awareness that change is in the air.

## DEMONSTRATING COMMITMENT

The most significant and profound way to elicit workforce commitment is by leadership clearly demonstrating the high value it places on the employees. This demonstration must be supported by decisive action—walking the talk. A work environment must be fostered and nurtured where people are empowered to contribute to ongoing improvement and learning and, at the same time, ensure accountability and fairness at all levels and with all members of the diverse workforce. Honesty must prevail, and open, two-way communications must be the way operations are conducted. Only then can a vision be shared and openly discussed. As communication grows, so will ideas and the innovative spirit.

When good ideas emerge, they must be rewarded. A good way to send a clear, motivational message is to budget and provide incentives for innovation. The traditional way of doing business rewarded people based on what was left over in the budget instead of making it a priority in the budget. Everyone must understand that this requires some tough decision-making, but the organization must look beyond the immediate fiscal year if the intent is to develop a committed performance culture. This is an investment, and if leadership adopts a "day trader" mentality, the workforce will respond and perform in kind, i.e., react to the daily "fires" and pay little attention to the long-range future. This also applies to leadership's willingness to invest in training and learning experiences that lend themselves to a learning culture. The future comes with an investment. Is leadership willing to commit?

Rewarding innovation, however, is only part of the picture. Employee rewards and recognition must become part of the culture. The traditional way of looking at recognition must change if it is going to be performance-oriented. What must now be a priority is rewarding achievements that contribute to the goals and objectives of the performance plan.

If the budget is to continue to drive all decisions, then only a certain amount will be set aside for awards, which further translates into a quota or percentage of salary for each employee. This is not rewarding performance; it's simply allocating what's left over, if any, to those who "may" be performing.

How many of us had to endure the "there's only so much for awards this year" philosophy, so that being a supervisor also meant having to be a mathematician and an accountant all rolled into one? And, if the budget didn't allow for any monetary awards, the employee became the victim regardless of how well the organization performed. Employee performance and organizational performance were not related. The logic may be understandable, but what happens is that everyone becomes focused on a small amount of money rather than the bigger picture of accomplishing something for the organization and achieving results. If it's not in the performance plan, it shouldn't be rewarded, which has implications for how the plan should be developed.

Recognition and rewards have to be rethought totally in a performance culture. It's about more than money, and it's about more than individuals. It's about a total organizational or corporate effort. That may require teams of various types, and it may require many different types of recognition, many of which need not involve money. Simple recognition before one's peers can have tremendous influence. A certificate citing the accomplishment of an objective, or a team award for contributing to the organization's success, can provide motivation for everyone.

The major thrust of an award system is to promote teamwork and performance to achieve goals and objectives, not to scramble for a small pot of money. A performance culture says we all win, instead of winning meaning that someone else must lose.

## THE WORKPLACE ENVIRONMENT

Establishing a culture of commitment also goes beyond training and recognition. If employees are indeed given high value, attention must be devoted to their health, welfare, safety, and overall well-being. Lip service may say "employees first" or "we're all family here," but backing it up with an environment that says the employee is "high value" and "we care" demonstrates proof of leadership's intentions and goes a long way toward establishing organizational commitment.

This is not about plush, luxurious offices and settings. It's about having enough and the right kind of equipment to facilitate getting results and effectively pursuing the goals, objectives, and ultimately the vision of the organization. More importantly, it's about conducting business in an environment that encourages performance rather than creates obstacles.

## BEING AGILE

One of the core values and concepts highlighted in the Baldrige criteria is agility. For the organization to be agile enough to respond to a rapidly changing environment, the human capital of that organization must be agile as well. This agility should allow for freedom of thought and action within a framework of performance. That cannot occur unless the workforce is committed and operating on principles and values.

In April 1995, the General Accounting Office sponsored a symposium of 32 leaders from across the government and the private sector to discuss approaches to managing people and how those approaches changed as their organizations transitioned to a performance culture. Eight interrelated principles emerged that had commonality: they required agility from everyone and established commitment for the transformation process:

- Value people as assets rather than as costs.

- Emphasize mission, vision, and organizational culture.

- Hold managers responsible for achieving results instead of imposing rigid, process-oriented rules and standards.

- Choose an organizational structure appropriate to the organization rather than trying to make "one size fit all."

- Instead of isolating the "personnel function" organizationally, integrate human resource management into the mission of the organization.

- Treat continuous learning as an investment in success rather than as a cost to be minimized.

- Pursue an integrated rather than an ad hoc approach to information management.

- Provide sustained leadership that recognizes change as a permanent condition, not a one-time event.

I would add a couple of my own:

- Teach the workforce to focus on the customer.

- Develop an understanding that everyone is part of a performance system, not parts working independently.

It must be emphasized that this is not a hit-or-miss proposition. Trying to apply just a few of these principles will not work. This is not about picking and choosing. This is a total, systematic approach that must include all parts of the system.

The human capital part of that system must be viewed in the same way. The human capital dimension is made up of many parts as well, and these parts must be integrated and working together if results are going to be achieved. The human dimension is the operational body that facilitates and ensures that all parts of the system work together.

## MEASURING THE WORKFORCE

Traditionally, the "people" aspect of an organization is viewed as the "soft side," or subjective component. That may have been the way things were in times past, but to assess objectively how well the organization is doing with its most important asset, its people, measures must be established that are deemed critical to the success of the organization. These measures may vary as the environment changes or the needs and requirements of the organization change.

Data that can have significance and have proven successful include:

- Size and shape of the workforce, including the distribution of employees by pay level, attrition rates, retirement rates, projected eligibility by employee pay level, and ratio of managers to employees

- Attrition rates, retirement rates, and projected retirement eligibility of agency leaders

- Skills inventory, including current and potential gaps in skills, distribution of skills by demographic cohort, and level of education of the workforce

- Dispersal of performance appraisal ratings, such as the mean, mode, and standard deviation of scores

- Average time required to fill vacancies

- Acceptance rates among job candidates to whom positions are offered

- Number, size, and costs of bonuses, incentives, and other awards

- Results of employee satisfaction surveys and focus groups

- Information from exit interviews

- Information technology expenses, such as equipment costs, contractor support, upgrades, and training

- Statistics on grievances, EEO complaints, and findings over time

- Number of cases handled or resolved via alternative dispute resolution (ADR) programs

- Organization's total human capital cost in dollars as a percentage of the total operating budget

- Percentage of operating budget spent on recruitment

- Costs of promotions, grade increases, and within-grade increases

- Percentage of operating budget spent on training and the amount per employee

- Organizational performance data that compare various human resource data with organizational performance.

The data collected from the human element of the organization will be relatively meaningless unless they are viewed in the context of the overall system in which the organization is operating. For example, data from exit interviews or employee satisfaction surveys are of little value unless they are validated with existing organizational information. Transition often causes, and should cause, unrest, so employees may be voicing their dissatisfaction with change.

Another example is data on budget percentage spent on training. These are meaningless data until they are compared with organizational performance. How has training impacted performance? It is only by viewing data as part of the overall system that the data become information, perhaps even knowledge. Information that's used to map trends of three or more years can provide an even more complete picture of how the organization is doing and the impact one area has on another.

Taking the actions outlined in this chapter will go a long way toward establishing commitment. It doesn't happen overnight, but once the workforce develops an awareness of the different ways of functioning, they'll begin to realize that this change may be more than just talk. Moreover, when they see the effort to collect data on the employees and realize that data are an integral part of the performance reviews, they'll be much more accepting of the commitment to change, and their resistance will diminish accordingly.

# Chapter 6
# OFFSITE II

The second offsite should take place within six months of the first. Prior to the offsite, the results of the initial assessment should be reviewed. A summary of this review should be distributed to the executive leadership and the directors. A list of performance gaps by Baldrige criteria category should be distributed along with the review. The memo accompanying the review should explain that the gaps identified in the initial assessment provide a starting point for the next offsite. This indicates where planning must begin to shore up gaps in the performance management system.

Keep in mind that this is just the beginning. Realistically, the performance management system is in its initial stages and is rudimentary at best. Nonetheless, it's a start. It's the beginning of transition.

Everyone should be asked ahead of time to prioritize the gaps in order of their importance. This will provide immediate areas of focus as the offsite begins. The strategic planning team can analyze everyone's input and use it to build the agenda. The same logistical requirements and procedures that were followed for the first offsite plus any additional suggestions from the feedback should be followed for the second offsite.

By now everyone has a good idea what to expect and should arrive ready to go to work. A read-ahead packet outlining the agenda and schedule of events should be distributed at least two weeks prior so everyone can make arrangements and be adequately prepared.

Participants should be informed that this offsite will further refine the strategic map that has been conceptualized and outlined at the first offsite. While many strategic planning endeavors stop at merely identifying mission, vision, and goals, the heart, soul, and brains of the plan are now to be formulated. It is during this offsite that specific, measurable, long- and short-range objectives with associated metrics will be identified.

Everyone should also be aware that the plan will be further deployed via action plans to everyone in the organization. While the development of action plans is not necessarily offsite material (although activity areas or teams can conduct their own offsite meetings as appropriate and necessary), business participants should know that measurable objectives will require that action plans be associated with them and will be expected to develop them for their own activities back at the office.

## IDENTIFY KEY PROCESSES

During the earlier analysis of the mission, customers were identified and their requirements outlined. Those requirements were focused into key result areas, i.e., those areas in the organization that will optimally affect customer satisfaction. Government organizations, especially the military, have clearly defined missions. A good mission statement outlines an organization's purpose—its essential reason for existence. This is where the key processes of the organization reside and ought to be identified.

It is very important that this step not be overlooked or taken lightly. This is a focal point and a validation of what's most important. The question should be asked, "If we stopped doing something, what would it be that would cause us to go away?" Once that "something" is identified, the mission becomes clear. The key processes will also emerge. Government organizations in particular tend to gravitate into stovepipes and details, thus losing sight of the big picture and their main reason for existence. The initial assessment audited those processes (if they were identified) and surfaced those gaps that lessened the capability for mission accomplishment.

Developing the process management structure must begin at the mission level and becomes key in the building of a performance management system. Key processes and those necessary for support establish the framework for efficiency, effectiveness, and continuous improvement. The process management structure frames the operational arm of the organization.

## IDENTIFY KEY SUCCESS FACTORS

Key or critical success factors are those that define an organization's existence; in other words, they define the main things the organization must do in order to be successful. What must be done to succeed/excel at the mission? The key processes that are derived from the mission hold the answer to that question. It may not be obvious in the beginning, but those processes will lead the organization to what's essential. A brainstorming session on what's critical may be useful at this point and should be done with the mission and key processes always at the forefront. This will help distill what's truly important versus what simply may be busy work that's being done simply because it has always been done.

Once a list of factors that are key to the organization's success is developed, it must be prioritized. Keeping the mission in the forefront will also greatly assist with this process. Brainstorming can quickly yield a long list that needs to be consolidated or prioritized into the three to five most important factors; otherwise, the process will bog down.

Once the key success factors are determined, it's important for everyone to have a clear understanding of what each factor means and its implications for the organization. This discussion and clarification will be of great help later on when measurement takes place and metrics have to be selected and assigned. Also, when the plan is deployed throughout the workforce via action teams, a general and consistent understanding of what's critical will be very valuable.

Performance planning and management cannot occur without identifying those factors that are key to an organization's success. For example, the Sensors Directorate of the Space and Missile Defense Command views the factors that are key for its success as:

- Competing for customer funding

- Becoming more Army-focused

- Aging workforce

- Maintaining an intellectual edge

- Enhancing technology.

The Army Corps of Engineers, Huntington District, views its success as depending on:

- Investing in people

- Meeting or exceeding customer expectations

- Meeting emerging regional and national needs

- Improving partner and supplier performance

- Ensuring organizational effectiveness.

The United States Army, as part of its transformation to the Objective Force by 2020, has identified the well-being of its human dimension as critical to the success of that transformation. This corresponds with National Security Presidential Directive 2 (February 15, 2001), in which the President of the United States highlighted the quality of life of our nation's service members and their families as a principal priority of his administration. The factors that are critical to the success of well-being in the Army are:

- A competitive standard of living

- Pride and sense of belonging

- Enrichment of personal life.

The General Accounting Office (GAO) has listed several factors that are key to the successful implementation of GPRA and the success of government organizations in general:

- Strong leadership

- Clear goals and performance measures

- Building human capital

- Linking programs and processes to customer satisfaction results

- Basing decisions on sound data.

## IDENTIFY KEY INDICATORS

Once the key processes and key or critical success factors have been identified, the key indicators must be developed. Key indicators paint a picture of how well the organization is performing with regard to the critical success factors. If a determination has been made regarding what's key to success, then it makes sense to take extra care and time to ensure that those critical elements are responsibly measured.

A common mistake organizations make is that they try to measure what's currently in place, with no analysis to determine whether it's important to the organization. This is a very important issue that must not be overlooked. What this is all about is transitioning to a new way of doing business. Therefore, it makes no sense to apply metrics to factors that aren't related to the organization's success. This gets down to actually applying the new way of thinking.

Likewise, assigning a measure to everything in the beginning is not necessary—it's not even desirable. The key indicators are just that: indicators of what's critical for success. Therefore, a minimum number of measures should be identified, the "vital few" that will most clearly demonstrate the maturity and health of the organization. As the plan is deployed at all levels, the data generated will be voluminous but will feed into the "vital few" indicators, providing senior leadership knowledge about how the overall system is operating.

This, too, is a crucial step because it provides the basic framework for the all-important dashboard that will be developed later and refined as the organization's measurement system develops. This whole process must cascade from the mission, and each linked step must be followed. If linkage is not maintained down through implementation of the action plans and individual support forms, full deployment will not occur.

The question may arise whether the organization has enough of a system in place to go forward with this endeavor. The organizational self-assessment that was previously conducted will yield valuable information about the organization's current capabilities. Attention must be focused on closing those gaps and thus meeting customer requirements. The indicators should be assigned to depict how well the key processes are being performed. Accordingly, the key indicators for the success factors have been identified.

The Space and Missile Defense Command views its key indicators as:

- Improvement of effectiveness, communication, and task management

- Improvement of positive business referral

- Improvement of organizational awareness

- Expanded technology base and improved intellectual capital

- Increased customer satisfaction.

The Army Corps of Engineers, Huntington District, views its key indicators as:

- Empowered workforce

- Open communication

- Individual and organizational accountability

- Meeting customers' needs

- A learning culture that fosters teamwork

- Attract and retain a diversified, high-quality workforce

- Embody the Corps of Engineer's organizational values.

The United States Army has identified as key indicators for the well-being of the Force as:

- Readiness

- Retention

- Recruiting.

Success in these areas will indicate that the key success factors are being achieved, or at least are well on the way to being achieved. These indicators connect to the Department of Defense's Social Compact goals of:

- Quality housing

- World-class health care

- Underwrite family support

- Reduce work-life stress

- Support education

- Communication with families

- Employer support.

GAO views its key indicators as:

- Organizational mission and goals drive daily activities

- Transform the culture so that achieving results becomes the driving concern

- Program and process improvement on a continual basis.

## ASSESS CURRENT CAPABILITIES

Once the key processes have been identified, conducting a strengths, weaknesses, opportunities, and threats (SWOT) analysis for each process and subsequently for the whole organization provides the material needed to determine current capabilities. This is important because it can:

- Help develop a solid definition of current levels of performance and current focus on essential mission elements

- Show the need to address the efficient management of personnel and other resources

- Improve the use of effective monitoring indicators of both processes and outcomes

- Cause leadership to examine change rather than just report activity.

Key issues needing to be addressed and clarified are what the organization's current capabilities are to conduct required operations to accomplish the mission and meet customers' needs, and whether these operations can be conducted simultaneously.

To assess its current capabilities, the organization must:

1. *Define its current state.* The organization must know where it is currently before it can initiate quality improvement efforts in response to its strategic plan. For each key process, the agency should identify strengths, weaknesses, opportunities, and threats (through a "SWOT" analysis). The executive leadership should involve a cross-section of the organization in these assessments.

2. *Distinguish between current and future demands.* It is important to distinguish between the assessment of current capabilities according to present standards (current issues) and the expected demands or standards of

the future customer or environment (vision). A strong, clear image of the future and a clear picture of the desired or standard level of performance will expose gaps. Gap analysis begins after current capabilities are assessed and a vision of the future is developed. The gap that emerges between the present state and desired future state—whether it's the future state of effectiveness and efficiency of operations, achievement of the vision, or both—is what must be reviewed and analyzed.

## Avoiding Pitfalls

The greatest danger is complacency and contentment with current performance. This is especially true if current performance is measured against long-standing, outdated criteria that may not anticipate any of the future demands, changes, or adaptations needed for organizational survival. Further, the workforce may not accept transitioning to a performance management orientation and may want to stay where it is—a typical symptom of resisting change.

Another danger is using metrics in a way that makes the organization look better than it actually is. This is not about looking good but about being good. An example is estimating capability using "percentages" instead of actual numbers. It is easy to rest with a 99 percent success rate. It is harder to rest with the same performance measured in absolute numbers such as "five safety issues last year."

In absolute language, the true assessments of the systems are evident (i.e., results) and should not be hidden by the amount of work accomplished. Work quantity may be quite irrelevant because there may be little or no relationship between amount of work and results achieved. Old performance measures may be dealing with routine, easy, or non-mission elements. Performance is now redefined as part of a total system, and everyone must now be educated and trained in that system.

**Suggested Management Tools**

The following management tools may be useful in assessing current capabilities:

- A tree diagram to organize the relationships of KRAs, processes, assessments, and gaps/critical issues. (See Figure 6-1, Commonly Used Symbols.)

- Process decision program charting or process mapping, which breaks down what may seem to be a highly complicated procedure into a step-by-step methodology, thus opening the door for eliminating unnecessary steps and becoming more efficient. (See Figure 6-2, What Is a Process? and Figure 6-3, Process Mapping: Calling a Friend.)

**Questions to Ask to Move Forward**

Ask the following questions when auditing the key processes to determine current capabilities:

- Has each key process been assessed using applicable Baldrige criteria?

- Does each key process have associated measures? Are the measures valid and reliable?

- Have resources been identified and applied for each key process?

- Could each key process be combined with another key process or managed more efficiently by any other means?

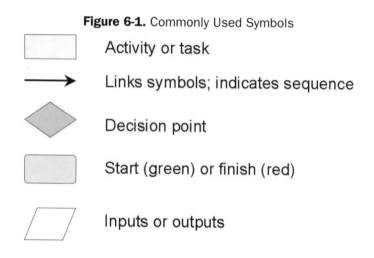

**Figure 6-1.** Commonly Used Symbols

Activity or task

Links symbols; indicates sequence

Decision point

Start (green) or finish (red)

Inputs or outputs

---

- Is there an accurate tracking system for the key processes?

- Have the strengths, weaknesses, opportunities, and threats of each key process been documented, discussed, and acted upon appropriately?

---

**Figure 6-2.** What Is a Process?

- Systematic series of steps, tasks, or activities that have inputs and outcomes (a beginning and an end)

- Using inputs, it produces either a tangible product or an intangible service as its output to a customer

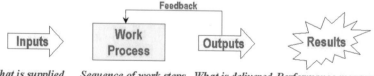

Feedback

Inputs → Work Process → Outputs → Results

*What is supplied    Sequence of work steps    What is delivered    Performance measures*

**Figure 6-3.** Process Mapping: Calling a Friend

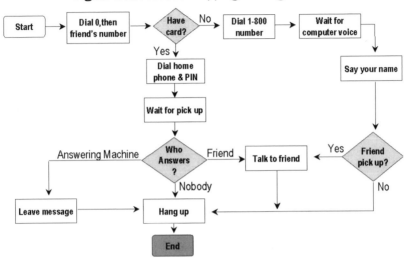

- What are the implications for the strategic planning process in how the organization deals with the strengths, weaknesses, opportunities, and threats associated with each key process? (Is the organization's strategic planning process designed to incorporate the improvements that have been identified in the SWOT?)

## PERFORM GAP ANALYSIS

Before undertaking gap analysis, the following inputs should be available:

1. Key processes and key result areas

2. Future vision and customer requirements

3. Current capabilities.

The previous assessment of current capabilities provided data that compare the current capabilities of each key process to the KRAs. The gap analysis generates data on what capabilities the organization needs in each of the key processes to reach the future state (the vision) and to identify performance gaps. It is a good idea to prioritize the critical issues before finalizing goals in order to remain focused on what is critical for survival or mission success, both for the organization and for its customers.

If there are numerous gaps, the organization needs to prioritize them. There will be too many trivial gaps unless the organization sticks only to the critical gaps associated with the KRAs and key processes and ignores the gaps that are not strategic. (Non-strategic gaps should be delegated to the normal continuous improvement processes and not dealt with during strategic planning.)

The gaps represent the critical issues the organization must address to be successful in its mission, and some of the gaps are the basis for senior leadership to set the near-term and long-term objectives. The gap analysis, in effect, becomes a reality check of the planning process to this point. If the gap between present capability and the future state is small and easily achievable, the leadership most likely didn't look forward enough in visualizing the future. Conversely, if the gap is large and overwhelming or unlikely to be achieved, then a readjustment of the future state is warranted. A balance must be struck so a most-likely scenario in achieving the desired end state can be developed.

The planning team may also find that, while the gaps are all achievable, there are too many to address simultaneously. If so, the earlier work with prioritization of KRAs, values, and environmental factors will aid in setting reasonable objectives for the organization. Once prioritized, they may be worked on systematically, depending upon availability of resources. Critical issues may address a range of subjects, depending on what business the organization is in; for example, product or service delivery, new technologies, training and skills, and regulations.

Some warnings need to be heeded, as there are some real world issues that might cause difficulties or confusion. Some managers will need to be supported or else they will think this is a "finger pointing" exercise, i.e., since this is "my" area, the identified gaps must be "my" fault. Likewise, some managers will assume that any "less than desirable performance areas" are a result of poor personal performance rather than an accurate picture of the system itself. This must be viewed as a systems issue and not a personal issue. Some managers will not see the connection of the issues across function or across support systems and will assume that a problem measured in another functional area is not a shared problem.

The gap analysis becomes the basis for setting strategic long-range and near-term objectives. The purpose of long- and short-term objectives is to determine how the unit will move from the present to the future. The strategic goals and objectives will become the basis for the functional action plans, so they need to be prioritized and sent out for feedback from organization personnel before they are finalized.

## DEVELOP GOALS

Goals are broad statements describing a desired future condition or achievement, without being specific about how much and when. Goals are directed at the longer term. They are the first level of specificity on how the unit plans to address the critical issues that were identified by gap analysis on the path to the vision.

A well-developed list of goals should reflect and be directly tied to the vision. The number of goals should be manageable. Too many goals may cause the organization to lose focus. Each goal will have at least one long-term objective, usually more.

Goals are essential because they:

- Give a sense of purpose people can use to guide their day-to-day work

- Identify more specific outcomes and define a pathway to the vision

- Taken collectively, force an organization to stretch toward better ways of doing business.

All personnel need to know the commitment, connectivity, timetable, and customer impact for strategic planning goals and objectives. This needs to be communicated throughout the organization. The goals that are developed at offsite II can certainly be changed or developed further at subsequent offsites. This first effort, however, should ensure that the goals cover the mission areas and provide a clear path to the vision. Once everyone is relatively satisfied that this has been accomplished, the group can move on to formulating the objectives.

## FORMULATE OBJECTIVES

Objectives are specific statements of shorter-term conditions or achievements that need to be accomplished to arrive at the goals. An objective includes measurable end results to be accomplished within specific time limits. Each objective is assigned to a person or group, or at a minimum a responsible office is designated for coordinating and collecting the data for performance reviews. The designation of a responsible office doesn't necessarily mean that the office is tasked to do all the work. It does mean, however, that the office is responsible for coordinating the effort with the various teams, collecting the data, and reporting out in the performance reviews.

Objectives should be definable, acceptable, attainable, and measurable; they should be further categorized into long- and short-term. A long-term objective should include as a minimum a three- to seven-year time frame, while a short-term objective outlines the next one to three years. An objective can be measured in terms of accomplishment or degree of accomplishment. Each objective should specify a date of completion, a responsible activity to report out on the performance during performance reviews, and the level of quality or standard at which the objective is to be accomplished.

Some organizations use objectives as equivalent to projects; in that case, the sponsor or champion of the objective would either act as the project leader or would appoint a leader. Caution should be exercised that the requirements of "metrics" are met. In other words, a danger exists that the objective is viewed as a simple task to be completed, with no concern for the level of quality. Remember, objectives should also be measured in terms of quality.

There is no precise point at which the second offsite should conclude. Remember, this process must bring everyone along, and each area must be covered to everyone's satisfaction. The general direction of the process, however, should get as far along as possible in developing that roadmap. The components of the roadmap include, of course, the mission, vision, values, key process identification, and key indicators. It must be re-emphasized that an environmental scan needs to be conducted prior to mission development, and most definitely before the development of organizational goals. If goals can be developed, strategies outlined, and long-term objectives established during offsite II, so much the better. If that point can be reached, then the basic framework for the plan is in place.

The most desirable outcome of the second offsite is to have all the long-term objectives established for each goal. As mentioned, long-term objectives should encompass a three- to seven-year time frame and consist of three measurable components. There should be at least one long-term objective for each organizational goal. The objectives should reflect expectations developed during the plan-to-plan step, and relevant issues should be raised for review by the organization's planning team. Performance gaps that were previously identified as part of the assessment should be considered part of the objective development process. This allows for the opportunity to correct problems that are systemic in nature and impede performance.

An example of how long-term objectives can be developed to support an organizational goal is seen with the Colorado Army National Guard. One of the Guard's goals is to meet or exceed Department of the Army readiness standards. The Guard has broken down this goal into objectives, or "chunks," that enable it to work on the goal from different aspects and various parts of the organization. Some objectives in support of this goal are:

- Improve duty military occupational specialty quota from 70 percent to 80 percent by FY 05.

- Obtain 90 percent accuracy in the personnel database by June 2003.

These objectives are specific and, along with others in support of this goal, provide a means to a desired end state.

A longer-range view can also be adopted. For example, in developing a plan for the well-being of the force, the Army has looked 20+ years into the future and planned for the living conditions of its personnel. The stated goal is to "provide a competitive standard of living for all soldiers, civilians, and their families." One of the supporting objectives is stated as: "by the end of FY 23, provide and maintain all barracks complexes for eligible permanent party soldiers and trainees, commensurate with equivalent facilities in civilian society." This objective is certainly in the long term.

Backing into the present, mid-term objectives were established as "steps" to achieve the broader, long-range objective: "By the end of FY 08, provide and maintain all barracks complexes for eligible, permanent party soldiers commensurate with equivalent facilities in civilian society." In support of this objective, certain actions were identified as necessary to accomplish the objective, e.g., "fund all barracks upgrade projects to standard by FY 03" and "centrally fund initial issue furnishings to 100% for all renovation/construction projects by FY 02."

Having one or two long-term objectives for each goal provides further guidance and directions for building steps for deploying the plan into the heart of the organization. With appropriate measures already tied to the long-term objectives, the measurable short-term objectives can now be established.

## WRAPPING UP OFFSITE II

As a final wrap-up to offsite II, the Baldrige criteria should be reviewed in light of the organization's purpose. The Baldrige criteria provide a framework of transition to a performance management system. This review should cover how this system consists of the driver—senior leaders clarifying the mission, creating the vision, and establishing the values, goals, and measurable objectives designed to meet or exceed customer requirements.

The plan establishes the framework in which performance can take place. It, along with leadership, drives the system. The system is the set of well-defined and well-designed processes that accomplish the quality and performance requirements. The system is focused on results and provides a basis for channeling action, measuring progress, and moving the organization forward to the vision. It is important that this concept of a framework and a system oriented toward performance be reinforced on a regular basis, particularly during the performance reviews and the offsites.

# Chapter 7

# DEPLOYMENT

Deployment is all about converting what has been laid out in the goals and objectives into action planning throughout the organization. This is where the transitioning to a performance-based way of operating can get difficult. Up until now, much of what has been occurring is meetings at a higher organizational level and putting thoughts on paper. Other than making the workforce aware that changes were on the way, nothing has been done that has direct impact on the employees' work lives. This is about to change.

Category 2.2 of the Baldrige criteria specifically addresses the deployment of the strategic plan into daily action planning and related key performance measures/indicators. Where it becomes binding is that the criteria call for an explanation of how resources are allocated to ensure the accomplishment of the plans. This is a major turning point, because this sets the conditions for the strategic plan driving the budget versus the budget driving how the organization plans for the future. Additionally, the criteria ask for a description of the human resource plans that are derived from the strategic objectives and action planning.

This heralds the real aspects of culture change. The criteria are requiring the workforce to transition to a performance orientation. This change affects everyone and does so in many different ways (see Chapter 8, Human Resources).

## FINISHING DEVELOPMENT OF THE OBJECTIVES

It isn't necessary to establish short-term objectives at offsite II. As long as the long-term objectives have a designated responsible activity, the short-term objectives can be established back at the office. This, however, will require considerable coordination because more than one activity may have ownership of a short-term objective. There is considerable benefit to this because teamwork is now being fostered.

There will be many more short-term objectives than long-term. Each long-term objective may have as many as 10–12 short-term objectives as steps to achieve results in the long term. An organization typically develops too many short-term objectives in the beginning, because the tendency is to become immersed in the trivial, thus running the risk of a management problem. Since there is no "correct" number, the guidance for setting short-term objectives should be that they lead to the accomplishment of the long-term objectives and can be linked to specific action plans for further development.

When setting objectives, the organization should deploy the long-term objectives to the short-term and subsequently to action plans. Experience has demonstrated that structured deployment results in realistic linkages, less duplication and wasted effort, and cooperative cross-functional relationships.

## OBJECTIVES AND PROJECTS

Distinguish objectives as you would assignable projects. An objective can be accepted more readily as a project and can be part of a performance assessment system for a manager. Assurances must be made that the projects meet the requirements for objectives and are focused on goal accomplishment. Most managers would feel that a stand-alone goal statement is too broad, cannot be measured, and leaves too much interpretation for accurate assessment of a project for which they are responsible and accountable. It must be cautioned, however, that objectives don't merely become task lists for managers to dole out to the workforce in higher quantities. Employees will quickly see through this and feel betrayed by the whole process; true ownership of the organization's goals will never be realized. Further, and most importantly, the organization will fail to buy into the strategic direction mapped out by the vision and goals.

## DEVELOPING ACTION PLANS

Action plans are documents that outline step-by-step actions to be taken by the action team. They support the short-term objectives and are the "active" component of the strategic plan. They define roles and responsibilities and can be used to track implementation. (See Figure 7-1, Creating Action Plans.)

**Figure 7-1.** Creating Action Plans

| What | Why | How |
|------|-----|-----|
| A document that defines the actions to be taken, the person(s) responsible, and the time frame for completion | To define roles and responsibilities and provide a tool for tracking implementation | –Define actions<br>–Gain commitments<br>–Agree on deadlines |

*Steps in Developing Effective Action Plans*

1. Identify actions based on the strategic planning team's work.
2. For each specific action, identify who will be responsible for getting it done.
3. Discuss and agree on completion deadlines with each person responsible for completing the action.
4. Put the whole plan in writing, showing actions, responsible persons, and deadlines.
5. Ask yourself, "What can go wrong with this action plan?"
6. Build in additional steps or actions to keep the things that can go wrong from derailing the plan.

The deployment process is a breakpoint for the organization. It derives action plans, monitoring methods, milestones, team assignments, and integration with budget cycles. Transferring the objectives of the organization is a critical step in making the future real and putting the destiny into the hands of the people doing the work. This requires that leadership clearly demonstrate its commitment to the process.

At this point in the strategic planning process, top management deploys the objectives to working groups to develop action plans. This is the point in strategic planning that ties all activities of the organization to the strategic plan. Linkage is essential; it's the glue that causes the organization to be focused. It links the day-to-day activities to the organization's KRAs and key processes, goals, and objectives. These action plans prescribe the specific method or process to achieve the results called for by one or more objectives. They outline in detail the part each individual must play in the performance journey.

If an objective is reviewed by the working group or team for appropriate action, the proposed action should be thorough and comprehensive. One method that helps provide specificity and clarity is the establishment of charters. A charter can be used by an action team or improvement group to get started and to provide scope and direction. Charters are written commitments by management that specifically addresses resources and boundaries.

Charters can be used to provide clarity and more clearly define team roles and functions. This is where priorities can be listed. The priorities should clearly outline the cost of each level of objective accomplishment. Potential problem areas should be addressed by covering the "what if" provisions in the event that the primary plans cannot be executed. This includes an environmental scan of each undertaking.

Development of the action plans necessitates defining the sub-processes and tasks that support and align to the key processes. If metrics do not yet exist to measure the sub-processes, they must be developed at this time. The development of metrics may be difficult in the beginning, but it's essential if measurement is going to occur. The proposed plans can then be communicated back to the senior leadership to see if this investment is acceptable to the organization. This cascading, two-way communication may result in:

- Reassessment of the priority of objective

- Approval of the recommendation

- Modification of the objective.

Metrics must have a built-in "trigger" or in-process review threshold at which the project implementation team must report back to senior leadership (e.g., a resource-expenditure level, a minimum-progress level). The in-process reviews form the basis for overall organizational performance reviews. The data collected and used for these in-process reviews can and should be used to develop more global information for higher level performance reviews.

## RELATIONSHIP TO OBJECTIVES

Action plans should be focused on and linked to the objectives and strategies that have been developed earlier. (See Figure 7-2, Relationships and Linkages.) Otherwise, all the actions (operations) that occur at the worker level will lack direction and generate much meaningless data. The action plans should address the objectives on an annual basis. Each action plan should be designed for accomplishment during that work year at a minimum. If it can be accomplished sooner, so much the better.

**Figure 7-2.** Relationships and Linkages

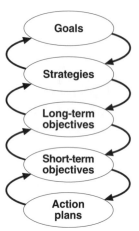

Goal statements are broad, action- and results-oriented *descriptions* of what the organization must excel at to fulfill its vision.

Strategies tell *how* to achieve the goal.

Long-term objectives quantify specific targets or *levels of performance* required to achieve the goal. Three components are *quality standard, specific date to be accomplished,* and *lead/ responsible office.*

Short-term objectives quantify specific targets or *levels of performance* within a shorter time horizon. Short-term objectives support and are derived from long-term objectives. *Also have three components.*

Action plans detail specific *tasks* to achieve strategies and long- and short-term objectives (and, therefore, goals.)

An action plan should be viewed as the work the employees are currently involved with. It's the operational part of the organization. A short-range action plan should address successes that are achievable in the short term. Longer-range action plans may be developed and reviewed on an annual basis for inclusion in the employee's support form and annual performance review. (See Figure 7-3, Aligning for Performance.)

Action plans can be adjusted to the objectives so that good integration can occur. Gaps between the objectives and what each individual employee is responsible for (individual support forms) should be addressed and eliminated, or at least minimized. Action plans are most effective if they're designed for accomplishment annually but can be adjusted to fit with the shorter-range objectives and link to individual support forms.

All the action plans in an organization should be reviewed at least annually. Action planning becomes the day-to-day business of the organization, and a periodic review provides an opportunity for adjustment. The best time to review and adjust action plans is during the quarterly performance re-

**Figure 7-3.** Aligning for Performance

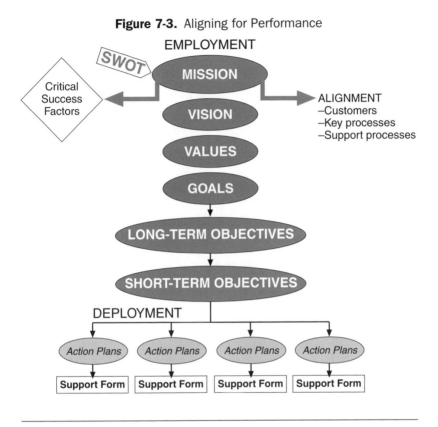

views. During these sessions, a quick analysis can be made to determine whether the actions being taken are effective and are leading to the accomplishment of the objective.

The Army Corps of Engineers, Huntington District, elected to define its action planning in terms of initiatives (see Appendix C). Each initiative or set of initiatives supports a strategy and has a specific date targeted for completion. While this approach may be somewhat different from the typical mission–vision–goals–long-term objectives–short-term objectives–action plan format, it is certainly workable as long as the terms are well defined and everyone com- pletely understands how the concept translates to the real world and everyone's personal performance requirements.

The Army Aviation Center at Fort Rucker, Alabama, has broken down its goals into specific key objectives, which are further broken down into key action plans/tasks. For example, key objectives under the organizational goal of "training" are: (1) develop a long-range training plan, (2) provide program training for each budget year, (3) execute training plan as outlined, (4) sustain staff levels to train the load, and (4) provide professional development leadership training for staff.

Fort Benning, Georgia, has developed a human resource plan as part of its strategic plan. The human resource plan has as one of its goals "recruit and maintain a high quality workforce." This goal is supported by several objectives that, when collectively accomplished, will serve to reach the goal. The objectives are: (1) promote a safe, caring environment, (2) fill jobs in a timely manner, (3) provide career and promotion opportunities, (4) tie individual objectives to mission essential tasks, and (5) enhance management and labor partnerships.

Action planning can also take the form of defining an overall set of actions used to implement the strategic direction of an organization. This type of action planning forms the umbrella and integration tool that initiates the "action" for how the goals are to be accomplished. This type of action planning puts into actionable language the plan for performance and success.

An action plan of this type is usually associated with large organizations and links the conceptual with the day-to-day operation. The Army's action plan for well-being falls into that category. It outlines the actions that need to occur so that the human dimension of the Army is part of the overall transformation process and receives priority consideration as the Army moves to its planned Objective Force 2020.

This type of action planning is a good example of how a framework is used to cause change and promote continuous improvement during the change process. The change is taking place on a much larger organizational level, and the well-being of the human aspect of that change is being kept in primary focus. The action plan for the human dimension outlines the way as the entire organization engages in a much larger transformation endeavor. Of equal importance is the linkage of the organization's overall plan with its parent organization, the Department of Defense, and how the strategic direction is integrated throughout. The well-being action plan maps the way for how human capital is going to take part in the future and provides a means to measure how well that is being accomplished.

## MEASURABLE PROCESSES

Every organization should have key and supporting processes identified. An action plan should be developed around processes that can be measured, analyzed, and improved. These processes can be viewed as a series of steps, tasks, or activities that have inputs and outcomes—i.e., have a beginning and an end. Using inputs, a process produces either a tangible product or an intangible service as its output to a customer.

Excellent organizations define key processes and key process measures based on customer requirements. They also identify key support processes based on those key customer requirements. What is crucial is the link between the process improvement initiatives and the organization's strategic plan. This link is where the operation of the organization becomes systematic. Key supporting processes are linked to key processes, which tie into the overall direction of the organization. This is also where the strategic direction (vision and goals) converges with the organization's operation (mission and processes). This is the point at which true, holistic performance occurs. Both aspects or components must be present.

Imagine a high-performance automobile functioning perfectly but not knowing in which direction to go. Conversely, imagine a clear strategic direction mapped out to a well-defined destination, but a poorly functioning vehicle that's unable to get there. Both function and direction are vital for performance.

Once the performance structure is in place, improvement is the next step. Improvement initiatives for key and support processes can take place through many different methods; the most widely used are process mapping and benchmarking. The whole system can be incorporated into a plan–do–check–act cycle of continuous improvement. (See Figure 7-4, Overall Strategy.)

---

**Figure 7-4.** Overall Strategy

- Identify and align installation key processes/key supporting processes
- Design performance metrics around processes to measure results
- Refine systematic information and analysis architecture
- Conduct quarterly performance reviews using performance metrics
- Execute performance improvements

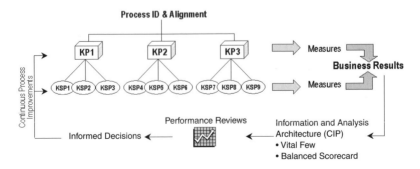

## FUNCTIONAL INTEGRATION

As action plans are developed, functional groups should understand and accept the principle of plan integration. This is where many organizations encounter real problems. If the workforce is not properly prepared for integrating the plan both vertically and horizontally, there will be resistance. In traditional, stovepiped organizations, employees are generally very comfortable in their existing paradigms. Integration means being dislodged from that paradigm and placed into a less structured way of doing business.

Integration should have impact throughout the organization. Integrated plans can focus and maximize use of the organization's resources. This begins a process of effectiveness and efficiency that cannot be realized through traditional functional stovepipes. Integrated action plans can preclude a reorganization effort; in fact, this is how an agency should align itself for performance. Typical, traditional reorganization efforts need not occur.

## TOP MANAGEMENT BRIEFING

After action plans have been developed, top management must be briefed to gain feedback, buy-in, and resource commitment. It's important that action plans be specific and linked to measurable short-term objectives. Senior management must have total visibility regarding how the objectives of the organization are being carried out via the action plans. In a performance management system, this now becomes how the organization operates and functions.

## GUIDELINES FOR ACTION PLANS

An action plan is the specific method or process for achieving the results called for by one or more short-term objectives. This could include improving current processes, designing new processes, or incorporating several processes into one. Cross-functional groups carry out action planning.

An action plan should include: functional integration instructions dealing with the nature of the task, roles and responsibilities, milestones, measures, standards or quality levels, resource identification, feedback mechanisms, success criteria, "trigger" points, and charter. In other words, action planning should contain certain components that are ingredients of performance. The level of formality depends on the size and complexity of the actions being undertaken as well as the size of the organization. At minimum, a record should be maintained reflecting what has been done.

The strategic plan will not be dynamic or contain any power unless it is deployed throughout the organization—that is, the plan cannot be employed until it is deployed. This is also a paradigm shift. Traditionally, plans are viewed as a formal document seen only by top executives at high-level meetings. Performance plans must be accessible by everyone and used on a regular basis. Formality is not the issue; utility is.

The operational arm of the organization, its human resources, must have ownership of the plan if it is to succeed. It does not belong only on a senior executive's desk. Each short-term objective must be linked to specific actions that each group and each individual must be working on daily to move the organization forward. It becomes the business of the organization. The plan conveys into daily activities and tasks those critical factors that are reviewed for performance.

Each process owner carries out the applicable action plans to move the organization to greater heights of mission accomplishment and closer to its vision. It is senior leadership that drives the planning process; thus, it is senior leadership that must ensure that the plans are communicated and deployed throughout the organization. How thoroughly deployment occurs can and should be part of the performance reviews.

Action plans become part of each employee's performance support form and, subsequently, performance rating on at least an annual basis. More of how this can be accomplished is addressed in Chapter 8, Human Resources. Of primary importance is that direct, cascading linkage be established to the measurable objectives. This more clearly defines the system and establishes accountability and ownership.

## THE PUBLISHED PLAN

Everything that's needed for drafting the document for publication now exists. The fundamental plan should include an introductory page with a signed letter and picture of the senior leader of the organization. This is a great opportunity for the senior leader to articulate where the organization is going and how it's going to get there in a performance management framework. This narrative can more clearly define the vision and outline the organizational direction. It's the senior leader's opportunity to set the tone on one page.

The actual vision statement should follow, with leadership's philosophy about the desired end state of the organization: What does the organization aspire to be? This integrates with the core values and concepts of the Baldrige criteria, specifically "visionary leadership." This is a good place to outline how the organization links to other government organizations, specifically higher headquarters and those most affected by the operation.

The next page should include a description of the strategic planning process, including a diagram depicting how it has occurred, how it is currently taking place, and how it will occur in the future. The results of the environmental scan could be included here as well. This will help the workforce understand more clearly the steps that have been undertaken to arrive at the current state; it will also engage the readers in the process.

The next pages of the plan should begin with the mission statement, which includes a discussion of what the organization does and what it is all about. This should be followed by the values page. Values set the conditions and organizational behaviors that are to be employed in the journey to the vision. This is another great opportunity for the senior leader to outline the organization's expectations and directly influence the behaviors that are expected. Instead of a list of "do's" and "don'ts," explaining the organization's values can do much to generate enthusiasm, organizational spirit, and character-building as the culture begins to transform.

Finally, the heart of the plan is the goals and supporting objectives, both long- and short-term. The strategies for achievement of each goal should be included.

There is no need to go any deeper into the organization with the published planning document. Specific action plans and further deployed tasks that are included on the support forms do not need to be in the published plan. That becomes the work of the managers and action officers and can be retained in their respective work areas.

Deployment involves the workforce; thus, the deployment process must integrate with the organizational framework of the strategic plan and the human resources plan. When action plans and subsequent tasks are outlined in the employees' support forms, consistency is important. Having the organization's direction, strategy, goals, and measurable objectives in one published document will do much to provide that consistency. The plan becomes the focal point of the road map that adds purpose to the employee's work life.

# Chapter 8
# HUMAN RESOURCES

Organizations frequently devote much time and energy to developing a sophisticated strategic plan, yet give little or no consideration to their human resources. The leadership—with the customer foremost in mind in the strategic planning process—is the driver for the performance system. Achieving results depends on the organization's workforce working in and on organizational processes.

Category 5 of the Baldrige criteria addresses the approaches used with employees to achieve consistently effective performance. These approaches range from recruiting and selecting the best people for the organization to jobs that are designed to promote efficiency, agility, and employee development. The criteria ask for evidence that all employees are treated as business partners and have high value. Creativity, innovation, and energy directed toward the objectives for optimum results are what should be incorporated into employee incentive and recognition methods.

The core values of the Baldrige criteria stress a well-executed approach to employee learning, both on a personal level and in terms of how that translates into organizational learning. Visionary and caring leadership attempts to foster a learning culture aimed at achieving the highest levels of organizational performance.

The criteria ask for how the organization embeds learning in the way it operates. Learning experiences are not just other events that happen in addition to the normal day-to-day operations but become an integral part of daily work practiced at all levels of the organization, from executive leadership through all activity levels and into each employee's personal daily business activities. This environment provides increased opportunities for root-cause problem-solving and knowledge-sharing throughout the organization, as well as increased potential to affect change geared to performance. It also leads to learning circles that continuously incorporate new ideas and experiences.

Organizational and personal learning are closely interrelated and are synergistic in the sense that they dynamically contribute to one another. As an organization furthers its learning, the customer ultimately benefits through new, improved products and services with reduced errors and cost. Efficiency and effectiveness are enhanced, and the organization's overall responsiveness is improved.

The more organizational learning is supported and encouraged, the more opportunities are created for personal learning and practicing new skills. Personal learning increases employee satisfaction and versatility and enhances opportunities for employees to learn from one another and across functional areas, thus creating a more innovative environment. This adds value to both the employee and the organization; it also provides sustainability while positioning the organization to make a contribution.

A learning culture leads to organizational success. Thus, it is to an organization's advantage to place a high value on its employees. This requires commitment to more flexible work practices and consideration of a more diverse workforce that includes home life and personal needs. Leadership must openly demonstrate its commitment to providing recognition and compensation opportunities beyond what is normally offered, knowledge-sharing that is tied to organizational goals and objectives, and encouragement of risk-taking. Commitment is also demonstrated by moving training to a high priority and allocating resources to ensure that it happens. Placing a high value on the employees and demonstrating this attitude through actions in the transition to a performance-oriented organization results in a situation where both the employee and the organization win.

It's not enough merely to create a few initiatives for employees to learn more. That will not lead to a learning culture. The organization must develop a systematic approach to learning that permeates throughout. That systematic approach must then be deployed to all employees and linked to the goals, objectives, and action plans—i.e., tied closely to the strategic plan. Everyone's support form should directly link to action plans at the activity level, which in turn link to measurable short- and long-term objectives. This brings the organization's plan into everyone's work life, thus making it real for the work force and investing everyone in the organization's performance.

Change is inevitable, and it is occurring even more rapidly as technology both drives and leads us into the future. The rapidly changing environment for organizations has forced new ways of thinking and doing business. It has also left organizations with significant gaps, most of which affect or are affected by the workforce. This is especially true for organizations that have not embraced change and not taken advantage of the opportunities. Instead, they find themselves facing more work with fewer people. The workforce's technical skills are lagging, and resources for training have become scarce. Limited learning is occurring because everyone is just "hanging on" and skill sharing is a rarity because everyone is focused on tasks at hand.

This situation hampers performance. Human capital is the organization's greatest asset. What is done to develop that asset could very well be the key to the organization's future.

The vast majority of these issues cannot be dealt with, or perhaps even recognized, until the workforce becomes part of the planning process and part of the plan itself. Thus, a good strategic plan should have as one of its goals a clear statement about the human dimension. This organizational strategic plan goal should then become the mission of the human resource plan. This highlights leadership emphasis and importance placed on the workforce. This also greatly assists with organizational alignment and plan deployment, as well as giving everyone ownership while enhancing opportunities for organizational effectiveness and efficiency. This "employs" the plan—gives it viability—and, before a plan can be deployed throughout the organization, it must be employed.

Plan viability begins to take place when activities within the organization are assigned responsibility for achieving objectives. Activities, in turn, develop action plans for various teams that work on (and in processes that eventually provide) a product or service. From the human resource learning point of view, cross-functional teaming enhances learning and performance. Individuals with different skills and backgrounds form a team to bring a wide range of viewpoints to accomplish a task. They collaborate on common work issues and learn from one another. By operating in this manner, the workforce acquires greater knowledge of the complexity of the organization, business issues, and decision-making processes.

## GETTING STRATEGICALLY ALIGNED

The human resource plan must align the workforce with the organization's operations, goals, and objectives. This alignment must include more than the day-to-day work, but also the entire training and learning activity with the organization's big picture, i.e., the organization's business strategy. With today's dwindling resources and limited training dollars, training and learning must be linked to performance and results. This is a step-by-step process that involves building several components into the human resource plan that will assist bringing the workforce to a performance orientation:

1. *Review the organization's strategic plans and objectives.* With an integrated, deployed strategic plan, this review should be relatively easy. The important aspect of this review is to understand and confirm the linkage from objectives to the action plans and each employee's support forms.

2. *Determine how you contribute to agency plans and performance requirements.* What is each employee's core expertise? What do they each do best? Draw the relationship between each group's function and the organization's mission, goals, and critical success factors. Examine the ways the workforce is expected to perform and the outcomes produced. Are there potential new ways of leadership, support, or participation?

3. *Plan learning that supports the ability to contribute to organizational objectives.* Check the annual training plan to identify priority training programs that involve the employees. Determine if your organization has key positions in mission-critical areas that need continuing professional education. Find out if your employees can explain the organization's business strategies and the specifics of their own group's performance. Identify the competencies necessary to learning activities that build and strengthen them.

4. *Focus on learning that addresses areas of performance weakness.* Review the results of your organization's past performance using the results of the last self-assessment. What are the strengths and weaknesses, and where are improvements needed? Most importantly,

what learning can be done that will result in closing the gaps and providing the biggest payoff in measurable results?

5. *Create learning objectives that tie into business outcomes.* Whenever possible, set up learning that directly relates to your organization's critical success indicators. For example, if the organization is measuring cycle time, or output, or customer satisfaction, try to build learning activities or select training courses with related objectives. This helps ensure that the changes in your employees' performance are the ones desired and the ones measured.

6. *Support the transfer of learning into performance and results.* On average, less than half of what is learned is actually applied on the job. There is no automatic transfer of new skills into new job behavior. Leadership should foster an environment that gives employees a chance to practice new skills, values innovation, and rewards improved performance.

The human resource plan should take steps to integrate training and development with all the other human resource functions—recruitment, retention, creation of new positions, work systems, and performance management systems—to align total performance requirements with the organization's mission, goals, and objectives. When all human resource requirements and priorities have been integrated—i.e., when it is known what level of effort will be needed to move the agency forward for each career area, for retraining efforts, for introducing new systems, for reorganization and reinvention, for leadership—managers gain valuable information and insight into the kinds of learning that are strategic. This in turn promotes consistency across all managers striving to link learning to performance and results. Thus, the organization's strategic plan is employed and deployed. It now is viable and has organizational life.

## DEVELOPING A TRAINING PLAN

There is a straightforward way to avoid the "first-come, first-served" mentality that plagues many government organizations in allocating their training dollars: develop a training plan. Such a plan is extremely useful for organizing thinking about investments in formal training. With limited dollars to go around, managers need an aggregate perspective to find balance, establish priorities, and separate merely good ideas from business imperatives.

When learning and training are planned for as an organizational unit, powerful advantages are gained and results are obtained. With an annual training plan, you can:

• Train to major performance gaps existing in the organization

• Make a connection to the organization's strategic objectives up front

• Target training areas of greatest need and biggest payoff

• Find the best and most cost-effective ways to get training.

The basic steps in developing a training plan for your organizational unit are:

1. *Define learning needs linked to strategic plans.* Identify your contribution to your organization's mission, strategic goals, and measurable objectives. If there are gaps in your performance relative to the goals and objectives of the organization, this is an indication of where to start. Check into the introduction of new technology and new ways of doing business, both internally and externally. Technology both pushes and creates opportunities for organizations to move into the future.

2. *Review other information to identify needs.* Organizational performance in relation to learning needs can be highlighted by employees, customers, and other stakeholders. To ensure that career programs are preserved, professional education requirements must be clearly outlined. A determination must be made whether the organization has full knowledge of and is oriented to the strategic plan.

3. *Validate your list of needs.* Ensure that all the needs are learning needs and determine whether training is appropriate to meet those needs. Does accomplishing the training goals contribute to the overall solution? The learning requirements should be ranked in order of importance to mission accomplishment and in terms of what should be funded first.

4. *Determine the best strategies.* Make "business case" decisions based on your resources (time, money, and agency programs and assistance available to you) and potential payoff, especially as it relates to overall organizational performance. Consider formal learning options with the following alternatives:

- Classroom vs. on-the-job

- Onsite vs. offsite

- Customized vs. off-the-shelf

- Contractor vs. in-house instructor

- Technology-based delivery (computer-based training, satellite broadcasts) vs. classroom instructor delivery.

Consider informal learning strategies for individual and organizational learning. The first step in this process is learning the performance management system your organization is working with.

5. *Identify potential sources for learning.* Numerous sources offer potential learning opportunities. Recognized vendors, partnerships with other organizations, and colleges and universities are good places to get started. Also check into possible collaborations with other organizations.

6. *Estimate costs.* Include tuition, travel, per diem, facilities, contracts, and special equipment in the cost estimate. The costs must be weighed against projected costs for different strategies and sources. The cost data must be retained so returns on investment as related to organizational performance can be calculated.

7. *Set priorities.* Select the critical areas that most need addressing, especially as they relate to the mission. Then prioritize to the areas that will provide the biggest potential payoffs. Finally, determine the organizational funding level and where the line must be drawn.

8. *Determine how to evaluate results.* It's all about results. Identify the measurable outcomes you expect to have and link outcomes and the business strategy for your organization. Finally, build the organizational scorecard in as simple a manner as possible to track progress.

9. *Share your plan with employees, customers, and other managers in your organization.* A plan—whether it's a strategic plan or a training plan—only has value when it is deployed throughout the organization. Generate understanding and promote "buy-in" of the plan as well as leadership by example by demonstrating commitment to learning for results.

10. *Execute, deploy, and monitor.* Assign responsibility to implement the plan. Assign a person to collect evaluation data, including data for baseline measures. This will enable you to track your group's contribution to the agency's strategic goals. Document success stories to use as models for the rest of the organization. Make additions and adjustments, i.e., calibrate the plan as necessary. Finally, continuously provide opportunities for employees to apply their learning on the job.

Remember that the training program should be designed to meet the performance requirements outlined in the strategic plan. At the same time, the organization is building a learning culture—one that shares knowledge and promotes and rewards innovation. This is investment in human capital.

## CREATING A LEARNING CULTURE

A learning culture doesn't just happen because someone wishes it. All levels of the organization, especially the managers of processes, are crucial to the process of learning and the development of the learning culture. A learning culture has as its beginning systems thinking that promotes communication and the sharing of knowledge across traditional boundaries. As an organization adopts a systematic approach in the performance journey, efforts should be made to focus on establishing a learning culture.

Managers are in a key position to involve employees in setting both activity and personal goals that contribute to the overall human capital investment. As the systematic approach develops, opportunities emerge to structure the chance to learn, provide tools and ideas, and offer support. This is where meaningful change occurs.

Organizations are changing rapidly and on a global level. No longer is it desirable to have just one marketable skill.

The value of being multi-skilled is that more learning is brought to the organization, and employees can move more easily across functional boundaries and to different work processes. Employees who are motivated will emerge to lead work teams, work projects, and cross-functional teams. Once employees are immersed in the performance management system, they will be more proactive in writing their own individual development plans, setting goals for themselves, and building the pathway to achieve those goals.

A learning culture creates the initiative whereby employees seek training and development programs, as well as assignments that are both career-enhancing and focused on results for the organization. These employees soon develop a mentorship mentality and serve as coaches to those less senior or who have greater learning needs. Problem-solving shifts from reactive to employing organization learning strategies geared toward preventing problems and situations that adversely affect performance.

The challenge for managers is to promulgate this culture by creating an environment in which employees feel free to make suggestions, take risks, and actively seek out learning activities. Senior leaders must encourage work and communication across organizational boundaries and reward and offer incentives to the workforce to experiment and innovate. It is only through an open climate that encourages an interchange of ideas and information that learning initiatives that produce results can be identified.

The learning environment must be sustained if it is to become a true culture. This can be accomplished by ensuring the linkage of the human capital dimension to the organization's strategic planning process, i.e., the development of the mission, vision, and values. The human dimension must be recognized as a critical success factor for the organization and treated as such throughout the performance journey. Investment in human capital that includes training and development that support strategic organizational objectives must become totally integrated into the planning process—not an afterthought that simply uses whatever is left over in the budget.

Integrated learning leads to performance, so flexible structures and processes must be designed that facilitate learning as employees work in the organization's processes. Measuring the effectiveness of training and development as they relate to overall organizational performance is essential for sustaining a learning culture. Every employee should feel ownership of the organization's performance and share in the results.

# Chapter 9

# PROCESS IDENTIFICATION AND MANAGEMENT

An organization has little hope of continuously improving performance if it hasn't identified its key processes. Improvement in performance is highly dependent upon becoming more efficient and more effective. Efficiency has to do with removing roadblocks and barriers to streamlined operations, whether in the area of production or service. Effectiveness deals with optimizing the results of the organization given what's critical for success and based on measurable objectives.

The first order of business in designing the organization in accordance with its key processes is to analyze the mission and make sure that the key processes include all aspects of mission accomplishment. Once that's ensured, how the processes are to be managed must be outlined. The key processes to be managed must be effectively designed, and they must have a prevention orientation, a linkage to supplies and partners, a built-in operational performance evaluation for continuous improvement, and organizational learning. The question to continually ask is: Is the organization optimally designed for performance? Arbitrarily selecting processes that seem to link to mission or appear to be what the organization spends the majority of the time doing is not the way to go.

This is all about getting better and improving results. Caution must be exercised to avoid regressing to business as usual. The organization must be viewed as one overall, cohesive system made up of various connective parts focused on performance. The key organizational processes must be selected with this concept foremost in mind.

What are the main components of a process that optimize performance? Flexibility, reducing cost, and reducing the cycle time for delivering products or services to the customer are ingredients for efficiency and effectiveness. In today's fast-paced environment, flexibility is crucial. How well is the organization positioned to adapt responsibly and quickly to changing customer requirements? A change in public policy, national strategy, or economic environment, for example, can drastically alter an organization's strategy, and even its mission. These changes can have great impact on how an organization determines its customers, the customer's requirements, and how it designs its processes to optimally meet those requirements. Flexibility may mean partnerships, outsourcing decisions, and agreements with contractors and suppliers to optimize results. Since we are identifying the processes that are key for organizational success, it's critical to select key measures for these requirements so that performance can be improved.

The initial question "What does your organization do?" must be answered. The reason is that the organization must be designed around the customer requirements and the key processes needed to meet those requirements. This will vary by organization because each organization has different customer segments and thus different requirements. Factors to be considered in designing requirements include safety, long-range performance, impact on the environment and impacted community, supplies and partner capability, sustainability, and regulatory and legal considerations. This will involve (at least in the beginning) detailed mapping of those processes in order to gain a full appreciation and understanding of how the organization should function. Once the key processes are mapped, they can be reengineered or recalibrated to improve efficiency and performance.

## PROCESS DUPLICATION

How an organization designs itself around processes requires a good look by senior executive leadership. The management harness for process management and how it is designed has much to do with how efficient that organization is. Clearly identifying key processes at the onset helps prevent duplication later. That means that processes can now be designed to specifically address requirements and be built to support one another.

This is in marked contrast to having processes that are parallel to one another and duplicate functions. Thus, by conducting a thorough process design analysis, duplication can be avoided, and many similar functions and processes can be consolidated. Obviously, this requires a description of the process, the specific requirements, how performance is measured relative to the process, and how performance is maintained. Measurement points in the process should be identified as early in the process as possible to minimize cost and error. Remember, the purpose is to design the prevention of problems and errors into the system as opposed to reacting to problems later, which is wasteful and inefficient.

## STANDARD LEVELS OF PERFORMANCE

An organization that's serious about customer satisfaction and performance results will establish a standard of performance for the total organization. This standard should be established based on customer requirements and be communicated to all areas of the organization, thus initiating standard-setting behavior for each activity. These standards lose their meaning, however, if customer input is not an ongoing consideration. Therefore, the organization's key processes should be designed to meet those requirements established by customer input. If the requirements or standards are not being met, then the process must be reviewed for applicability, efficiency, and effectiveness.

## IN-PROCESS MEASUREMENTS AND CUSTOMER INTERACTIONS

It may not be best to wait until the results are in before the process is calibrated to improve performance. Keeping the customer in the game is crucial. The first question to ask is: Is the process designed so that critical points are identified to determine if the process is on track to produce the desired results? The key processes should allow for critical points for measurement, observation, and customer interaction. These interaction and review activities should occur at the earliest points possible in the processes to minimize problems and costs that may result from deviations from expected performance.

When deviations from standard or expected performance levels occur, corrective action can be taken to restore process performance to the original requirement and specification. This corrective action could involve several aspects of the organization (e.g., technical adjustments may have to be made, the workforce may have to be reallocated). This is not a reactive measure, but a focus on the root cause or source of the deviation, thus solving the problem permanently. Not only is the corrective action applied to the process in question, but it can be shared across the organization for use in other processes.

## PROCESS IMPROVEMENT AND PERFORMANCE

What this is all about is improving performance—not only to improve quality for the customers but also to improve organizational performance. In addition to making root cause corrections, many process improvement initiatives can be employed. For example, successful strategies can be shared across the organization. Process mapping can also be used to identify impediments or roadblocks to efficiency.

Benchmarking may be of great value as well. Using someone else's ideas in process design and implementation is an efficient and effective way to improve performance. Initiatives such as these can lead to redesigning the organization's processes and thus improving performance.

## SUPPORT PROCESSES

Support processes do just that: support the key processes of the organization. They are primarily internal to the organization and must meet particular organizational requirements. Those internal requirements are in large part determined by the overall organizational requirements. Support processes (which may include finance and accounting, technology support, personnel, and administration assistance) must be linked to the key processes if performance requirements are to be met. How well these support processes are linked to what the organization actually produces in goods and services, and how well they're integrated internally, determines the effectiveness and efficiency of the organization.

The same process improvement initiatives can and should be employed with the support processes as with the key processes. The possibilities for improvement are endless.

## SUPPLIER AND PARTNER PROCESSES

Your organization may have developed standards and requirements for performance, with expected results. It makes no sense to purchase goods or services from suppliers or partners that are below the standards you've set for your organization. Why pay someone to provide inferior quality? Therefore, it is imperative that your organization's requirements and standards be clearly stated and serve as the driving force or baseline criteria that your organization uses in purchasing and partnering for goods and services.

The relationship and communication methods that are in place enable your supplier/partner to understand fully what you require and how well it performed on the basis of those requirements. This is no time to dwell on the status quo. Innovation and out-of-the-box thinking will help lead to unique and proactive relationships with partners and suppliers, which will in turn lead to high levels of performance. Information technology can create whole new ways of thinking and put whole new perspectives on supplier and partner relationships. How this information technology is used for improved performance for your organization and for suppliers can definitely lead to a win-win situation.

Process is defined as a systematic series of actions directed to some end—a specific, continuous action or operation. A series of actions connotes a linkage to a set of activities designed for the purpose of producing a product or service for a customer. It's in this design of sequence where a predetermined desired outcome can begin to be shaped and controlled so that these results achieve or surpass the desired level of quality or standard of service.

An organization will have a great number of processes, and while identifying and outlining them is a first step, how the processes are organized and managed as part of an overall performance system is key. While a specific process is designed to produce a specific result, how an organization manages its processes is the main component of performance, i.e., achieving the desired results. Process management from a total organizational perspective is integral to the development of an overall system.

The system that the organization develops and operates in must determine those processes that are key to its existence. These key or crucial processes form the operational framework that creates the opportunity for evaluation and learning. The development of learning and continuous improvement cycles (i.e., plan–do–check–act) can now take place and facilitate organizational growth and maturity.

## PROCESS MAPPING

Process mapping is a graphic representation, or flowchart, of the steps involved in a process. (Processes can be shown as one consecutive operation, but actually involve several subprocesses involving several people conducting the operation simultaneously.) A graphic depiction of a process helps provide a clearer understanding of the various steps and pathways involved in the process. A map allows viewing inconsistencies, bottlenecks, and redundancies. This ability to view the flow of an operation from beginning to end enables opportunities for improvement to emerge—and ultimately leads to increasing customer satisfaction.

Inputs and outputs are generally depicted by parallelograms linked to the step where they are used. Tasks, steps, or activities within the process are symbolized by rectangles, and decision points are usually diamonds. Start and stop points are depicted by rounded rectangles. Arrows are generally used to link symbols and to indicate direction and sequence. The example in Chapter 6 (Figure 6-3) depicts a simple process map outlining the steps that could occur in calling a friend. Please note the start point and end point and the various options for direction that occur at the diamonds.

Ritz-Carlton has twice won the Malcolm Baldrige National Quality Award for service. This is in large part due to the hotel's attention to detail in all operations and how it specifically maps each step of its operations to optimize efficiency and effectiveness to ultimately satisfy the customer.

Process mapping can be very beneficial. It clearly depicts the steps involved in any activity, requiring a start point and a finish point; thus, everyone involved has an opportunity to see what's involved in achieving a desired result and to refine or make improvements to the process. This is how efficiency is realized, and it is where analysis for efficiency begins.

# Chapter 10

# PERFORMANCE MANAGEMENT SYSTEM

The main purpose of the Malcolm Baldrige National Quality Award criteria is performance excellence. This is accomplished by using the criteria as a basis for organizational self-assessments, which allow organizations to look at themselves through the lens of a strategy-driven performance system. Once the framework is in place and the organization has developed some basic understanding of the system and its components, the performance practices and capabilities can be readily employed.

The organization can continue to use the criteria as a working tool to understand and manage performance. The organization can design itself for continuous improvement and use the system to guide planning and training. The criteria are designed to help organizations enhance and improve that performance by delivering ever-improving value to customers as well as improving overall organizational effectiveness and capabilities.

## CORE VALUES AND CONCEPTS

Every organization, regardless of what business it is in, is interested in results and performance. The criteria provide that framework and are built on a set of core values and concepts (see Chapter 2) that provide a foundation for integrating the requirements to attain performance excellence. It is imperative that the core values and concepts be understood as the foundation of the total performance system. They provide the overall philosophy that must be embraced if a performance management system is to be established and maintained. These core values must continually be emphasized, reinforced, and made a part of the organizational culture.

## ALIGNING FOR PERFORMANCE

The performance system, composed of seven categories (see Chapter 2), must function as a system—that is, all the categories must work together as components or parts to achieve results. The better the parts function together and in relationship to one another, the better the results.

Managing these components successfully requires synthesis and alignment. This goes beyond simply aligning according to the goals and objectives of the strategic plan and deciding what's critical. It means looking at the organization as a whole, determining the basic reason the organization exists and what's most important.

Alignment also refers to the key organizational linkages outlined by the requirements of the Baldrige criteria. Alignment means that senior leaders are focused on the future, have imagined that future by creating a vision for the organization, and have developed a direction and strategies for the organization while fully incorporating the customer's requirements.

The organization itself must align with the leadership triad. That alignment occurs with the linkage of the key strategies to the key organizational processes, i.e., those processes that are integral to the mission (see Chapter 4). The human dimension is what makes the organization operationally viable as the work force works in and on processes in teams and as process owners (see Chapter 8). Alignment of resources to address and engage in this systematic performance, i.e., resourcing the plan and strategic direction, furnishes the fuel for operation. How well that system is operating is demonstrated in results.

## MEASURING PROGRESS

Results and the performance required to achieve them have no meaning or relativity without a means of measurement or keeping score. Category 4, Information and Analysis, is the "brain center" of the organization, which essentially transforms the vast amount of data that the organization generates into more usable information, even knowledge, for leadership to view, monitor, and analyze. How the measurement system is designed and what measures are selected are the major components of an effective measurement system.

As noted, alignment is key because it forms the basic architecture in which the measurement system is used. The strategic plan is the map that contains the objectives, and the metrics must be derived from that plan. It makes no sense to measure something that's not in the plan, and, conversely, everything in the plan should be measured. Also, it is helpful to have measurement as part of comparative information, or standards. How well is the organization doing in relation to a predetermined level of performance? The established standards for the organization or program must link to the purpose of the program, i.e., why we exist.

Measurement and metrics can be a burden and can cause much frustration if not properly explained and presented in the context of the bigger picture and the overall organization. That is one reason it is so important to have linkage to the strategic plan.

Employees will naturally rebel at doing things a whole new way, especially if it looks like a lot of work. The reporting system should minimize the reporting burden by maximizing the use of existing data and making it as automated as possible. Discard any metrics that aren't needed and used for decisions. All sorts of things can be measured, but if something has no relationship to what's core to the purpose of the organization, measuring it serves no purpose. So start simple and use an existing framework that seems to work. Don't create something that's foreign to everyone. Getting started is what's most important; adjustments can be made later.

The measurement system must take into account specifics about daily operations, i.e., the efficiencies of supporting processes, as well as overall organizational performance. This is when it is important to have a thorough understanding of progress.

In the past, most government organizations viewed progress solely as meeting the requirements of the stated mission and responding to the various tasks that happened to be generated on a regular basis. Within a performance management system, progress is redefined. It includes moving forward on at least two different planes. The organization is no longer functioning on a single dimension, but rather is operating on two or more dimensions—on a much more global basis. The first consideration is how well the organization is continuing to become more responsive to the customer while increasing its efficiency and effectiveness, especially in light of the established objectives. Progress also means how well the organization is accomplishing its goals and objectives while moving toward the vision. At minimum, progress now includes an operational and a strategic aspect.

A performance measurement system that demonstrates the relationship between specific process efficiencies and overall performance (which includes progress toward a vision) is well into the continuous performance improvement cycle. Just having a system in place is not enough, however. How that system is working, i.e., how well the parts of the system are working together to yield results, is of primary importance. The system must continually be reviewed for reliability and kept current with changing needs.

The President's budget director, Mitch Daniels, Jr., has stated that the executive branch of the U.S. government has developed a management scorecard that will be used to rate each agency's performance. The budgeting process and the allocation of dollars will consider the agency's performance prior to finalizing the budget. Further, the scorecard will clearly depict how well the respective agencies are meeting the President's goals. These goals are outlined as standards for success in the areas of: Human Capital, Expanding E-Government, Competitive Sourcing, Financial Management, and Integrating Budget and Performance. The standards, by area, are as follows:

### Human Capital

- Agency human capital strategy is aligned with mission, goals, and organizational objectives: (1) integrated into budget and strategic plans; (2) consistent with OPM's human capital balanced scorecard; and (3) complies with standards for internal accountability systems to ensure effective merit-based human resource management.

- Agency has a citizen-centered organizational structure that is delayered and oriented toward performing the mission assigned to it.

- Agency (1) sustains a high-performing workforce that is continuously improving in productivity; (2) strategically uses existing personnel flexibilities, tools, and technology; and (3) implements effective succession plans.

- No skill gaps/deficiencies exist in mission-critical occupations.

- Agency differentiates between high and low performers through appropriate incentives and rewards.

Changes in agency workforce skill mix and organizational structure reflect increased emphasis on e-government and competitive sourcing.

### Expanding E-Government

- Strategic value: All major system investments have a business case that meets the requirements of OMB Circular A-11 (Exhibit 53, Form 300).

- IT program performance: On average, all major IT projects operating within 90 percent of Form 300 cost, schedule, and performance target.

- E-government and GPEA implementation show department-wide progress or participation in multi-agency initiative in three areas:

    (1) Citizen one-stop service delivery integrated through Firstgov.gov, cross-agency call centers, and offices or service centers.

    (2) Minimize burden on business by reusing data previously collected or using ebXML or other open standards to receive transmissions.

    (3) Intergovernmental: Deploying E-grants or Geospatial Information one-stop.

- Obtaining productivity improvements by implementing customer relationship management, supply chain management, enterprise resource management, or knowledge management best practices.

## Competitive Sourcing

- Completed public-private or direct conversion competition on not less than 5 percent of the full-time equivalent employees listed on the approved FAIR Act inventories.

- Competitions and direct conversions conducted pursuant to approved competition plan.

- Commercial reimbursable support service agreements between agencies competed with the private sector on a recurring basis.

## Financial Management

- Financial management systems meet federal financial management system requirements and applicable federal accounting and transaction standards as reported by the agency head.

- Accurate and timely financial information.

- Integrated financial and performance management systems supporting day-to-day operations.

- Unqualified and timely audit opinion on the annual financial statements; no material internal control weaknesses reported by the auditors.

## Integrating Budget and Performance

- Integrated planning/evaluation and budget staff work with program managers to create an integrated plan/budget and to monitor and evaluate its implementation.

- Streamlined, clear, integrated agency plan/budget sets forth outcome goals, output targets, and resources requested in context of past results.

- Budget accounts, staff, and specifically program/activities are aligned to support achieving program targets.

- Full budgetary cost is charged to mission accounts and activities. Cost of outputs and programs is integrated with performance in budget requests and execution.

- Agency has documented program effectiveness. Analyses shows how program outputs and policies affect desired outcomes. Agency systematically applies performance to budget and can demonstrate how program results inform budget decisions.

The scorecard will show spending priorities by agency and display the management scorecard in green to show that goals are being met, yellow to show that some are being accomplished, and red to show that the standards are not being met and improvement is still needed. It should be noted that *any* item not being met in an area would cause a red light. (See Figure 10-1, Federal Government's Management Scorecard.)

The initial assessment has been completed, and it was no surprise that almost none of the standards were met and the scorecard was nearly all red. This is only the beginning, however, and is a part of an ever-evolving performance improvement process. Daniels acknowledges that it will be difficult to deploy throughout the federal government as programs may have problems identifying what is a fair measure of program performance, but he goes on to say that difficulty can't be an excuse for ignorance.

It is appropriate that a warning be issued at this point. This executive branch management scorecard with its core criteria

**Figure 10-1.** Federal Government's Management Scorecard

**2001 Baseline Evaluation**

| Agency | Human Capital | Competitive Sourcing | Financial Management | E-Government | Budget/ Performance Integration (R=red light Y=yellow light G=green light) |
|---|---|---|---|---|---|
| Agriculture | R | R | R | Y | R |
| Commerce | R | R | R | Y | R |
| Defense | R | R | R | R | R |
| Education | R | R | R | R | R |
| Energy | R | R | R | R | R |
| Environmental Protection Agency | R | R | R | Y | Y |
| Health and Human Services | R | R | R | R | R |
| Housing and Urban Development | R | R | R | R | R |
| Interior | R | R | R | R | R |
| Justice | R | R | R | R | R |
| Labor | Y | R | R | Y | R |
| State | R | R | R | R | R |
| Transportation | R | R | R | R | Y |
| Treasury | R | R | R | R | R |
| Veterans Affairs | R | R | R | R | R |
| Agency for International Development | R | R | R | R | R |
| Corps of Engineers | R | R | R | R | R |
| Federal Emergency Management Agency | R | R | R | R | R |
| General Services Administration | R | R | Y | R | R |
| NASA | R | R | Y | R | R |

*continues*

**Figure 10-1.** Federal Government's Management Scorecard

| Agency | Human Capital | Competitive Sourcing | Financial Management | E-Government | Budget/ Performance Integration (R=red light Y=yellow light G=green light) |
|---|---|---|---|---|---|
| National Science Foundation | R | R | G | Y | R |
| Office of Management and Budget | R | R | R | R | R |
| Office of Personnel Management | Y | R | R | Y | R |
| Small Business Administration | R | R | Y | Y | Y |
| Smithsonian | R | R | R | Y | R |
| Social Security Administration | Y | R | Y | Y | R |

could be viewed as a self-contained performance management system. This is definitely not the case. This scorecard in no way justifies the abolishment of the performance criteria that were necessary to produce the information on the scorecard. The scorecard reflects the results of an agency employing performance criteria (Baldrige or the President's Quality Award criteria) to meet the President's goals and standards. Another way to look at it is that the Baldrige criteria develop, evaluate, and continuously improve the system that must be in place to deliver the results found on the scorecard.

Another good example of measuring progress and incorporating functional and strategic elements of an organization into a single set of metrics can be found in the U.S. Army's evolving Well-Being Program. The Department of Defense is one of the "gauges" on the President's dashboard or scorecard, and the Army, in one if its programs, has begun the process of developing an objective measurement system.

Well-being depicts the human dimension of Army transformation over the next 20 years, and is linked strategically to quality of life and readiness of the Force in general. The challenge was to measure quality of life and its improvement in the future and at the same time demonstrate the impact that this state of well-being was having on readiness.

The measurement architecture the Army established to measure the progress of well-being is called the Well-Being Status Report, or WBSR. A "scorecard" of the Army's human dimension shows the status and progress of all the quality-of-life aspects for all Army personnel, uniformed and civilian, and their families. Further, it provides a gauge on the Army's senior leadership dashboard as to how well-being is contributing to Force readiness.

Following the "cascading" model of alignment from goal–objectives–actions–tasks, a simple formula was developed that yields a result or an easy-to-read rating. For example, metrics (f) = objective status/compared to a standard = progress. Therefore, if (f) is fitness facilities, and the objective status is 60% of the standard (which is to have state-of-the-art fitness facilities at every Army installation), then a "progress score" is readily available.

It is important to keep in mind that metrics are assigned at the objective level, and the tasks and actions feed into those objectives. The objectives are stable and should not change, nor should the standards. The only exception is when the objective has been met or the standards exceeded. Then, and only then, should the bar be raised. The actions, and especially the tasks, can be modified whenever overall objective performance is reviewed, as long as they are changed with the caveat that their contribution to the objective is being optimized. Fully using technology, progress can be viewed on a real-time basis.

Objectives can also be aggregated to demonstrate progress for a particular category. For example, if the category is facilities, then objectives that have been developed for fitness facilities, recreation, barracks, family housing, etc., can be consolidated to depict a facility "score" for a particular installation, or, for that matter, the whole Army. Further, a gauge could be developed on the dashboard of senior executive leadership that would indicate how facility status is affecting overall readiness. A powerful tool is one that can provide real-time access to status, show progress, and, over time, give some measure of predictability.

## ANALYSIS AND REVIEW OF PERFORMANCE

Having a means for senior leadership to monitor and analyze the organization's overall health and maturity is crucial if the strategies are to be used as pathways to the vision. The requirement to conduct performance reviews is in category 1.2 of the Baldrige criteria. The strategies may have to be altered or adjusted as the information dictates. Facts and data, in and of themselves, have little meaning outside the context of a prioritized, systematic setting.

This performance review forum is where the actual performance and its analysis are linked with the organization's strategic plan. This linkage ensures that decision-making is based on relevant information. Relevance, as it pertains to performance, is both operational and strategic and is directly related to the maturity and sophistication of the measurement system (i.e., how accurately do the results portray what is actually occurring in the organization?) Depending on the sophistication of the system, that information becomes knowledge.

Overall organizational performance reviews enhance leadership's ability to see cause-and-effect relationships between various process actions. This is part of the value of a total performance system. Further, there is increased opportunity for an analytical basis for decision-making as priorities can be reviewed for resourcing and changed as appropriate.

Performance means more than progress toward goals and vision. Performance also means how well the organization is functioning in the here and now. Therefore, the analysis portion of performance reviews is focused on examining the quality and effectiveness of the operation. This examination or analysis might include:

- How product and service improvement correlates with customer satisfaction and retention

- Effectiveness of problem resolution

- Trends in key operational performance indicators such as productivity, cycle time, and defect levels

- Relationships between employee learning and workforce performance

- Cost savings derived from safety, absenteeism, and turnover

- Cost of operation and comparison with competitors

- Process improvements and efficiencies as they relate to operational costs.

Performance reviews could also include a condensed environmental scan and a quick look at the organization's strengths, weaknesses, opportunities, and threats. While this is certainly a major item for strategic planning offsites, it may be valuable to set aside a little time to do this at performance reviews, especially when the organization is in the early stages of transition and is establishing a performance system.

## PERFORMANCE REVIEW SESSIONS

As the performance management system is developing and maturing, the performance review sessions are a great opportunity for senior leadership to instill learning and facilitate change. Review sessions should be held more frequently in the beginning, at least quarterly, so that major gaps can be readily addressed and the performance improvement philosophy remains viable and gains momentum. These review sessions should be mandatory for senior leaders and directors, as this is at the heart of what the leaders of the organization ought to be doing.

The reviews should be scheduled for at least four hours, and everyone should have a copy of the strategic plan. It also should be determined in advance as to how much of the plan, i.e., which goals and objectives, will be reviewed. A specific activity such as the strategic planning team or the resource manager should be designated as early as responsible for gathering the information for the review and method of presentation. It is very important to have a prescribed format that maximizes relevance to everything in the organization.

## CHARTOLOGY

As much information as possible should be provided on one review chart. The chart should tell the story. One of the best available formats to tell the story on one page is the "quad chart." The chart is divided into four areas or quadrangles, each providing information and collectively painting a comprehensive picture of performance. (See Figure 10-2, The Quad Chart.) As the quad charts are being developed, consideration should be given to using the charts as part of the organization's "dashboard." Leadership needs to have a quick view of how the organization is functioning, and, if the quad charts can be developed with the thought of creating a "gauge" on that dashboard, then the system can be developed much more rapidly.

The four quads on the chart are:

**Figure 10-2.** The Quad Chart

| | |
|---|---|
| **Goal:** Supports accomplishment of the vision. Broad, action and results-oriented descriptions.<br><br>**Agency strategy:** How the goal is to be accomplished.<br><br>**Long-term objective:** Supports accomplishment of the goal. Must be measurable. Has three components: *quality standard, specific date to be accomplished,* and *lead office.*<br><br>**Short-term objective:** Supports accomplishment of the long-term objective. Must also be measurable. | **Programmed/current status:** This is the metrics piece that measures the long-term objective or the supporting short-term objective. Show easy-to-read graph, chart, or timeline of target relative to suspense date. Include target or standard and applicable benchmark or competitive comparison. Indicate direction of "good" progress. |
| **Rating:** Red, Green, or Amber<br><br>**Actions this quarter:** List key actions that were taken during this reporting period.<br><br><br>*(Operationally define what red, green, and amber mean.)* | **Future actions:** Programmed actions or tasks that still need to be done to accomplish long-term or short-term objective.<br><br>**Inhibitors:** Any known circumstances or actions that will inherit or prevent accomplishment of the long-term or short-term objective (e.g., decisions, funding, time) |

- **Upper Left-Hand Corner**—This section of the chart outlines the pathway from the organizational goal, long-term objective, short-term objective, and strategy for how the objectives are to be met in the accomplishment of the goal. It is an immediate reference to what the organization is doing now as it conducts its journey.

- **Upper Right-Hand Corner**—This is the actual metrics piece that measures progress toward the long-term objective or the supporting short-term objective. What is shown is an easy-to-read graph, chart, or timeline of targets relative to the required date of completion. Included is the standard or quality level at which the objective is to be accomplished. For reference, an applicable competitive comparison from a like process, product, or service is included to depict how the organization compares with other organizations demonstrating superior performance. Finally, some indicator of the "good" or desirable direction is important to show whether the organization is headed in the right direction.

- **Bottom Left-Hand Corner**—This section indicates whether the organization is moving along at expected performance levels or is outside of performance limits (e.g., lagging behind expected timelines, not providing the product or service at the desired level of quality). The rating can be depicted using a color code such as red, amber, or green, but each color must be operationally defined for clarity purposes. Any "reds" would certainly merit leadership attention, as they may well indicate a performance problem.

- **Bottom Right-Hand Corner**—Specific future actions or tasks that need to be done to accomplish the organizational objective are listed here. This gives leadership some indication of the level of effort required by the activity or the overall organization. Also included in this section are any inhibitors to performance. These are any known circumstances or actions that will prevent accomplishment of the objective, such as funding, human resources, or higher level priorities. This will enable leadership to take actions as required to remove obstacles and to provide enablers to meet the objective.

Each quad chart is essentially data that can form a "gauge" whereby an area of the organization or a component of the "system" can be reviewed and monitored for performance. (See Figure 10-3, Sample Performance Reviews.)

Certainly it is not necessary to review the entire organizational system at each quarterly review, but it can be done if desired. A better approach may be to determine by priority: What are the most important indicators or critical factors for success for the organization for that year or that quarter? Has something emerged that requires a prioritized review now? These various components contribute to the makeup of the system itself—those parts that are vital to sustaining operations and thus meeting the customer requirements. Knowledge about where those components are located and what it means for your particular organization from a global perspective forms the systematic baseline from which improve-

## Figure 10-3. Sample Performance Reviews

**Goal:** Maximize the ability of the installations to execute their mission.

**Agency Strategy:** Champion installation BASOPS issues.

**LTO:** 1.A.1. Reduce Class A accident rate by 10% by FY 03. (SAFE)

**STO:** Evaluate level of Risk Management training in the schoolhouse/leader training.

**Programmed/Current Status:**

CLASS A-C Accident Rate/1000

| | | | | |
|---|---|---|---|---|
| 4 | | | | |
| 3 | | | | |
| 2 | | | | |
| 1 | | | | |
| 0 | | | | |
| | FY96 | FY97 | FY98 | |

→ MDI  → AMV  → Total

---

**Rating: AMBER**

**Actions This Quarter:**

• Quarterly review accident statistics (current levels, trends, Roadmap, safety memos).
• Increase Risk Management Training of leaders.
• Ensure safety is included as part of the commanders special staff.
• Commanders safety assessment.
• Safety Home Page/Bulletin.
• CG-Commanders Safety Assessment.

**Future Actions:**

• Study impact of waivers and review of high and medium risk training.
• Accident Prevention Awards.

**Inhibitors:**

• Do not have a reporting requirement for the status of Risk Management programs.

---

**Goal:** Maximize the ability of the installations to execute their missions.

**Agency Strategy:** Champion installation BASOPS issues.

**LTO:** 1.A.4. Conduct the Winning the Infrastructure War (WTIW) to achieve affordability by FY 05. (ENGR)

**STO:** Demolish 2.7 MSF in FY 99.

**Programmed/Current Status:**

Demolition

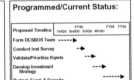

■ Goal ▨ Act □ Proj

---

**Rating: AMBER**

**Actions This Quarter:**

• FY 98 goal achieved.

• FY 99-03 plan defended to ACSIM.

• FY 1999 OMA funding letter included $36.6M for demolition.

**Future Actions:**

• Distribute FY 99 funds to installations.
• Review March 30 IFS data.

**Inhibitors:**

• Pressure to divert funds to other bills.
• Timeliness of fund distribution.
• Lack of HQDA support for renovation costs.

---

**Goal:** Maximize the ability of the installations to execute their missions.

**Agency Strategy:** Champion installation BASOPS issues.

**LTO:** 1.A.13. Identify each installation s wastewater & drinking water compliance requirements (for installations not planning to privatize the function), and program a buy-out by FY05. (ENVR)

**STO:** Develop resource requirements to prepare and implement a plan of action. Form DCSBOS cross-functional team to monitor and direct activities.

**Programmed/Current Status:**

| | FY99 | FY00 FY05 |
|---|---|---|
| Proposed Timeline: | 1stQtr 2ndQtr 3rdQtr 4thQtr | |
| Form DCSBOS Team | ----▶ | |
| Conduct Inst Survey | ▶ | |
| Validate/Prioritize Rqmts | --▶ | |
| Develop Investment Strategy | ---▶ | |
| Budget, Fund, & Execute | ------▶ | |

---

**Rating: AMBER**

**Actions This Quarter:**

• Developed Long Term Objective.

• Developed proposed timeline.

• Completed first scrub on water and wastewater compliance requirements during the Environmental Program Requirements (EPR) review.

**Future Actions:**

• Meet with involved Directorates.
• Identify team members.
• Work to flesh out general plan.
• Begin time/resource estimates.

**Inhibitors:**

• None identified at present.

ments can be made. The alternative is the status quo—or worse, regression. In today's environment, that may well mean extinction.

The strategic plan is the roadmap to the organization's future. The plan should contain as part of its infrastructure the information system that will measure progress to the plan. Therefore, the performance reviews, the design of the information, and the strategic plan should all be tied together. While it is important that this linkage exist, it may be unrealistic to review the entire plan every quarter.

The strategic plan is the simple, all-inclusive document that forms the basis for the performance (i.e., management) process. The quarterly reviews are snapshots in time when the organization assesses its progress overall and reports its progress on selected objectives that require attention. The process should include management of the entire plan and steer the course of the organization.

Reviewing objectives on a quarterly basis may leave gaps in the review process. Some objectives may need more frequent monitoring. For example, selected objectives may be crucial to some situation existing organizationally or to an important customer or stakeholder issue. Some of these selected objectives may merit monthly or even weekly tracking. These items are still a part of the plan and the review process, but merit a higher level of attention and leadership visibility. Items that are critical for the system's successful operation may be "gauges" that need to be viewed more often. This more frequent review contributes to plan viability and organizational agility.

The other component of a plan that must be considered on a regular basis is ensuring its deployment throughout the organization. Performance occurs at all levels; accordingly, performance reviews should occur at all levels. The director level, for instance, can conduct performance reviews for the objectives in the plan that pertain specifically to them or something in which they have a vested interest. That directorate-level performance review can and should be part of the various action plans that are being carried out throughout the directorate and are part of the total organization's plan and strategy. Some action planning can and should occur across the directorates as the plan and the performance management system become more integrated and cohesive.

The action plans should support the organization's objectives, especially in the short term, as they become the daily business of the organization. Action plans can be worked on by individuals or teams, depending on the nature of the action. As the performance management system gains in maturity and the organization's work becomes tied more closely to processes (see Chapter 6), then cross-functional teams are formed much more readily. This "cascade" makes the plan real for everyone in the organization and helps everyone actually contribute to the results.

The final step in deploying the strategic plan and making it viable is to ensure that everyone in the organization has a direct connection to the plan. This linkage can be effected through the employee's annual performance plan (support form). The various tasks listed as the employee's performance plan for the upcoming year can be tied to the various action plans derived from the strategic plan. Thus, an individual's performance can be tied to the organization's performance. All incentives, training, and learning opportunities can now be tied to measurable objectives. It's a win-win situation for both the employee and the organization as a whole (see Chapter 8, Human Resources). Performance now becomes a part of what everyone does; everyone knows where they fit in the performance picture and the contribution they're making to the performance of the organization. Everyone has a piece of the plan.

## A PROPOSED METHOD

While it's unrealistic to think that this dashboard will reflect 100 percent system accuracy, the dashboard itself must become a continuous process of improvement so that what is reflected in the dashboard and what is truly occurring in the organizational system are striving for 100 percent consistency. How can this be accomplished without rummaging through mounds of data? The graphic representation must correlate with performance measures that are established in the strategic plan.

A graphic representation is a target or series of targets. The organizational goals can be placed on one target, with each goal occupying a section of the target. This goal target could easily be the "master graphic" from which all other gauges can cascade and be accessed. This goal target could become the global monitor for the organizational system. Progress or performance to 100 percent completion of the goal can be depicted by a bullet strike (•) in relationship to the center of the target.

Using available technology, measurable objectives can be placed under each goal area, thus giving the organization monitoring capability. The target gives immediate access and visibility to the progress toward accomplishment of the objectives. Further, each objective owns its own space on the target and shows progress toward the 100 percent completion of that objective: The center of the target depicts 100 percent completion. Action plans that make up each objective can be displayed on subsequent underlying targets. Therefore, it's entirely conceivable to click on a specific goal and cause the display of the objective under that goal, and to click on a specific objective and cause action plans in support of their objective to be displayed.

The automated dashboard could theoretically cascade into everyone's performance evaluation form, thus giving everyone access and visibility of organizational performance. This method can be used to display total horizontal and vertical integration of where the organization is going and how well it's performing during the journey. (See Figure 10-4, Dashboard Using Targets.)

The targets can become the information architecture that all the data used for performance reviews (see Figure 10-2) could feed into. The targets can be adjusted and calibrated as the organization adjusts and calibrates its objectives and related measures. This adjustment can and should be driven by annual assessment results that reveal performance gaps and input from all organizational levels. Thus, the performance of the organization and the system to monitor that performance can continually become more accurate.

Another benefit of using a "targets" methodology is that correlations can be readily drawn between various objectives throughout the organization. Cause-and-effect relationships can be ascertained. This is crucial to performance because if

**Figure 10-4.** Dashboard Using Targets

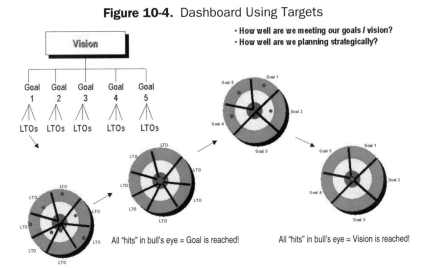

an organization is concerned about continuous improvement, it should be involved in more than just refining its processes for efficiency. The organization should be concerned about how these processes interrelate and affect results in various areas of the organization. This more thoroughly addresses the balance issue and enables an organization to design itself to prevent problems rather then merely react to them. This methodology also clears the way for maximizing responsiveness to the customer.

It's crucial to remember that the strategic plan is the map wherein all of this takes place. The plan is what drives the rest of the organization, but it is the rest of the organization and its monitored results that drive the improvement in the plan. Thus, everything becomes and remains viable. The performance system drives out stagnant stovepipe operations and bureaucracy.

The strategic plan can now be deployed more readily. This is an excellent way to promote a learning culture and get the workforce personally involved in the organization's performance. How well this is all put together into a functioning system—a functioning harmonious system—begins to define what performance is all about. The synergistic effect of all of the parts working together to achieve ever-improving results is every organization's ultimate goal.

# Chapter 11
## KEEP THE CUSTOMER IN THE GAME

At the beginning of the strategic planning process during the first offsite (see Chapter 4), one of the required tasks was to identify the organization's primary customers. This was not merely an exercise, but part of a process that helps define and justify an organization's reason for existing.

It's rather easy to identify with the concept of "customer." We're all customers, and the type of customers we are depends on our needs, wants, and requirements. How we feel as customers depends on our experience and the quality of the product or service we purchased. Were we treated well? Were our requirements met? Did the perceived value of the goods or service meet or exceed our expectations? If so, we probably were satisfied. However, if whatever we received fell short of our expectations in any way, we were disappointed or frustrated, and perhaps even angry—angry at the provider, and even angrier at ourselves for allowing someone to treat us in such an inconsiderate, shabby manner.

### CUSTOMER OR VICTIM?

As a customer, we would like to think that someone or some agency is going to give us something or do something for us in exchange for some type of tangible offering, usually money. All too often (and we've all experienced it), we get treated like a victim: Someone or some agency does something *to* us rather than *for* us, and we end up being deceived or cheated. We don't have to dig too far into the past to recollect an experience of victimization. My "favorite" experiences center around hotel and lodging accommodations.

I recall one experience where I arrived late at night (10 PM) and, after considerable research with the desk clerk, located my reservation (they had given my room to someone else). After finally getting into my room at 11 PM, I discovered that the air conditioning was not working. It was August, it was in the deep south, and it was hot. I called down to the front desk to either have it repaired or get moved to another room. The desk clerk (whom I had come to know very well by this time) said "no problem; we'll fix it...tomorrow." Of course, moving to another room was not an option because they had sold me the last one. So I requested a fan, because hot air that's moving feels cooler than hot air that's not. The desk clerk stated that I could have a fan for a deposit of $20. When I went down to pick it up, he discovered that the fans were locked in a storage closet, and he didn't have a key.

With my frustration growing by leaps and bounds, I resigned myself to lying in bed, afraid to move in an attempt to keep my body temperature as low as possible. Deciding to watch TV and perhaps doze off, I reached for the remote— only to discover that it was bolted to the nightstand, which was in turn bolted to the wall. Ordinarily this would not be a problem, except that the TV was on the opposite side of the room and my body was blocking the signal to change channels. So I had to get up and move out of the way if I wanted to make any television adjustments. So much for trying to stay cool.

I checked out early the next morning, and the "new" desk clerk made the fatal error of asking me how my stay was. I'm sure the 15-minute response I gave was not anticipated, nor were the 3+ pages of customer comments I filled out on a feedback sheet I managed to locate on a nearby magazine rack. And I never smiled once; those in the process of being victimized rarely do. I'll never be a customer there again.

At another hotel chain, I was coming in the lobby from my early morning run. I spotted the coffee maker over in the corner, but to my dismay there was only decaffeinated. When I brought this to the attention of the desk clerk, her response was "I can't tell the difference, can you?" Had I known my comment would have flown completely over her head, I certainly would have phrased it differently. I gave her an opportunity to make me a customer, but her lack of training and sensitivity made me a victim.

Sometimes the difference between being a customer and being a victim is a very fine line. I recall another experience where I left for my morning jaunt only to be greeted upon my return an hour later by the desk clerk with a bottle of ice-cold mineral water and a towel. This happened every morning, all week long. Whenever I visit this city, I make every effort to stay at that same place in order to relive that experience. Customer satisfaction? It was more; I was delighted.

A final story, and another lodging experience. After rinsing out my running gear, I laid it over a railing in my room to dry. When I returned to my room later that evening, I discovered that my clothes were no longer there. I immediately concluded that they had been stolen. However, when I entered the bedroom, all my running clothes were lying neatly folded at the foot of my bed. The maid service had washed, dried, and folded them.

These last two stories are great examples of how my needs as a customer were not only met, but anticipated and exceeded. The result was customer delight and guaranteed repeat business. Plus, I've recounted these experiences to numerous people who have since stayed at these hotels per my recommendations.

These examples clearly illustrate the difference between being victimized and being delighted. The first examples guaranteed no further business from me and everyone else I could tell. The last examples guaranteed not only my return business, but everyone else's I could tell. More importantly, the additional effort to achieve positive results was minimal.

## CUSTOMERS AND PERFORMANCE

The Baldrige criteria look to Category 3, customer and market focus, as the major input to the performance management system. Excellent organizations target specific groups or segments of customers and spend a considerable amount of time learning everything they can about them— what they care about, what they require, and what's truly important to them. A performance management system designs the organization or agency around what the customer wants in an effort to meet or surpass those expectations. Once all that is established, the criteria require that customer satisfaction performance be measured. Beyond that, the criteria ask what sort of strategies the organization has in place to listen to and learn from the customer. The better the customer is known and understood, the better the chance the organization has to satisfy and achieve positive results— thus, a comprehensive customer focus.

The argument is often made that government organizations are not in the free marketplace and therefore much of what the Baldrige criteria address does not apply. This is a matter of perspective, education, and experience. While it's certainly true that the profit motive does not apply as often in the government as it does in free enterprise, both the private and public sectors have much more in common than they have differences. Both have customers, and both are concerned with satisfying them as effectively and efficiently as possible.

Another argument posed by government agencies is that their customers are already decided for them. This is also a matter of perspective, because from a performance point of view this provides a great opportunity. This segment of customers is already established; much of the research to determine who they are has already been done. The agency could adopt the attitude of "being stuck" with this customer group or see this as a great chance to improve its customer service. All that needs to be done initially is to start asking what the customers care about.

This concept of serving the customer may require some getting used to for the agency. There is considerable diversity among government organizations regarding how they view customer service and performance. There is no "best" time to get started other than right away. Getting started simply means identifying the primary customers and taking the necessary steps to satisfy them. Once the process begins, there should be no turning back. The organization will never be the same, and if the continuous improvement process is embraced and implemented, then the organization will be redesigned to meet customers' needs.

This redesign must be a macro process consisting of: (1) inputs; (2) the processing system; (3) outputs, including results achieved; and (4) how customers' needs are being met and how their problems are being solved. This macro process must overarch the entire process identification and management system for the organization (see Chapter 9). Every step of this process must include a measurement component as a means to determine the performance level of each step. This measurement must then contain a feedback component that enables each step to use the information to make improvements.

Once this is accomplished, the customer grouping and segmentation process must be refined. While most government agencies have been "given" their customers, the identification process should take into account whether that customer group is indeed valid, or are some changes and adjustments required? Are we sure that the customers we've identified (or had identified for us) are the ones that are critical to the organization's existence? Further, can this large customer grouping be divided into segments that would enhance meeting those requirements?

There is no prescribed formula for accomplishing this, but there should be some logic to the selection and segmentation process that is tied to how the organization is designed to perform optimally. Each group/segment will likely have different needs and requirements, so the knowledge your organization is able to gather about customer groups will greatly assist in designing itself to achieve the highest level of performance. These listening and learning strategies must continually be refined and updated to keep current with changing needs, environment, and technologies (which may be a major factor in the strategic planning process). The type of organization and the types of customers may vary considerably, prompting a closer look at listening and learning strategies. These strategies will largely depend on your organization's key business factors, i.e., what is crucial for the organization's success.

If your organization has correctly developed its key processes, then the processes for determining what your organization's customers care about will be in place. The processes for building and enhancing customer relationships and developing new opportunities will also be established. These processes may be rudimentary in the beginning, but getting them identified is the first major step; refinement and improvement will come later.

A good example of how listening and learning from the customer can lead to a positive experience took place at Ft. Bliss, Texas, during the Army Teen Discovery Symposium. The host of the symposium (trained in customer service at

Disneyworld) anticipated every detail of the leaders' and facilitators' needs, freeing them up to concentrate entirely on the events at hand. All aspects were considered: room setup, snacks, lodging, transportation, communication, conference materials, etc. Conference presenters and attendees were made to feel special through strict attention to detail, from meals down to specially monogrammed t-shirts. All attendees' needs were anticipated, and reactive measures were nonexistent. There were no complaints and a multitude of compliments. That experience set a baseline or a standard for customer satisfaction that motivated everyone concerned not to fall below that standard and improve on an already tremendous experience that delighted everyone in attendance.

On a larger organizational scale, the Department of Defense was facing a dilemma in the late 1980s and early 1990s: a decreasing ability to deploy its service members due to a lack of available child care. Families where both spouses were on active duty or where there was a single parent had no available means for child care that was convenient, affordable, and consistent. This situation compromised the mission, because a large percentage of service members couldn't deploy, let alone report for daily duty. This was an internal customer problem that resulted from a lack of knowledge about customer requirements and not having any method in place to listen to and learn from the customer.

The Department of Defense's response was not only to meet customers' needs, but to continuously improve child care services in an effort to keep customers happy. Standards were developed across the various services for child care that exceeded the standards found in the private sector, resulting in consistency of care and a service that families could depend on. The concept of child care was expanded to include child development; in addition to providing quality care, a learning environment was established and continuously improved upon. Child development was expanded to include all youth, so an already good program further added to customer satisfaction. Generally, a positive, open line of communication and positive relationships have been established between the service providers and the customers, so that suggestions for change and improvement are always under consideration.

Customer satisfaction surveys indicate extremely high ratings for child and youth development programs in the Department of Defense. This is a classic example of a need emerging as a dilemma, and the response resulted in a program that continues to make customers happy on a continuously improving basis.

## CUSTOMER ACCESS

Government organizations vary widely in terms of the amount and degree of access they can allow their customers. Security factors and certain political considerations may limit customer access. This, however, is the exception, as most government organizations are public agencies whose primary mission is service in some form. Therefore, is the organization designed for easy customer access? That is, do the various customer groups feel comfortable about interacting with the organization on how to improve and change to meet their needs? Do the customers feel comfortable about complaining? This interactive process contributes positively to performance. How does your organization learn from this open, communicative relationship to better satisfy the customer?

Today's government organizations and agencies find themselves in a fast-paced, rapidly changing environment and cannot survive by being bureaucratic, closed, and self-absorbed. While they must always be mindful of the organizational human resource factor, the reason for their existence must be outward-focused. A traditional line and staff organization with boxes and lines depicting various levels of authority and the supervisory chain no longer applies. Of course, accountability is important, but so is responsiveness to the customer.

In today's environment, if the customer is not considered at all levels of the organization's operation, the organization may cease to exist. So it's not an either/or situation; it's a matter of how the total organization, especially the workforce, is designed to best respond to customers. The organizational configuration may not be neat and organized and appear self-contained. Just the opposite may be true—it may appear disorganized and chaotic. The key is whether it's responsive. Major components in customer satisfaction and loyalty are prompt, effective responsiveness and solutions focused on customer needs.

## PROCESS LINKAGE

A key concept in keeping the customer in the game is "actionable": How closely and directly linked is the customer information that's gathered from the organization's key processes? If a direct relationship exists, then that responsiveness should be on a glide path of continuous improvement along with all the other organizational processes. This is especially true for incorporating this information into the strategic planning process for priority-setting and resourcing those priorities. For true, effective, responsiveness to exist, and for results to be achieved, the information gathered and analyzed must be deployed throughout the organization. Not only does this increase the opportunities for customer satisfaction, but it also motivates the workforce by establishing a sense of real purpose and giving viability to the strategic plan.

## SETTING A STANDARD

An organization left to its own gut-level determination of how to achieve customer satisfaction will inevitably regress to functioning in a manner that is most comfortable rather than using a method that focuses on performance. That's one reason why it is sometimes easier to let bureaucracy take over and "hide" in its non-threatening environment.

This is where the value and importance of standards become apparent. An outside target or group of targets that is agreed upon and published provides an objective mark to shoot for that is hard to compromise. Standards help guarantee a level of customer satisfaction while helping prevent the organization's workforce from sitting back and letting bureaucracy take over. They provide a level that everyone can strive for that is a step closer to the vision while supporting the organization's values. Standards can and should be part of a system that is focused on performance and results.

Standards are of little use unless they are stated in a specific way and are quantifiable. Then the organization's performance can be measured against what it professes and plans to do. Tracking and measuring help ensure that standards are being used to improve performance. Gathering customer information and feedback is crucial, but simply obtaining customer survey information without reliable, valid internal measures for comparison is unscientific at best and may be misleading. If the organization can make the comparisons objective, it will be able to form a true picture about whether it is meeting customer requirements. This information can also be used to change and improve the standards as the customers' expectations change and, in all likelihood, are raised.

## THE CUSTOMER'S VOICE

How often do we see customer complaint departments in government organizations? In the past (and perhaps even to a large extent today), complaints were swept under the rug because, in a bureaucratic system, they would reflect adversely on how we performed our jobs. The responsive system seeks out complaints because they're viewed as information that can help the organization improve.

Once the attitude of hiding complaints is overcome, the process of using that feedback to improve can begin. However, it's not enough merely to react to complaints as they come in. That's still a reactionary form of management that, while perhaps solving individual problems, does little to improve the organization's performance. The questions that need to be asked are: Is there a process for handling complaints? Is the process part of the performance management system? Is it reviewed during periodic performance reviews?

Making complaint management a part of the organization's system of improvement is another component in the formula to get better. The organization establishes: (1) a method for recording, following up, and taking corrective action on each complaint; (2) a way to analyze the root cause of each complaint; and (3) a means to collect and aggregate complaint data from across the entire organization so that trends can be identified to help create opportunities for improvement.

Developing an effective customer complaint system can also help build positive and enduring relationships with customers. A customer who knows that your organization is doing all that it can to provide the best service possible will be much more loyal and tend to work with you instead of against you. It's also helpful, whenever possible, to do something special or out of the ordinary for customers to make them feel they're cared about. Most important, however, especially in a bureaucracy, is the organization's effort to keep the relationship hassle-free, thus making it as easy as possible to conduct business successfully. This is particularly important in government organizations because there may be little choice of whom you have to do business with; the fewer impediments and roadblocks, the easier it becomes to conduct business.

It's also easy in a bureaucratic organization to let things ride and to be content with the way things are—the status quo. This is no longer acceptable. Today's government organizations must continually ask themselves what they are doing to keep current with contemporary business practices and new, innovative ways of doing business. Technology is driving change at light speed. The more today's government organizations can take advantage of technological advances and leverage technology to the customers' advantage, the easier it will become to accomplish their missions.

# Chapter 12
# THE NEXT ASSESSMENT

In Chapter 2 we discussed how to begin the assessment process for your organization. It is extremely important that the first assessment be kept as simple as possible to avoid overwhelming the workforce. It should accomplish several things: (1) familiarization with the criteria and how they provide a framework for change, (2) introduction of a systematic approach to organizational management, and (3) a basic foundation for where the organization can begin its continuous improvement journey, highlighting the major gaps in performance that would prevent or inhibit the achievement of results. Thus, the first assessment introduces the concept of a performance management system and initiates the transition to a whole new way of thinking about the organization and how it functions.

Regardless of how the organization started to look at itself through the lens of the criteria, no assessment effort should be undertaken unless accompanied by a considerable amount of education about the criteria and how they translate into performance and productivity. At a minimum, a refresher is called for, and this refresher should be more than a simple waltz through the seven categories; instead, it should focus on how the categories link and work together synergistically, as a system. Otherwise, the categories may be seen as merely a series of chapters with little or no relationship with one another.

The next assessment must build on the previous one. Questions to be addressed include: How were the major gaps dealt with over the last period? Was any progress made in closing those gaps? If so, how much progress was made; if not, why not? Building on each assessment solidifies the continuous cycle of improvement while preventing the abandonment of initiatives because someone didn't want to devote the energy or thought they had a better idea. At any rate, the second time around for assessments requires more than a simple survey. Top-level management must be involved, and the assessment effort must now be intensified.

This assessment must be approached with the latest iteration of the strategic plan in hand. How is the organization doing in relationship to the plan? Is the organization on the course it planned? What adjustments need to be made? In all likelihood, looking at the plan as it was conceived in the context of where the organization is currently will be a real eye-opener. At a minimum, it will force senior leadership to step back and take a more global, holistic view of the organization, what it's all about, and where it's going. This is the point where decisions must be made about how to tackle the next assessment.

## BALDRIGE ASSESSMENT PROCESS

Applying for the Malcolm Baldrige National Quality Award requires a formal application package. The development of such a package is a major endeavor requiring the involvement of many in and across the organization. While an organization that's just getting started in this new way of functioning and looking at itself certainly isn't ready to compete, the exercise of developing an application has tremendous value and can be the next logical step in the performance maturation process.

The development of a draft application starts with the business overview. Senior leadership should write the business overview because it sets the tone for the whole assessment package and puts into perspective what's relevant and important to the organization and its performance. Most important, however, is that this is an opportunity for leadership to get involved personally in the assessment process—this can have great impact on the organization and how performance management is perceived and implemented.

The business overview is the starting point for the assessment process. It focuses the assessment on the key performance requirements of the organization and the expected or desired results.

The business overview comprises five sections: (1) basic description of the organization, (2) customer and market requirements, (3) supplier and partnering relationships, (4) competitive situation, and (5) business/organizational directions.

As one reviews each of these sections, it becomes clear that all these organizational components should be considered on a regular basis, or at a minimum, during the actual strategic planning and development process. In fact, once one is knowledgeable about all the components of a performance system and has some idea of how they all can work together and the potential they offer, the alternatives for managing an organization seem pale by comparison. This second assessment should consider all the components and be as thorough as possible, while taking into account that the organization's performance maturity level is still low.

### Basic Description of the Organization

As mentioned, senior leadership should be involved in writing the overview. The understanding of the core values and how they're applied to the organization has its linkage in this section. What is the organization all about and how is its culture defined by its reason for existence, its mission, and how it conducts itself in the accomplishment of the mission? That sets the tone. Information should then be provided on the organization's products and services, its size, customers and customer types, and other major users of the organization's products and services.

The human resource aspects of the organization should also be discussed here, because as the organization is being basically described, the workforce must receive primary consideration; in the final analysis, the workforce *is* the organization. The workforce should be addressed in light of existing equipment and technology, because advances will have a direct effect on the workforce, especially in terms of training and learning.

One of the key areas that government organizations must address is the regulatory environment. The bureaucracy is famous for regulations, many of which are in direct conflict with or inhibitors to performance. Describing the regulatory environment in the overview can help leadership focus on what is really necessary, and more importantly, what is inhibiting performance and can be done away with without legal ramifications.

Nearly all government organizations are sub-units or parts of a larger organization. The business overview addresses how those units are related to one another and how the work design affects the workforce. The description should also cover how the key processes relate to the other units and sub-units, and how they are aligned to enhance performance.

Corporate process identification and subsequent linkage and alignment have a major impact on many supporting processes down the line. Therefore, this initial construct is crucial. It is also crucial for senior leadership to have visibility early on in the assessment process, and what better time and place than in the business overview?

## Customer and Market Requirements

The concept of customers is relatively new to some government organizations. Until recently, a customer was someone who belonged to the free enterprise system and was directly related to the profit motive. Somewhere along the line, it was discovered that by satisfying its customers an organization could improve performance. Since then, the customer has been a growing consideration in the government sector. We've made the transition from not having customers to being told who our customers are (forced choice) to everyone potentially being a customer.

In describing customer requirements, senior leadership will discover early on that to identify and meet customer requirements, it is first essential to determine who the customers are by segment. That requires extensive research and broad-based thinking. This is not about being reactive, but rather about knowing the customers well enough not only to meet their requirements without continually asking them but to anticipate what they will want in the future. With senior leadership writing the overview and identifying the customers in the very beginning, the need to keep the customers foremost in the organization's priorities will always be present.

### Supplier and Partnering Relationships

Crisis often creates opportunity, and as downsizing in the government sector becomes more of a reality and impacts all of us, the need to develop and establish partnerships and business relationships becomes increasingly evident. Each sub-unit or activity within an organization can probably come up with numerous partnering opportunities that would not only benefit customers but also increase the organization's efficiency and effectiveness. If each activity can do this, senior leadership will have broad visibility of potential partnering opportunities, as well as candidates for partners within the organization.

### Competitive Situation

Government agencies and organizations also thought they weren't in competition with anyone, that they had an untouchable niche that was more or less quarantined from the private sector and that would never change. How wrong they were! In fact, the private sector views government at all levels as a very lucrative market and competes directly with the products and services offered by the government. Why? Because the private sector can compete to do it better, faster, and cheaper, and to offer more value to customers. Leaders of government organizations and agencies should have an opportunity, at least annually, to describe and assess this environment if their organizations are to remain viable.

### Business/Organizational Direction

The summation of the business overview should integrate the description of the organization with the direction it is taking in the future. This is leadership's opportunity to introduce the more formal assessment process and to demonstrate how they're scanning the real world environment so they can optimally control their destiny.

Business direction is all about the future and how the organization is doing new things to address that transition. This is where everything can and should be considered, such as new technology, changes in strategy, new partnerships/alliances, or any special or unique factors that must be addressed in planning for the organization's future. This sector of the overview lays the groundwork for the strategic planning development process.

## THE "DRAFT" ASSESSMENT

The initial survey started the process of looking at the organization throughout the lens of performance criteria. Now is the time to start focusing that lens. That means delving deeper into the criteria and responding to what they're asking for as it relates to your organization. At this stage of performance maturity, it's not about applying for or winning an award—it's about continuous improvement. The survey concentrated mainly on the categories and was focused at that level, but as the assessment process becomes more specific, attention must now be given to the 19 examination items and the 27 areas to address.

The organization, if it is to begin responding to the items, must describe what it does. That description must be a part of each category—that is, what does the organization do with regard to leadership, strategic planning, etc. If that description is not present, then it becomes impossible to view the organization from a diagnostic perspective.

## APPROACH AND DEPLOYMENT

One of the most difficult concepts to put into practice is the deployment of what the organization says it does. Government agencies in general, and bureaucracies in particular, claim what they are all about and do many things, but do those things really happen? Another way of putting it is, "Does the organization walk the talk?"

Deploying the approach is where the productivity cycle has its roots and where the continuous improvement journey begins. Responses to the various category items that lack information on how something is practically being accomplished are really nothing more than anecdotal information. They can be characterized simply as occurrences or events that are not necessarily related or linked to either the overall system or the intent of the strategic plan per se.

Categories 1–6 all contain both an approach and a deployment dimension, while category 7 is exclusively results. An organization with a perfect approach but with no deployment will never score above 300 points because the how question, i.e., the way in which the approach is being carried out, cannot be addressed.

When conducting an assessment and writing responses to the items in the criteria, it is vital to keep this concept clearly in mind. As the responses are written, it will become clear very quickly where the gaps in performance are. The basis for the feedback report to senior leadership will consist of where deployment does not exist. This may be very enlightening for senior leaders because they may become aware that what they intend for the organization and what actually is occurring are two different things.

An example is the requirement in Category 2 (approach) to develop a strategic plan and describe the process undertaken in its development. Most government agencies will have little problem with this requirement, particularly in light of GPRA, which requires that this be done. The problem arises in the plan's transition from its development to its actual deployment.

We are all familiar with the fancy plan that sits on the senior executive's coffee table but never makes its way to the workforce, where the work is actually being accomplished. In fact, very few plans contain the necessary transitional pathways or bridges to make them viable throughout the organization. Those "bridges" consist of measurable objectives and subsequent action plans that provide the avenues for deployment. Rather, the "plan" remains a fancy publication to be shown to dignitaries but with very little applicability and relativity.

Very sophisticated plans are being written today at the highest levels of government with no realistic, actual means of measuring performance. Therefore, the good intentions and good ideas remain only that: good intentions that never see their way into the organization and never become a result achieved. The expanded assessment must be undertaken with this in mind—how to use the feedback to more fully integrate the stated approach of the organization into what is actually being done on a daily basis.

## RESPONDING TO THE CRITERIA

To become more thoroughly engaged in the continuous improvement cycle and be more performance management-oriented, the items of the criteria have to be specifically addressed. It's not enough to simply provide a yes or no answer at this stage. It's important to respond fully to each item and each area. In describing what your organization does, try to show how the activities are part of an overall system as opposed to a segmented, stovepipe operation. If the approach you are describing is not systematic, that reduces the opportunity for improvement and learning dramatically. It also inhibits the organization from achieving a performance maturity level that can start yielding positive results.

Also in responding to the item, ensure that the "how" question is answered, i.e., how is the particular action being accomplished in different parts of the organization? Without deploying the approach, all that is occurring is talk, but no walk.

Is the organization focused and consistent? Does what was being described in the business overview as being most important and the direction the organization is taking remain consistent throughout the categories? For example, is the response to Category 2, Strategic Planning, consistent with what senior leadership sees as the future of the organization? Is the strategic plan deployed into measurable objectives, both long- and short-term, that can be formulated into action plans that can be accomplished? Even this is not full deployment; the objectives and action plans still don't have complete ownership by individual members of the workforce. The support forms of each employee should have delineated, designated tasks outlined for the full year (subject to adjustment, of course) that link to the measurable objectives of the organization. That makes the plan viable for everyone.

The workforce must now be viewed as part of the overall performance system, so the response to the items in Category 5 must incorporate the entire workforce and address how that workforce is part of the overall system. This relates directly to the human resource plan (see Chapter 8) and how the organization's workforce works in and on the processes to produce results. The expanded assessment should clearly address how this is accomplished.

We must keep in mind what is being assessed or examined. While performance results are ultimately what the organization is attempting to achieve (450 points), that is not possible unless a deeper organizational diagnosis takes place. That diagnosis must concentrate on the "why" and the "what," i.e., why results are poor in certain areas and what can be done to improve. This means knowing what the organization does and how it is done (see Chapter 9, Process Identification and Management). Identifying, defining, and mapping processes start to get at the question of how the organization achieves its results. The response to Category 6 should specify product, service, support, and supplier processes that are key to overall organizational performance.

## RESULTS

The "quad" charts used for quarterly performance reviews should provide the basis for the results attained by the organization. The criteria are focused on results—this is where it all should come together. The better organized and managed the performance reviews, the easier it will be to respond to Category 7. The results should link to what has been determined to be necessary or critical for success. The performance reviews should already be addressing what is critical as measurable objectives supporting each organizational goal.

It's not enough to just show a graph or chart and call it "results." There must be relevance to the direction and goals of the organization and a direct relationship to how the system is performing. The criteria guidelines outline four key requirements for effective reporting of results data:

• Trends, showing direction of results and rates of change

• Performance levels, on a measurement scale that has relevance

• Comparisons, showing how results compare with other selected organizations or entities

• Breadth and importance of results, showing the relationship to what's critical for organizational success.

A compact format is desirable to depict results. Therefore, the use of charts, graphs, and tables to tell the story is preferred. The less narrative the better, but trends that show a significant change should be explained. It should be noted that there is a danger of trying to put too much information on one chart or graph, thus causing confusion. Therefore, there is a certain "chartology" that can add to the quality of the assessment and contribute to overall organizational performance. (See Figure 12-1, Examples of Presenting Data.)

**Figure 12-1.** Examples of Presenting Data

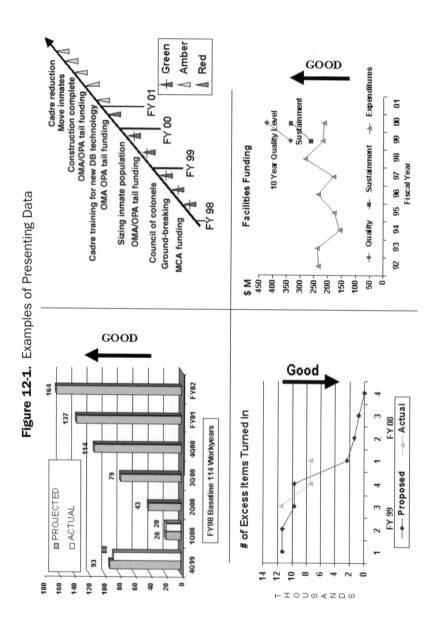

The second assessment, i.e., the expanded one, is a refined look at the organization through a more focused lens, i.e., deeper application of the criteria. Gaps will be exposed quite readily, but the gaps should be less profound this time. The initial performance survey probably showed where a major area was missing, or the category was not addressed at all (e.g., no strategic plan). The annual assessment process conducted through the lens of the criteria and in the context of a performance management system will engage the organization in continuous improvement and maturation.

# Chapter 13
# USING ASSESSMENT FEEDBACK FOR THE NEXT OFFSITE

The expanded assessment is the next step in the transition process to a performance management orientation. It is crucial that the assessment be used for maximum benefit. All too often, this is viewed as "another program" or something that's done "in addition to" normal business. This type of thinking will cause a slowdown or perhaps even a failure in transitioning to a performance management system. Leadership must continue to emphasize and insist on going forward with the transition.

Until now, this has been largely a learning experience for everyone. While learning must continue, it is time for managers to take the lead and begin application. During this process, some of the workforce will have become more familiar with the criteria and will have developed an avid interest. They may have become quite good at using the criteria and probably are interested in extra training. Leadership now needs to decide whether further training should be provided for these employees so that they can become the "resident experts" and lead the effort from within, or whether outside expertise should be called in to examine the assessment package and provide feedback.

While hiring the expertise may be easier in the beginning and cause less disruption to the workforce and overall operations, convenience now may exact a price later on. This pro-

cess must be all about transition and the development of a
learning culture (see Chapter 8) that is focused on performance. This can be viewed as an opportunity to get more of
the workforce trained in the criteria. Certainly, if the organization was competing for the award during this particular
assessment process, outside assistance could be considered—
but the assessment package is not going to be competitive
after just one year.

How the assessment package looks will not get you any
more points, so trying to be fancy in putting together an
assessment package at this stage of the game is a wasted effort. There are a few rules, however, that would have to be
adhered to if the package were to be entered into competition, and these rules actually assist in the accuracy of the
assessment. The total package is limited to no more than 50
pages, not including the business overview, which is limited
to five additional pages. The formatting and typing instructions are given in the Application Forms and Instructions for
Business, Education and Health Care booklet.

A workforce learning situation can be created if some
members of the organization who were not directly involved
in conducting the assessment are asked to examine the prepared package. This speaks to getting as many people as possible trained on the criteria in the beginning so the culture
change can be effected. This may be difficult at first because
many or all of the "criteria-knowledgeable" people on the
workforce may have been used to put the package together.

Getting as many trained as possible early on certainly has
value. I have been involved with several organizations that
have employed various methods in conducting assessments,
examining packages, and providing feedback. The outsourcing method gave one organization a quicker start and
resulted in a package that would grace a professional book-
shelf. The package even won several awards. The drawback
(which took a couple of years to surface) was that the excep-

tional quality and performance alluded to in the package was only partially deployed in the organization. Outsourcing the effort may have provided a quick start, but the lack of deployment left the organization with hollow quality and gaps in the continuous performance improvement cycle.

Another organization, which was very similar in mission, size, and structure, was much slower to start. It had limited resources and was unable to contract out the assessment. The organization did have several employees who were experienced with the criteria, however, and these employees spent their time training everyone and soliciting support. The first assessment was rudimentary at best, yielding a score of less than 150 points. Examiners from other organizations were asked to provide feedback, and before long the organization had identified several major gaps that enabled it to get started. The employees convinced their leadership that this was the right thing to do even though they weren't winning any awards. It soon became a total organizational effort, and the workforce started to get caught up in the groundswell. Each year the organization made steady improvement to the point where it eventually caught and passed the organization that had outsourced.

This organization has enduring quality and performance maturity that are part of all it does. The main reason is that the organization, i.e., the workforce, experienced it. The outsourced organization still has not grown by experience. I'm sure there is some spillover as many of the ideas were used by many of the activities, but the outsourced organization is at a relative standstill.

The implication is that it is preferable to conduct the assessment in-house and have the assessment package examined by people trained within the organization. This includes writing a feedback report that will be used to make improvements in the organization's performance system.

## THE FEEDBACK REPORT

Whatever method is used to provide feedback, this is a prime opportunity for the organization to learn and improve. In examining the assessment package and providing feedback comments, certain guidelines should be followed for purposes of consistency, clarity, and effectiveness. Everyone in the organization should have the opportunity to read the report, and every effort must be made to minimize personal interpretation (i.e., stick to using the criteria at all times to ensure objectivity).

Feedback entries should be made with the presumption of honesty on the part of those writing the assessment package. If clarification/validation issues arise, vehicles are available for dealing with them. A good feedback report begins with fully comprehending and understanding the package, so reading the package in its entirety before examining and writing comments is essential. It is also essential to read the package and write comments on an individual basis; there will be time for discussion in a group setting and consensus later in the process.

Of equal importance is reading the entire criteria booklet to get an overall orientation to the criteria and how the responses are to be evaluated. The examiner should become thoroughly familiar with the item format, with a specific focus on the basic item requirements and the specific areas the assessment package needs to address. The notes at the bottom of each item can clarify key terms/requirements and outline specific linkages with other system areas.

The actual assessment package examination should begin with a copy of the package and criteria side by side so that every thing that's being read can be related specifically to the criteria. Then, sentence by sentence, paragraph by paragraph, the examiner should go through the assessment package and determine whether the requirements of the criteria are met.

The examiner should record the findings in complete, grammatically correct, narrative sentences that respond to how the item requirements were responded to in the criteria:

- *Strength*—Addresses most of item requirement

- *Significant strength*—Completely addresses item requirement

- *Opportunity for improvement*—Does not address most of item requirement

- *Major performance gap*—Omits or fails to meet item requirement

- *Site visit issue*—Response to an item that needs further clarification and can be resolved onsite.

Here are some helpful feedback comment guidelines:

- *Use complete, grammatically correct sentences.* Leave nothing to the imagination and no room for interpretation. Many people may be reading the same comment, so it's up to the writer to help ensure that they all read the same thing.

- *Comment only on the requirements of the criteria.* The criteria are self-contained. There are no other requirements beyond what the criteria are asking for. The organization's task is to tell how it is responding to the requirements.

- *Focus on process, approach, deployment, and/or results.* Categories 1–6 require that the responses to the items describe the approach and how that approach is deployed across and throughout the organization. Category 7 requires that the organization report what happened as a result of the various processes managed by the organization.

- *Avoid being judgmental.* Words like "good," "bad," "best," "worst," and "effective" are relative in nature and little can be done with them in terms of measurement, comparison, or action.

- *Maintain a polite, professional tone.*

- *Avoid jargon and acronyms.* Most of the workforce will at some time read the feedback report. It's unrealistic to think that everyone will know what is meant by certain phrases or abbreviations that may have specific meaning to the writer.

- *Answer the "so what?" question.* Try to foresee the impact the feedback comment will have. If the comment is written in such a way that no action can take place by the activity it's meant for, then the "so what?" question obviously has not been answered. If, however, the comment can be acted on, i.e., be used to improve or change the organization for the better, then the "so what?" question is satisfied.

- *Ensure that strengths do not conflict with opportunities for improvement.* Care must be taken that a comment that mentions what an organization does well and addresses the item or area of a category does not oppose a comment that is mentioned as an opportunity for improvement. That having been said, it's also important to remember that in categories 1–6, the criteria refer to both an approach and a deployment dimension. Therefore, it's entirely possible to mention a strength in the approach area while highlighting an opportunity for improvement in the deployment area of the same item. In fact, whenever comments can be written that provide discernment for the organization regarding its approach vs. what is not or has not yet been deployed, the organization will be more fully engaged in a continuous performance improvement cycle.

The scoring guidelines in the Baldrige criteria clearly outline that no more than 20 percent of an item's point value is available if no deployment is evident. That is why it becomes crucial to differentiate between what's been accomplished in terms of approach and what remains to be accomplished in terms of deployment.

- *Be clear and accurate.* In writing feedback comments, assume that if the feedback doesn't relate to the criteria, it doesn't relate. Therefore, it's important that the comment convey the thought/message the writer intends, plus speak to the item and area to address in the criteria.

## TOP 10 FEEDBACK MISTAKES

The feedback to the performance package is written with the intent that it be used to improve the organization. An assessment has true value, but that value multiplies considerably with the comments in the assessment package. The following are the ten most common feedback mistakes:

1. *Regurgitation of the words from the criteria.* While the criteria are universal in nature, the feedback should be organization-specific and worded in such a way that helps the organization improve.

2. *Using examples instead of describing response.* The criteria wording must be integrated into the response in some way that is simply not a repeat of the words. There is a danger in filling the comment with nothing but examples, thus diluting the power of the comment.

3. *No examples to help illustrate a comment.* Conversely, a comment without examples bypasses organizational ownership and leaves the organization wondering "how does this apply to me?"

4. *Lack of specificity.* Broad generalities tend to gravitate toward the "so what?" area, not giving the organization anything tangible to act on.

5 *Showing only a few examples.* A balance needs to be achieved so that the organization has information that pertains to and is focused on improvement.

6. *Too many expectations.* This is a new process, and the learning curve is quite high in the beginning. Raising the bar to what may seem unachievable to the newly conceived performance organization may be just as dangerous as doing nothing. A good approach is to focus on the major requirement of the item first. The numerous details found in the notes should be reserved for refinement once the foundation for performance and improvement is in place.

7. *Responding with a prescription.* The criteria are the same for everyone and have universal application. On the other hand, every organization is different, so telling them what to do and how to do it is not the intent or purpose. If the writers are internal to the organization, they may have some opinions in this regard, but it is always best to remain a purist and let the organization do its own application. This is why it's eventually best to have examiners (note: not *assessors*) from outside the organization so that maximum objectivity is ensured. This should not, however, be an excuse for not getting started.

8. *Not responding to the area to address.* The criteria are formatted in a way that best gives credence to a systematic method to improve productivity/performance. The categories begin with the broadest, most general of items and wind their way down to notes that are very specific. Feedback that doesn't specify a particular area to address may not be helpful and may cause confusion for the reader.

9. *Use of too many acronyms.* The purpose of the feedback is to communicate with maximum clarity and help the organization improve. Using acronyms may lead to misinterpretation or misunderstanding and is therefore in conflict with that purpose.

10. *Overusing industry or quality jargon.* Using language that is specific to one particular agency or activity may cause confusion. The feedback must help everyone learn, and using what could be perceived as pretentious language may be a hindrance.

## USING THE FEEDBACK FOR THE NEXT OFFSITE

The expanded assessment and accompanying feedback will create a different perspective of the organization for the senior leadership. Using the assessment results for maximum effectiveness is the next step in the journey of continuous improvement. The feedback report should largely drive the agenda for the next offsite and should be developed and incorporated into a cyclical process for the organization. The expanded assessment and feedback will cause senior leadership to take a fresh look at the entire organization and make adjustments wherever they deem necessary.

Doing nothing implies that the organization had it totally right from the very beginning. A realistic and viable approach is that perfection can never be attained, but quality can always be improved. Leadership may want to relook at everything, but this time through the lens of a performance management system.

Using the assessment results and feedback to optimum advantage may start with several questions:

- Is the mission statement correct? Does it accurately reflect what we really do? Is the mission statement consistent with the organization description found in the business overview? Is the organization's mission clearly stated and concise enough to be memorized by the workforce?

- Have the customers been correctly identified? Customers are the reason for the organization's existence. Accordingly, all planning must be conducted with customers in mind. Segmenting the customer base will further the refinement effort. Steps can now be taken to design the organizational system and all its components to satisfy customers.

- Is the vision clear and inspirational? Now that everyone has had time to reflect on the original vision, it's likely that some ideas have surfaced about how to improve that vision so it better defines the aspiration of the organization while inspiring everyone to go for that aspiration. A clear, inspirational vision that rallies the workforce can do wonders for productivity and performance.

- Are the values what the organization stands for? Values are the road signs that guide the behavior of the organization on the journey to the vision. The workforce has had time to reflect on the values decided on at the first offsite. The expanded assessment may provide more material for thought and discussion about whether these values are the ones everyone wants to live with.

- Are we happy with the goals? Are there enough goals? Are there too many? Do the goals responsibly provide steps in the stairway to the vision? They should be broad, general statements drawn directly out of the mission that can be seen as steps. Certainly, goals can be altered and changed as the organization reassesses itself and continues to become more effective and efficient.

- Do the objectives support the goals, and are they measurable? This is where performance begins to be clearly defined because it's where metrics enter the picture. While the mission defines what the organization does, the objectives are at the forefront of determining with increased specificity how well it is being done. The just-completed expanded assessment will reveal all sorts of gaps in expected performance, even to the point of whether the objectives are valid. The results (Category 7) will show how well the organization is performing in relationship to the objectives. We are now getting to the heart of the performance matter and where the assessment and feedback can truly move the organization down the road in the performance journey. The material from the last performance review should be available for the offsite.

- Are the organization's performance objectives deployed into action plans? Deploying the plan is what gives it life. A dead plan is one that simply sits on a coffee table for show. The upcoming offsite should be prepared to review whether the workforce is working on actionable items that directly relate to the objectives of the organization and whether their performance is evaluated on that basis.

- Are the assessment results realistic? The strategic planning offsite should at the onset include a SWOT analysis in light of the assessment feedback. The SWOT analysis can be part of a total environmental scan that takes place early at the offsite to ensure that the assessment and the feedback are realistic given everything that needs to be considered. What do the next couple of years look like for this organization and similar organizations? What is the political climate? What is bound to change, and what may change? Do we need to adjust in any way to accommodate what we know and what we anticipate in conjunction with the results we're currently achieving? Putting all this together at the beginning of the offsite will provide additional focus.

- Have the organization's processes been identified? Now that the assessment results have oriented the leadership to get strategically aligned, the processes that the organization is involved with must be identified as part of the organizational structure (see Chapter 9). A relook is in order, because this is where an organization becomes more effective and learns how to be more efficient. Related to this is designing the organization's work around the identified key and supporting processes, thus precluding the "need to reorganize."

## THE BUSINESS OF PLANNING

The feedback report identified and crystallized many gaps in the performance system by category. Tackling all these gaps at once would be overwhelming. Besides, it would be impossible to resource everything at once. The assessment results can be used best by choosing five or six major projects—those having the most impact—and prioritizing them for accomplishment in the upcoming year.

Everything cannot be done at once, but now is the time to "move out." Senior leadership must now make these choices and commit to resourcing them. That includes ensuring that training and learning take place to support the organization's direction.

## MAKING IT HAPPEN

Now that the assessment feedback has been reviewed and analyzed, the organizational direction and alignment reviewed for sufficiency, the processes identified to define how to design the work, and the choices made on what the organization is going to do, next on the agenda is operationalizing the choices. This is the "inputting" phase of the overall organizational process that leads to outcome, or results. This is where the organization's strategy becomes integrated with its operations. Making it happen involves assigning the prioritized choices to the identified processes.

This now becomes what the organization does to a large degree. This becomes how the organization operates. Full implementation occurs when action plans are developed and integrated into the processes, and every employee's support form contains tasks that can be directly linked to the mission of the organization. Now everyone has a direct stake in the organization's success. Now the plan can be employed because it is deployed.

# Chapter 14

# PERFORMANCE MANAGEMENT AND CONTINUOUS IMPROVEMENT

All of the components of performance management should now exist in the organization at some level and to some degree. The entire transitional process that the organization has been involved with from first planning to plan, to conducting a review to determine a baseline, to using the results of that review at the first offsite and subsequent offsites, has exposed the organization to all the necessary tools and has begun a process that will result in a performance organization. The challenge is putting everything into practice in a combination that works best.

The first thing to be aware of is that transition is never complete. This is not a "before and after" scenario. Those adopting that mindset will be sorely disappointed. The change will be more gradual, and it's more about charting a different course than waking up to a new organization. Nonetheless, resistance is to be expected. Within every organization there are the very few who lead, the majority who go along with change, and those "toads in the road" who are uncomfortable with a new way of doing business and prefer things the way they were. It's this last group that presents leadership with their greatest challenge.

As with any change, resistance will occur and leadership will be tested. This is when the temptation to wave the white flag and surrender looms large. Stay the course. Research has demonstrated that the "toads in the road" will eventually either convert or leave. What's important to remember is that these few should not dictate the future of the organization.

Another aspect to keep in mind is that this is a maturation process that involves many ingredients, many of which have yet to be thought of and are yet to be experienced. It is important to have an awareness that these things will occur and not to be thrown off course when they do. It is equally important, however, to take full advantage of the new tools made available and use them to continue the transition because they will help the organization improve performance and facilitate growth. The challenge is to use those tools in a way that optimizes performance.

Leadership must now understand that they're at the helm of a system—one that is synergistic and is made up of working parts to produce results. It is no longer about stovepipes and adding up the sum of those stovepipes to define performance. Instead, it is about how this system can optimally respond to the environment of customers, stakeholders, other reports, partners, and all who are impacted by the system and have a vested interest in the organization. It is also about how well the system takes care of its viability—the people who operationalize and nurture it and move it along on its journey.

The core values and concepts of the criteria form the basis of how the organization conducts that journey. They are the foundation on which the system must be built. Otherwise flaws will emerge that will compromise the system's performance.

The system, guided by leadership (Category 1), uses the organizational map (Category 2) to chart its course and set the conditions of operation necessary to achieve its purpose: customer satisfaction (Category 3). The operational part of the performance system, the workforce (Category 5), which carries out the processes (Category 6) to produce results (Category 7), must synchronize with the leadership's direction and purpose to make the system work. And how well is it working? The various gauges that provide a dashboard of performance indicators (Category 4) enable those in the organizational cockpit to monitor the system's performance. The better and more accurate the gauges, the easier it is to operate the system.

## MAKING IT WORK

Accept the reality that the system may not function as well as you want it to in the beginning. It will be a rudimentary system needing numerous adjustments. But there are certain fundamentals driven by the core values and concepts of the Baldrige criteria that should always be in place, i.e., institutionalized, if performance and productivity are to occur. The organization must be strategy-driven as opposed to budget-driven. The organization's resources must be applied to the performance journey, as opposed to the journey always being in a reactive mode to the budget.

While it is reality that resources may be limited, a resource prioritization process should be in place so that the journey can continue. No one wants their trip to have to end because of a lack of resources. Alterations and detours are acceptable—they can be incorporated into the strategy—but termination is not.

To achieve the desired end state, the organization must continuously improve. Otherwise, the journey may end abruptly if someone else is performing better than you are and everyone hitches their wagon to the brighter organizational star. You may be viewed as not being needed any longer. Therefore, it is imperative that the plan–do–check–act cycle of continuous improvement be incorporated into everything the organization does, and at all levels. This cycle of planning and continuous improvement gives everyone, as well as the organization as a whole, an opportunity to set targets, assess progress, identify performance gaps, and plan a strategy for closing those gaps. That's how an organization moves forward and becomes more efficient and effective in the process.

The leadership of most organizations has an idea how it wants to operate, i.e., they all have an approach. A common problem, however, is deploying that approach. Leadership's philosophy and intent remain only words if there are no means by which that intent can be deployed to produce performance results, let alone undertake a journey of continuous improvement. This is where alignment within a performance framework comes in. For performance to occur, everyone in the organization must have a part to play in the performance scenario. Therefore, everyone's support form/ employee evaluation form must in some way link with the measurable objectives of the organization. Everyone should have a part to play in the organization's performance. This fosters ownership and facilitates empowerment. Aligning for performance is a crucial element in performance management.

## THE TOTAL SYSTEM

For a total performance picture to be painted, all factors weighing into or contributing to that performance must be considered. This performance picture has more than just one or even two dimensions. It's a system that has height, width, and breadth—one that focuses on achieving a desired end state (vision) while continuing to get better at what the organization does (mission). (See Figure 14-1, Desired State: The Future.)

The strategic component of the system contains various measures, or "roadmaps," indicating progress toward the vi-

**Figure 14-1.** Desired State: The Future

sion. Included on the strategic side of the organization are corporate status reports, standards, strategic goals, and objectives. On the mission or operational side are process management and costing measures and operational objectives. The strategic and operational results converge to form the senior leaders' dashboard, an indicator of how the overall organization is doing, both strategically (avoiding the iceberg) and operationally (meeting or exceeding customer expectations). Taken together, the result is performance and a desired end-state.

Another dimension has to do with the interrelationship of the mission and vision so that the cause-and-effect relationships can begin to be determined. Thus, prevention and predictability can be a part of the performance picture.

A final dimension of the total performance system is a continual awareness of the environment as a major input into what the organization does and where it is going. Technology—and how it drives change—serves as a good example of an environmental condition affecting an organization. An environmental scan is essential to ensuring that this performance dimension is always visible.

To illustrate the need to consider all components of a performance system, the maiden voyage of the Titanic can be used as an analogy. The system, the ship, was certainly working well—the best in the world to date—and the customers, the passengers, were certainly satisfied. In fact, they were delighted. The failure was, of course, not considering the environment and keeping a watchful, measured eye on the desired end-state. There was a lot of frantic maneuvering at the last minute, but it was too late. The changes that needed to be integrated and implemented were much too drastic to avert disaster.

## THE STRATEGIC PLAN AS THE FOCUS

The document that should be used to focus the organization on this total performance picture is the strategic plan. The plan should bring it all together so that everyone has a holistic view of the organization in the performance framework. The plan should encompass the vision, with its goals and measurable objectives cascading down to action plans and tasks as one side of the performance picture. Accomplishment of the mission with optimal efficiency and effectiveness, i.e., process improvement, is another side. How these two aspects are affected by environmental influences and impacts defines the third dimension.

The integrative dimension is an ongoing process that incorporates the other three dimensions to determine comparisons, correlations, and cause-and-effect relationships. This is a formidable challenge, but one that must be undertaken if the organization is to be totally performance-oriented. Identifying and clarifying those dimensions is the first step in achieving balance with all the factors involved in the performance scenario. The focal point bringing it all together is the strategic plan. The next step in continuous improvement is to develop a set of gauges that responsibly reflect what this multi-dimensional performance system is doing—a set of gauges that represent a dashboard of system indicators.

## THE COST OF CONTINUOUS IMPROVEMENT

Thus far, we have been dealing primarily with transitioning from a traditional, bureaucratic type of organization to one that is performance-oriented. This transition requires a framework to facilitate change; thus, the use of the Malcolm Baldrige criteria to provide that framework. The criteria provide not only the parameters in the context of a system for change to occur, but also a means for assessing the maturity of that system and progress toward achieving the organization's goals.

We've also discussed performance in relationship to a system, i.e., a group of parts working together in synchronization to produce desired results. This system functions on two dimensions or phases as a means to continuously improve. These dimensions are approach and deployment. The approach dimension deals with how the organization is established or designed to provide optimum results. Deployment is about delivering on the mission: how well the organization carries out what it intends to do. The entire performance system is geared to accomplish the mission in the best way possible. The culture that is developed so the people of the organization can make it all happen is a crucial ingredient.

Every organization has an opportunity to excel. It is quite amazing that so few government organizations aren't continually acting on that opportunity or challenge. The ones that have pursued those opportunities and acted on those challenges are in various stages of performance maturity, and a sticking point for most is deploying what they intend to do. The government is quite good at the approach dimension; a lot of time and effort is expended on structure. When it comes to empowering everyone to act out what the organization intends to do, however, they run into trouble.

One of the main reasons this happens has to do with a control issue. Leadership in a bureaucratic environment is generally reluctant to relinquish control, so it creates a structure that has control built in. This makes it very difficult to deploy the organizational intent or mission, and it compromises the core value of agility. Therefore, what usually happens is that good ideas come and go; they move in and out of the organizational structure, but few, if any, of these ideas ever get deployed.

Another reason that makes it difficult for government organizations to fully deploy their intent involves the distance that's placed between the workforce and the financial aspects of the agency. This "distancing" compromises a sense of ownership that is required if true performance is to occur. This is in sharp contrast to the private sector, where viability is directly related to making a profit. Results must be achieved, or the company will cease to exist. In a government organization, that is not usually the case. In fact, financial performance means something altogether different.

In the government, agencies are rewarded if they execute 100 percent of their budget during the fiscal year. Budget execution thus drives the planning. If a large amount of unexecuted funds remains at the end of the third quarter, the agency will respond by funding projects and supplies to execute quickly to ensure everything gets spent. This all but kills any incentive to be more efficient. In fact, any savings realized by efficiency are usually taken up by the higher level and redistributed to those who are performing poorly. Thus, poor performance gets rewarded—the incentive is negative.

A slightly different scenario involves the development of an unfinanced requirement (UFR) list so that any money withheld at a higher headquarters level can be distributed to make up for what was not financed earlier in the year. This is a "fall in line" reactive type of drill that involves little planning and is also contrary to performance.

This type of fiduciary philosophy is in direct conflict with performance management and is a major inhibitor in the government's effort to transition to performance management. No fiduciary responsibility is deployed throughout the workforce. The human resource entity is detached and disassociated from the financial performance of the organization. There is no incentive to be good stewards of resources or to be efficient.

This is where cost management and activity-based costing enter the picture. If everyone has a share in the organization's efficiency, then everyone will have the opportunity to contribute to continuous performance improvement. Costing is the other component of deployment; quality products and services must be deployed, but costing provides the consistency and staying power for the quality journey. Activity-based costing is a major tool that can be used to measure efficiencies.

Until recently, the concern for how much things cost resided only at the top levels of the organization. Responsibility for costs and efficiencies never reached the level where work was actually being accomplished, where the processes were being implemented. There may be a lot of rhetoric regarding cost cutting and cost savings, but that usually translates into cutting back or doing more with less, not being more efficient. Cuts and reorganization—as opposed to process orientation and alignment—do not lend themselves to a most efficient organization.

Empowerment equates to responsibility, and if the responsibility is never deployed, neither are the efficiencies and the motivation to improve. If applying costs to activities was ingrained into the numerous activities and processes were clearly defined, government studies to determine efficiencies and most efficient organizations (A-76 studies) would not have been nearly so traumatic. The cost of conducting A-76 studies and the resulting outsourcing that occurred far exceeds what it would cost to employ process management and determine the cost of conducting the various and numerous activities in the government sector.

Activity-based costing and the management of those processes (activity-based management) are performance functions and should be part of the performance system. Only when processes are clearly defined and costed can continuous improvement take place. Most government organizations have not reached that point.

Activity-based costing training is readily available through numerous sources, so the "how" will not be addressed here. What will be addressed is how to think about costing in the context of a continuous improvement culture. Category 6 of the Baldrige criteria is where to find process management as part of the total performance system. The criteria ask for how the organization has defined its key and support processes as well as supplier and partner processes. Once the processes are designed and defined, the next step is to determine measures to assess how well these processes are operating. Any number of metrics can be applied, but eventually costs are going to have to be determined because they are the most universal method of communicating efficiency.

The hardest part is getting started, so it is usually best to start with processes that are simple and easily defined. That will alleviate much frustration and enable the workforce to believe it can be done. Plus, once a few simple processes are costed, they can be used as a model for other areas. To succeed, a process orientation and a drive for becoming better, faster, and cheaper must become part of the culture.

Applying a cost to the process is the next step as a means to determine a baseline. Once completed, targets for improvement can be established. Then, strategies can be developed for reaching those targets. The gap between the baseline and the desired target is the efficiency gap that everyone should be focused on for closure.

Once all the processes and accompanying inputs and outputs are outlined and applied costs are in place, the continuous improvement journey can become real. A vital part of the performance management system is now in place. Improved results can now be expected, striven for, and achieved.

This has profound implications for leadership in making decisions for performance improvement, not cutting and reorganizing. Costing involves the customers more directly in the process and partners them up with the organization itself. They are now recipients of the improved quality of products or services that are being delivered, in a timely manner, and at a reduced price. In a word, the customer is experiencing *value*.

Costing also has a major impact on the strategic planning process. In previous chapters, we discussed how strategic planning must consider not only the strategic, i.e., how to guide the organization to its vision, but the operational as well. The operational vector of the planning process is where the costing component has its genesis and applicability. It is important to realize, however, that there's another component to quality that must not be overlooked. It is the maturing organization that continuously improves and that consistently delivers high-quality products and services with few or no defects.

A satisfied or delighted customer is one who has expectations met or exceeded. A customer also wants to know that the quality of the product or service is not compromised for any reason. Consistency is the component of quality that is also the product of continuous improvement and the result of using costing as a means to determine efficiency and effectiveness.

# Chapter 15
# CASE STUDIES

GPRA prompted some government organizations and agencies to begin quality initiatives and even embark on a quality journey—a journey based on continuous improvement and performance. In testimony before the Subcommittee on Oversight of Government Management and Restructuring, J. Christopher Mihm of the General Accounting Office pointed out that for federal agencies to make the major improvements in mission-related results envisioned by GPRA, they must undertake management and process improvement initiatives, including quality management. He noted that it's really all about results. The projects must initiate change and produce results.

Following are some actual case studies of how certain government organizations have begun to embrace the quality journey and establish a foundation or framework for change to more of a performance-oriented system. Several of these examples naturally fall into a category of the Baldrige criteria and are described in that manner.

## LEADERSHIP

For GPRA to be implemented successfully, leadership must be clearly committed and set a clear, visionary direction of where the organization is headed. This vision must be clearly communicated, roles in accomplishing the vision must be clearly defined, and everyone must be held accountable in the fulfillment of those roles. Mihm testified that four leadership practices were found to be central to initiating change.

First, leadership empowered the workforce and established enabling practices and processes that allowed that empowerment to be effective. Second, leaders employed a wide range of tools to assist the workforce in their performance endeavors. Incentives and accountability were aligned with organizational goals. Third, leaders invested in human capital, viewing training as a contributor to results rather than as an expense. Finally, leadership integrated the improvement efforts from all aspects of the organization, both from within and from other agencies.

Mitch Daniels, Jr., the President's budget chief, cited three major programs that are "green" on the President's scorecard: (1) the National Weather Service, which has doubled its warning times for severe storms; (2) the National Science Foundation, which finances scientific research with low overhead costs; and (3) the Women, Infants, and Children's program, which devised measures to track improvements in the health of the people it serves. While these programs are still clearly in the minority, they are at least in existence and have the attention of the President of the United States.

The U.S. Army Operations Support Command (OSC) has established a Senior Advisory Board of Directors, which serves as a body for strategic direction and resource decisions. The OSC Commanding General chairs the eight-member board. All members are committed to represent the interests of the entire OSC and are not advocates for their functional organizations or individual installations. The Board of Directors identified the four major processes that make up the existence of OSC, determined and approved the process owners, and established key focus area champions.

This Senior Executive Board chartered six Quality Management Boards to begin implementation of the Total Army Quality philosophy. The six Quality Management Boards are directly linked to the President's Quality Award criteria (the government equivalent of the Baldrige criteria). They have empowered the organizations through integrated process teams to carry out process improvement initiatives. The integrated process teams have established objectives that are aligned with OSC's mission and key processes.

The Quality Management Boards conduct in-process reviews to monitor progress. The strategic vision and direction of the OSC is communicated and deployed throughout the organization and becomes an operational reality via the process teams. Further, OSC conducts well-advertised open forum meetings on a bimonthly basis to encourage open communications and new ideas. These meetings are scheduled well in advance, and read-ahead packages are distributed. Minutes for each meeting are published on electronic bulletin boards and Web pages for easy access by all OSC employees.

The U.S. Army Dental Command (DENCOM) has undertaken major initiatives for change and quality improvement throughout the Army Dental Care System. DENCOM senior leadership launched the Dental Care Reengineering Initiative and established a Web-based reporting system, the Corporate Dental Application. These initiatives have become and remain the preferred vehicles through which senior leadership addresses the corporate vision, values, and performance. The Dental Care Reengineering Initiative began as an experiment and now is the standard organizational philosophy for improving clinical efficiencies and business practices.

The key concepts of the reengineering effort were published in the *Clinical & Administrative Handbook* in April 1999. The initiative was deployed throughout the Army's dental clinics, and in May 1999, the Taylor Dental Clinic at

Fort Campbell, Kentucky, was awarded the Vice President's Hammer Award in recognition of its success in streamlining operations, empowering the staff, improving customer service, and reducing costs. Simultaneously, the Taylor Dental Clinic improved readiness and the effectiveness of the soldiers at Fort Campbell by steadily and continuously improving dental fitness by more than 100 percent. This is a true success story of leadership deploying its intent throughout the organization.

Category 1.2 of the Baldrige criteria addresses organizational performance reviews. Performance reviews are deemed a leadership responsibility because they provide the opportunity to monitor the organization's performance on a regular basis as well as make necessary changes and take any appropriate actions.

At the Tank-automotive and Armaments Command's Armament Research, Development, and Engineering Center (TACOM-ARDEC), senior leaders are personally involved on a regular basis in reviewing performance—both from an overall organizational perspective and from a more specific business unit perspective. Several systematic reviews are conducted, including the quarterly Systems Measurement Review, the Monthly Executive Council, and the weekly Top 10 Reviews. Review findings that indicate a need for process changes are referred to the appropriate System Owner—the senior leader for the process—who works the issues within the organization's system process priorities and budgetary considerations, up through one of the applicable Quality Management Boards, for resolution, incorporation, and implementation into TACOM-ARDEC's process system. A knowledge database is used to capture the information and share/deploy it throughout the organization. This is a great example of how to use performance reviews as an opportunity to improve overall organizational performance.

A final example in the leadership category can be found at Fort Hood, Texas, with its implementation of the Continuous Improvement System (CIS). Until a couple of years ago, Ft. Hood operated in a very traditional manner, highly structured, with each function completely separate. They embraced the principles of Total Quality Management (TQM) by leadership setting a visionary direction, with a focus on customers and empowerment of the workforce. The key leaders instrumental in getting the organization started in this direction left, and they soon realized their approach was not a system, nor was it deployed. They established the CIS, which embraces the principles of TQM and complements the chain of command. It focuses on significant processes for mission accomplishment, facilitates cross-functional integration, and is driven by the needs of the customer.

The CIS is composed of an Executive Steering Committee, a Senior Quality Board, and four Quality Management Boards. The Executive Steering Committee is chaired by the Commanding General and sets the strategic direction of the organization. It meets quarterly to review performance, and annually to align Ft. Hood's strategic planning to achieve long-range goals. The Senior Quality Board is the action arm of the Executive Steering Committee, and it guides and integrates the activities of the four Quality Management Boards. The key process owner in each area chairs the appropriate board and conducts quarterly performance reviews. Directorates and sub-units review their performance results monthly. The CIS is a systematic approach that is deployed and operational.

## STRATEGIC PLANNING

Category 2 of the Baldrige criteria addresses the development and deployment of the organization's strategic plan.

Mihm's GAO testimony emphasized the importance of a clear understanding of what is to be accomplished and how progress is to be measured. This is a central principle of TQM and performance-based management: the establishment of clear goals and performance measures, i.e., strategic planning. The organization's plan should be the driver for daily operations and the determining factor for the budget.

As part of its management reform initiative to improve federal performance, GAO followed Mihm's testimony with a performance and accountability report for the years 2000–2002. In this report, GAO outlined four strategic goals, addressing four critical performance areas: (1) provide timely, quality service to Congress and the federal government to address the emerging challenges to the American people, (2) provide this same service to respond to security threats and global challenges, (3) support the transition to a results-oriented accountable federal government, and (4) maximize GAO's value by being a model organization for the federal government.

These goals are broad-based and cover the waterfront with regard to GAO's expectations and responsibilities for the future. Objectives and supporting actions can and have been developed for each goal. GAO is transitioning to a performance-oriented way of operating and is being driven by the strategic planning process and the resulting strategic plan.

There is still a long way to go across federal and government agencies, but there are indications that performance-based management driven by performance plans is taking place in various sectors of the government. Appendix B contains actual strategic plans that have been deployed and are used as the organizational roadmap and driver for the operation.

Other case studies and vignettes provide good examples of how organizations viewed their future and how they developed plans to make that future a reality. The Army Research

Laboratory (ARL) was the only research laboratory to be designated a pilot project under GPRA. As part of the pilot, ARL developed a business planning methodology that provides a useful tool for managing the research enterprise, as well as developing a model for any laboratory to comply with GPRA and produce strategic and performance plans.

The ARL business plan consists of four volumes that are constructed and reviewed in senior staff quarterly meetings. The meetings are scheduled to coincide with the Defense budget cycle. Volume I, the strategic plan itself, projects 15 years into the future and lays out long-range ARL strategic goals. These goals articulate and are based on national defense requirements. Volume II is the long-range plan, which describes how the strategy will be resourced and shows the linkage to each strategic goal. Volume III is the actual performance plan, which is the upcoming fiscal year's actions specifically addressing the utilization of resources for the upcoming fiscal year. Volume III is developed at the quarterly meeting of the senior ARL staff and adjusted at subsequent quarterly meetings. Volume IV is the annual performance report, which summarizes the performance of ARL and tracks progress toward long-range strategic goals laid out in Volume I.

The U.S. Army Armament Research, Development, and Engineering Center uses a disciplined, overarching strategic planning process that serves as a very effective management tool. The Associate Technical Director for Systems, Concepts and Technology is the owner of the strategic planning process and the corporate strategic plan.

Twice yearly at the Board of Directors meetings, the senior managers review the overall corporate strategy. They revise the action plans on an annual basis to adjust for changes that have occurred during the last year as a result of changing customer requirements and executive-level decisions that may have impacted organizational operations and direction. This formal planning process yields four distinct but interrelated sets of documents: the corporate strategic plan, four system owners' plans, 20 business unit business plans, and a corporate performance plan. The process uses all input, both formal and informal, analyzed by the cross-functional strategic planning cell.

Major changes always involve specific guidance from senior leadership that is augmented by additional information from random work groups and business unit managers to ensure a complete, accurate corporate picture. This is followed by a thorough SWOT analysis to evaluate risks and options and to determine optimum market position. The "new" corporate strategic plan sets the stage and provides the necessary framework for system owners and business units to develop their plans.

The Board of Directors formulates a Commanding General's/Technical Director's strategic intent and six corporate objectives. These objectives and intents are communicated to the workforce through electronic mail and storyboards placed throughout the workplace. These strategic objectives are adapted and integrated into the business plans and the employee Total Army Performance Evaluation System. The strategic plan is now ready to execute.

Strategic plan execution is tied to performance measures and subsequently tracking that performance. Tracking performance requires a systematic, planned method that is best met by quarterly performance reviews. The key, corporate-level objectives cascade down in a logical manner from the corporate strategic plan to the system owners and the specific business unit.

Quarterly performance reviews are formal and are conducted by senior management. The reviews track the key metrics established in the corporate strategic plan. Program reviews, which contain the program metrics (such as cost, scheduling, performance, and other technical and programmatic issues). Action planning takes place at the team level, and team members are empowered to manage/improve specific processes. Good alignment increases the opportunity for better performance.

## CUSTOMER FOCUS

Category 3 of the Baldrige criteria focuses on the customer. Knowing the customers, their requirements, their likes and dislikes, and what they expect from your organization is the first step that must be taken to satisfy them. Customer knowledge means doing the necessary legwork to listen and learn in order to get that information.

Operations Management International, Inc. (OMI), is employee-owned and runs more than 170 wastewater and drinking water treatment facilities in 29 states and 8 other nations. Nearly 95 percent of OMI's customers are U.S. cities, counties, and other public entities that have outsourced the operation and maintenance of their plants. Providing clean water and efficient wastewater services fulfills basic human needs that can become very sensitive very quickly, so a close listening and learning relationship with the customer is crucial. That is why OMI is admittedly obsessed with quality; in fact, the company has dubbed its overall process model "Obsessed With Quality." This is a significant and symbolic mantra, because if quality is being compromised in any way, the customer will immediately be impacted and respond. That is why customer focus heads the list of OMI's four strategic objectives.

All OMI employees are authorized to address customer issues. They are encouraged to think and act like company owners and are rewarded for making decisions and taking actions that will improve customer satisfaction. A defining element of OMI's culture is exceeding customer expectations, and most of what occurs in that culture is oriented toward accomplishing that goal. OMI has developed a variety of listening approaches such as surveys, focus groups, and market research to learn from their customers and continually improve the customer relationship. (OMI has numerous examples of quality initiatives that fall into other categories of the Baldrige criteria; some of those will be highlighted later in this chapter.)

The Aberdeen Test Center, in an attempt to facilitate cooperation and customer satisfaction, designates employees or representatives as executive agents and places them at key customer locations. These executive agents are fully focused on meeting the needs of the center's key customers. This initiative is directly linked to resourcing, because the Aberdeen Test Center gets 70 percent of its command operating dollars from its customers. Since customers decide where they will bring their testing for execution, the command must have a keen and responsible customer focus.

As a part of determining customer satisfaction, Aberdeen mails a questionnaire to each customer for whom a test is completed. This feedback is closely monitored. If any rating is received that is inconsistent with quality, Aberdeen responds expeditiously with immediate action or a plan to correct the shortcoming.

Medical services is another area where basic customer needs are usually at the forefront and require a fast, agile response. An example of how customer complaints were received and responded to can be found at the William Beaumont Army Medical Center in Ft. Bliss, Texas. The pharmacy center was receiving a high complaint rate for prescription-fill wait time. The medical center responded by installing a robotic prescription filler and adding several service windows. The result was a reduction in waiting time of 55–60 percent and a higher rate of customer satisfaction.

## INFORMATION AND ANALYSIS

This category deals with measurement of the organization's performance. This measurement involves more than data recording, but also must take into account the correct framework or architecture for data to be ported into so that data can become useful information or knowledge. Major decisions have more credibility when they are based on knowledge rather than raw numbers.

Mihm's statement to Congress addressed the need to have accurate, reliable, and timely data upon which to make decisions. He went on to say that significant progress is needed across all agencies in this regard. Most of the fiscal year 2000 annual performance plans reviewed by his office provided only limited confidence that performance information will be credible. Further, they lacked the information on the actual procedures that agencies were using to verify and validate their performance information.

The Department of Transportation (DOT) has used a balanced scorecard for the last four years in measuring its procurement function. The department is using the lessons learned from that experience to apply the concept to its human resources management function. The model presents a balanced scorecard that links performance measures from five perspectives: financial, customer, internal business, innovation and learning, and employee empowerment. Key measures are identified for ten performance goals.

The team developed a variety of mechanisms to support data collection, including customer, employee, and manager self-assessment surveys. Human resources strengths and weaknesses identified from the data collected and analyzed will be used in identifying best-in-class practices, as well as formulating action plans for improvements. As noted in DOT's quality submission to acquisition quality initiatives,

DOT's procurement community views its balanced scorecard effort as "a real management tool that can empower managers, supervisors, and line employees to improve performance. The scorecard provides a point of departure for process improvement and benchmarking. It allows the organization to accelerate the process of change and accomplish breakthrough improvements. The links to improving individual performance can be substantial."

The Deputy Chief of Staff for Base Operations Support (DCSBOS) at Headquarters Training and Doctrine Command (TRADOC) has developed a corporate database for quick and easy access to the multiple databases available for decision support. The database was developed to support and accomplish a DCSBOS strategic goal outlined in its strategic plan: "Achieve Information Dominance—The Right Information at the Right Time."

Prior to development of the corporate database, there was no structured information library for integrating, viewing, and analyzing current or historical data from various sources. DCSBOS had data stored in many different kinds of reports, with different naming conventions and unique file formats. The corporate database makes information available to other users through system links. Program managers own and maintain the functional data. The database also uses geo-based technology to integrate geographic, tabular, and other information types in a user-friendly interface. It provides support to TRADOC installations, establishes a corporate memory, and reduces decision-making time.

The corporate database continues to be developed and refined. When the second phase of the system is complete, the corporate database will also be able to process business rules and develop "what if" scenarios on a real-time basis.

The Tank-automotive and Armaments Command-Armament, Research, Development, and Engineering Center

(TACOM-ARDEC) measures organizational performance using the Systems Measurement Review, a process that replaces standard review and analysis with a systems approach. The highlights of the Systems Measurement Review are: top leadership review of integrated performance, all systems integrated throughout the organization, linkage to strategic plans, peer review, benchmarking from industry and government, and a forum for customer feedback. The review is paperless and is available to everyone through the Internet.

In the review, system owners design performance measures and present them to top management and other system owners. They strive for cross-functional integration, focus on the customer, track process improvement, facilitate corporate decision-making, and motivate the organization to continuously improve. The Systems Measurement Review Team, trained in measurement methods and the Baldrige criteria, updates the TACOM-ARDEC measurement plan, which is the organization's systematic way of planning, evaluating, and improving quality measurement. Driven by system owners and customers (who have direct input to the system owners), the review includes data on operational performance, financial performance, markets, human resources, products, and customers. The Systems Measurement Review ensures consistency and validity of measures and gives decision-makers full access to quality data and performance trends.

## HUMAN RESOURCES

Mihm's testimony also addressed the fact that high-performing organizations know that the development and effective management of their human capital is essential to achieving results. Success is possible only when the right employees are on board and are provided the training, tools, structures, incentives, and accountability to work effectively. High-performing organizations gather and use all pertinent employee-related data such as employee skills and satisfaction. Such measures are tied to unit and overall organizational performance.

Mihm noted that federal agencies still have much room for improvement in making this vital link between their human capital planning and their mission-related goals and strategies. He further testified that most of the performance plans reviewed by his office did not sufficiently address how the agencies will use their human capital to achieve results. This suggests that one of the central attributes of high-performing organizations—the systematic integration of mission and program planning with human capital planning—is not being effectively addressed across the federal government.

To fully address the human capital issue, actions have to be taken that form the basis of a performance culture. A best practice case study can be found with Lockheed Martin Electronics and Missiles in Orlando, Florida. The company adopted the concept of performance management teams in 1985 to continuously improve the quality and reliability of its products and services, reduce cost and cycle times, enhance productivity, and ensure schedule compliance to maximize customer satisfaction. That means that quality has to be assigned top priority, and performance management teams must work toward that end and be totally committed.

Lockheed Martin has created a culture wherein this performance orientation can take place. Performance is monitored and measured at the team level. Teams are composed of work groups from various areas of the company (e.g., manufacturing, production, procurement). Where appropriate, customers are also members of the team. Teams meet once per week, review performance metrics, identify action items to improve product and service quality, and develop improvements to enhance overall efficiency. Participation is mandatory and is a major part of the performance appraisal process. The reward system is based on team recognition such as team of the month, team of the year, and various other team awards.

OMI, in its "obsessed with quality" culture, works hard to cultivate empowerment and innovation among its employees. Associates are "paid to think," and OMI backs up this claim with extensive training opportunities. Everyone is given plenty of opportunity to apply what they learn: All employees are authorized to improve job designs, respond directly to process problems, and address customer issues. Empowerment is reinforced by reward and recognition systems that encourage employees to think like company owners.

OMI has doubled its expenditures on training and learning. Training plans are regularly updated and are part of every evaluation, which occur every six months. Employee motivation, morale, and satisfaction are tracked regularly through focus groups and surveys.

Personnel systems in the government are notorious for bureaucracy. Numerous studies have reported the problems, and in some cases, action is being taken. Army Research Laboratory (ARL) is now in the second year of the implementation of PersDemo. The system is designed to make ARL more competitive in recruiting and retaining high-quality technical talent and to allow superior achievements to be recognized through a pay-for-performance system. One of the principal characteristics of the new system is the replacement of the entire General Schedule (GS) with a pay-banding system that consists of three or four bands for the various occupational families. This allows managers greater flexibility in making offers to prospective new employees and in promoting high performers.

Under PersDemo, the performance appraisal system is structured so that true performance is measured. The funding pool for awards and raises is allocated so that top performers get significant rewards, and under-performers receive little or no recognition. PersDemo has also greatly simplified automated classification and eased the processes for discipline and classification.

The Communications-Electronics Command Research, Development and Engineering Center, as an initiative to develop a learning environment, offers several types of developmental assignments to promote its employees' professional growth. Positions can include: a two- to three-year assignment as a science advisor under the Army Materiel Command Field Assistance in Science and Technology Program; an assignment at Army level with the Secretary of the Army for Research, Development, and Acquisition; or a one-year assignment with the Deputy Chief of Staff for Intelligence, the Defense Intelligence Agency Central Measurement and Signature Intelligence Office, or the Assistant Under Secretary of Defense.

Many other developmental opportunities are also available. These various opportunities allow the organization to make the most effective use of the workforce and broaden the participants' perspectives within the organization. The result is a learning environment that considers the broader corporate perspective.

Category 5 of the Baldrige criteria also asks about employees' well-being and satisfaction. TACOM-ARDEC's Total Fitness program was first deployed as an executive fitness program. It was very successful and was subsequently extended to all employees; currently, more than 70 percent are actively participating.

The Total Fitness program offers extensive resources contributing to the overall well-being and health of the workforce. Fitness facilities include an aerobics studio, a cardiovascular exercise studio, a cardiac rehabilitation area, and a health risk assessment center. Other wellness programs offered are classes on nutrition, weight reduction, stress management, smoking cessation, holistic wellness, and high blood pressure management. Support for these various programs is enhanced by a gymnasium, swimming pool, ball fields, tennis courts, fitness trails, racquetball court, and golf course.

## PROCESS MANAGEMENT

Processes are what an organization is involved with to produce an outcome. This outcome is built on many outputs that are the result of supporting processes. All processes should be working toward meeting customer requirements and accomplishing the mission. How all this is being managed by the organization is addressed in Category 6 of the Baldrige criteria, process management.

When Mihm testified before Congress, he went through the Baldrige criteria category by category. For Category 6, he highlighted the importance of understanding how processes and strategies relate to achieving results—a system oriented toward performance. An organization cannot improve performance and customer satisfaction if does not know what causes current levels of performance and customer satisfaction, i.e., what are the key and supporting processes and how are they functioning?

Mihm testified that government agencies have much work remaining in this area. Many agencies have developed goals and strategies but have not taken the next and necessary step indicating specifically how the strategies will contribute to the expected level of performance. An analogy may be made to a Hollywood set: The front of the building is there and it appears as though it's a real building, but there's nothing inside. Those that have identified their key and supporting processes and have organized their operation in support of organizational goals get results.

OMI, a 2000 Malcolm Baldrige Award recipient, did just that. They viewed their organization as a system and identified four strategic objectives—customer focus, business growth, innovation, and market leadership—and subsequently identified/developed processes in support of those objectives. Improvement initiatives were selected in support of the strategic plan and crafted so that each initiative contributes significantly to achieving one or more objectives and key customer requirements. These initiatives (26 in 2000) were each assigned to a team led by a senior leader. Team charters were developed, with parameters of operation outlined and timelines for completion established. The system is now ready to operate, and, once that occurs, performance can be monitored, reviewed, and analyzed.

Every year the entire set of critical processes is reviewed, and the processes are ranked for their impact on progress toward strategic objectives. Existing processes are modified, adjusted, and strengthened as necessary to improve. Measures are also reviewed to ensure an accurate assessment of organizational health.

Letterkenny Army Depot in Chambersburg, Pennsylvania, established a shop stores contract with a local vendor to handle the purchase of common material and supplies used by the Department of Public Works. Previously, material purchases had been handled through the Installation Supply Account and the Directorate of Contracting for procurement actions, then shipped to the Defense Logistics Agency for distribution. These purchases required formal, bureaucratic procurement actions, which required time and cost. The procurement of an item often exceeded the actual cost of the item.

The shop stores contract is a firm fixed-price, indefinite-quantity service contract awarded to a single vendor who maintains a supply facility within a 15-mile radius of Letterkenny Army Depot. The contractor provides supervision, management personnel, equipment, and supplies to maintain the supply facility. The shop stores contract has streamlined the process for obtaining materials and supplies. As a result, customer service and satisfaction have greatly improved, costs have been reduced by more than 50 percent, and deliveries have been nearly 100 percent on time. The contract essentially eliminated the bureaucratic, cumbersome requirements for sole-source procurement as the number of buyers has been reduced from nine to one, and layers of management and paperwork have been eliminated.

The Center for Army Analysis (CAA) has identified 12 critical processes encompassing its major functions. Process action teams, consisting of representatives of internal process suppliers and customers as well as process experts, monitor each process during the course of executing normal work to identify potential problem areas and opportunities for process improvement. CAA's leadership team, consisting of the director, senior leaders, and supervisors, reviews progress at least annually.

The 12 processes have been greatly streamlined, and the quality of data inputs has markedly improved. Features have been added that enable analysts to see relationships and gain insights not previously discerned and made it possible for the center to provide real-time, quick-response analysis to support Army decision-makers. CAA output has increased dramatically. This is a classic example of how an organization aligns its processes to support objectives and ultimately the mission, thus greatly enhancing performance.

Process management and improvement can positively impact all types of organizations. The staff of Madigan Army Medical Center at Ft. Lewis, Washington, realized that the task of dictating records of patient care was making heavy demands on their physicians' time and taking away from patient care.

The Patient Administration Division's Transcription Service conducted an analysis of the existing procedures and discovered specific high-volume surgeries and treatments that took an extraordinary amount of time but varied little from physician to physician. The transcription service developed a standardized template that individualizes each procedure, thus saving huge amounts of time for dictation and transcription. The doctors' dictating time went from 10–15 minutes to 2 minutes per patient. This resulted in an 80 percent increase in productivity and the savings of one full-time person per year.

Madigan expanded this initiative, and the medical center now has 57 templates that are being used consistently. This is an example of how a process change saved time and resources while increasing service to the customer.

Category 6 also addresses supplier and partner processes. Government organizations have traditionally believed they had to be "self-sufficient" in their operations, i.e., they had to develop their own programs or their own systems rather than relying on an outside source. That thinking has changed, and a classic example of how an organization dramatically improved by partnering with an external partner can be found at Ft. Bragg, North Carolina.

In 1997, Ft. Bragg's energy costs exceeded $32 million per year. Its energy partner, Honeywell, developed a long-term energy plan that incorporated both supply side and demand side opportunities. Forty-nine energy savings projects were identified, and most of those have been implemented. Savings realized are being reinvested into the program, and new initiatives have generated energy worth over $2.6 million. Projects have been awarded with a value of over $10 million.

This partnership led to the development of the Postwide Energy Center. The center makes it possible to operate, monitor, and troubleshoot the performance of the major energy centers and 6,000 buildings throughout Ft. Bragg from a central location. This high-value initiative demonstrates the need and potential benefits of exploring opportunities beyond organizational or agency boundaries.

## BUSINESS RESULTS

Results are the reason an organization exists. Improving performance and managing for performance are really focused on achieving desired results. Business results as addressed in Category 7 of the Baldrige criteria have five aspects or areas of concentration: customer focus, financial performance, human resources, supplier and partner, and organizational effectiveness. A balance of these five areas in light of the organization's mission is necessary to achieve and maintain a performance orientation.

GAO certainly had results foremost in mind when the agency developed the Performance and Accountability Plans and accompanying Performance and Accountability Reports to provide Congress and the American people a better-performing government. The four strategic goals and underlying objectives responsibly cover all the areas addressed in Category 7 of the Baldrige criteria:

(1) "Provide Timely, Quality Service to the Congress and the Federal Government to Address Current and Emerging Challenges to the Well-Being and Financial Security of the American People."

*Supporting Objectives:*

—the health care needs of an aging and diverse population

—a secure retirement for older Americans

—the social safety net for Americans in need

—an educated citizenry and a productive workforce

—an effective system of justice

—investment in communities and economic development

—responsible stewardship of natural resources and the environment

—a safe and efficient national physical infrastructure.

(2) "Provide Timely, Quality Service to the Congress and the Federal Government to Respond to Changing Security Threats and the Challenges of Global Interdependence."

*Supporting Objectives*:

—responding to diffuse threats to national and global security

—ensuring military capabilities and readiness

—advancing and protecting U.S. international interests

—responding to the impact of global market forces on the U.S. economic and security interests.

(3) "Support the Transition to a More Results-Oriented and Accountable Federal Government."

*Supporting Objectives*:

—analyzing the federal government's long-term and near-term fiscal position, outlook, and options

—strengthening approaches for financing the government and accounting for taxpayer's dollars

—facilitating government-wide management and institutional reforms needed to build and sustain high-performing organizations and more effective government

—recommending economy, efficiency, and effectiveness improvements in federal agency programs.

(4) "Maximize the Value of GAO by Being a Model Organization for the Federal Government."

*Supporting Objectives*:

—cultivate and foster effective Congressional and agency relations

—implement a model strategic and annual planning and reporting process

—align human capital policies and practices to support GAO's mission

—develop efficient and responsive business processes

—build an integrated and reliable information technology infrastructure.

Although these goals and objectives are in themselves not measurable, GAO has developed performance measures and targets for each objective and each fiscal year. The results are clearly laid out, indicating whether a particular objective or set of objectives was met. On closer examination of the goals and objectives, it becomes apparent how the framework is established to produce performance results across the spectrum, i.e., a balanced set of indicators that, if accomplished, will accomplish GAO's mission to support Congress in carrying out its constitutional responsibilities.

The question arises, however, of how fully deployed this performance plan is. Certainly GAO is headed in the right direction, but is this performance orientation implemented and integrated throughout the government? There may be pockets of implementation, but clearly, it is not fully deployed. Looking across the spectrum of federal government, it's easy to see how the intent of GPRA was understood and taken seriously at the highest levels. As we work our way down and through the various agencies and organizations, however, it is apparent that some chose to ignore it, while others were preoccupied with other matters. Results are what GPRA is all about. While deployment is sporadic, some organizations got the message and have adopted a continuous improvement mentality—and results are being achieved.

Lockheed Martin Electronics and Missiles in Orlando, Florida, adopted the performance management team concept in 1985, but a change in culture was necessary for these teams to effectively operate and facilitate performance. That change was accomplished, and Lockheed Martin is now working with a focus on quality and results. The company has had no negative government audit findings for over six years. It was U.S. Army Missile Command Contractor Performance-certified in 1990 and ISO 9001-certified in 1994. Production scrap and rework have been reduced more than 70 percent, resulting in production budget underruns. Total program cycle time has been reduced by an average of 36 percent on major systems, and there has been mission success on all programs. This is an organization that saw the writing on the wall and acted accordingly. The company is now reaping the benefits of how it organized and decided to operate.

OMI is also results-oriented. The company had a contract renewal rate of 95 percent in 1999 and boasts the industry's top rank in the average length of customer retention. OMI has won more than 100 federal and state awards for excellence in the area of environmental protection in the past five years (more than half of these in the last two years).

ARL has developed an extensive customer interaction process that provides information (results) on how it's doing. The process is called the Performance Evaluation Construct and involves getting information from fellow distinguished scientists and engineers as part of a peer review, feedback from ARL's customers and stakeholders, and the lab's own internal assessment of performance.

The government is famous for spending huge amounts of money for items of lesser value or buying things it doesn't need or already has. In FY 1999, the Defense Logistics Agency continued full deployment of the Standard Army Retail Supply System by maximizing redistribution of available stocks to satisfy customer demands, as opposed to purchasing new supplies. The result was a satisfying $30 million worth of supply requirements through inventory redistribution, providing a higher than average material return credit for turn-ins and earning a $9.1 million profit that was used to satisfy other unfinanced requirements.

The Army has implemented a Risk Reduction Program where high-risk behaviors are identified that have a detrimental impact on soldiers' and families lives and readiness. Army installations are in various stages of deployment with this program, but Ft. Hood, Texas, has it operational and is achieving results. Data are collected and, using the information system designed for Risk Reduction, an "acceptable" level of risk is identified for each of 14 identified risk factors.

Quarterly reviews by senior leadership have precipitated decisions and actions that have caused a dramatic increase in program participation and a huge reduction in high-risk behaviors. This plays a vital role in the overall readiness of the force stationed at Ft. Hood. It's an example of how human resource results fit into accomplishment of the mission.

Military organizations have recognized for some time the importance of partnerships and the need to "team up" with various programs and practices in the private sector. It has only been since GPRA, however, that data reflecting the positive results of these partnerships are maintained. Category 7.4 of the Baldrige criteria asks for that data.

Fort Lewis, Washington, teamed up with the U.S. Department of Agriculture Forest Service to conduct a forest ecosystem study using various harvesting methods. The installation has a viable and active timber harvesting program that uses selective cutting to work near areas inhabited by endangered species. Over the last five years, Fort Lewis' Forestry Program has consistently generated money for the Army, averaging $2,500,000 more than the cost of running the program. In 1995, Fort Lewis received the Nature Conservancy's Public Service Award for its effort to conserve natural resources. Forty percent of these annual timber sales revenues are provided to the state of Washington for use in its public education program. This is an example of a partnership that produces results.

Category 7.5 of the Baldrige criteria asks for organizational effectiveness results. In other words, what has the organization done to get better at what it does, and are there results that substantiate this improvement? An example of organizational effectiveness can be found at the Wuerzburg Dental Activity in Wuerzburg, Germany. This dental activity has 12 subordinate, geographically separated dental clinics. An incentive program was implemented that targeted the core requirements of each clinic and the fulfillment of those requirements. The program considered numerous factors: collections from patients who pay, budget execution, monthly reporting, mandatory training, physical conditioning, soldier training, and education.

For FY 1999, the Wuerzburg Dental Activity returned $10,000 in collectibles to two clinics. These clinics were allowed to use the returned funds in ways that drive further quality improvements, including workforce rewards and improvements to the work environment. The program encourages managers to focus on best business practices and aligns the interests of the subordinate units with the overall command objectives to ensure that military and civilian staff have the skills to meet the requirements of the Army's healthcare mission in Europe.

These case studies are examples of organizations that are meeting the criteria in certain categories or individual items of the Baldrige criteria. This is not to say that these examples indicate that a performance system is in place; they may be only "pockets of excellence." Nonetheless, viewed in the full context of the intent of the criteria, the case studies offer insights into what "system" means, as well as the difference between approach and deployment. The bottom line is that all the parts must be synchronized and work together—that is the dynamic that defines performance.

# Chapter 16
# CONCLUSION

This book has outlined a process by which organizations can transition from a bureaucratic, stovepiped way of functioning to a performance management system with a focus on achieving results. That is the spirit and intent of the 1993 Government Performance and Results Act. Each chapter builds on the previous, and while it may be possible to skip steps in the transition process, you will find that each chapter provides the necessary foundation for the next step. Each step must be addressed not only in transition, but also in the implementation of the continuous improvement cycle.

The Chief Financial Officers (CFO) Council recognized the significance of GPRA early on, and in 1995 formed a GPRA implementation committee to improve financial management in the U.S. government. The CFO Council examined the collective experience of federal agencies, the private sector, academia, state and local agencies, and local and foreign governments in how they managed for results. Their review (in the CFO Act as amended by the Government Management Reform Act of 1994 and the Federal Financial Management Improvement Act of 1996) is a good summary of what has been outlined in some detail in this book.

**Start wherever you are.** Most agencies do not yet have a measurable strategic plan in place, but every agency measures something and has some way to quantify performance.

Use those existing performance measures to begin to link to broader, strategic goals. Those goals, in turn, can be further developed as the external functions that provide a product or service are identified. These identified functions are essentially what the organization does—its mission. The hardest part is getting started, and getting started may involve overcoming uncertainty and fear of failure. That is why learning the criteria addressed in the early chapters is crucial.

**The importance of senior management commitment.** Leadership must drive the change. It won't happen on its own. It must be more than just talk; there needs to be some behavioral demonstration of leadership's commitment. Leadership needs to create an awareness of the GPRA requirements and their implications for changing the culture; provide training to effect that change; ensure that decisions are in line with the organization's mission, vision, values, goals, and objectives; and hold managers accountable for achieving performance goals, i.e., results.

**Put it into practice.** For a transition to occur, the workforce must believe it can really happen, so making it real for everyone is a priority. GPRA offers a framework to get started. A more definitive framework is offered with the Baldrige criteria. Included in the criteria are sound management principles and business practices that enable performance planning, budgeting, assessment, and continuous quality improvement. Training everyone in GPRA and use of the criteria will deliver the message that the organization is serious and intends to follow through on the talk.

**Linkage.** It is a well-synchronized system that achieves performance and produces results. A "system" in the performance management world refers to the linkage of all the parts that have an impact on performance. Organizational goals, quantifiable, measurable objectives, annual performance targets, performance measures and reviews, and performance indicators all must have relevance to one another and support achieving the mission and strategic goals.

**Integration.** One of the biggest problems with a bureaucracy is duplication of effort. A performance management system requires that process be identified and subsequently mapped so that everyone can readily identify where they operate in the organization and make a difference. The integration of these key and supporting processes and an understanding how they work together and complement one another will increase output, achieve desired outcome, and produce desired results. The better the integration and "meshing" of these processes, the better the performance.

**Simplicity.** Bureaucracies can become very complex. A well-synchronized performance management system should be simple and easily understood by all. Bureaucracies lose their utility as they grow in complexity; a highly efficient management system stays basic, continuously prioritizes for importance, and keeps performance measures simple and focused only on those indicators necessary to achieve results. Attempting to track everything is a waste of time and will just create another meaningless bureaucracy. Collect only the data that have meaning relevant to achieving desired results.

**The customer.** Chapter 11 highlighted the need to keep the customer in the game. The organization's desired results should reflect satisfaction of the customers' and stakeholders' requirements in concert with accomplishing the mission. Performance measures should not only be easy to understand for the workforce tasked with producing results, but the customers and stakeholders should be able to understand the various measurements as well.

**Training performance will change the culture.** Developing an understanding of performance measures and the performance measurement system is not a one-time event. Training in the system is an ongoing process that should continue to improve the knowledge level while helping everyone feel more comfortable with a new way of doing business. Regularly scheduled on-the-job training on the Baldrige criteria, strategic planning, balanced scorecard, process mapping, etc., all lead to familiarization and empowerment, thus getting everyone to contribute. Regularly scheduled performance reviews (at least quarterly) provide a great learning forum and can facilitate culture change quickly. Chapter 2 addresses conducting a self-assessment using the Baldrige criteria. The self-assessment process will also greatly contribute to a learning environment.

**Information management system.** Category 4 of the Baldrige criteria is viewed as the "brain" of the overall performance management system. How the organization builds that brain is very important to the reliability and viability of the system. Attention must be paid to the architecture so that the data being imported go to the right place and are tied to the appropriate objectives in support of the goals. The information management system should act as a synthesizer and transform the collected data into information and even knowledge so that the decision makers have high-level visibility, as opposed to having to wade through details. The information management system should assimilate and analyze the details so they make sense from a global perspective.

Transitioning from a traditional bureaucratic organization to one that is performance-oriented is not easy. However, there may be no choice but to do so. It's truly a paradigm shift in all respects. What must be cast out are old ways of thinking, such as vertically structured organizations where performance is defined as the sum of that vertical stovepipe. What must be driven out is reacting to an annual budget that enslaves the workforce to an annual cycle of the same old thing happening year after year based on the amount of money given to you. What has to be eliminated is the paradigm of thought wherein everyone's performance is based upon the next higher level opinion of you, which may have nothing to do with reality. Leadership's personal agendas must no longer drive the organization.

A step-by-step process for transformation is depicted in Figure 16-1, Eight Steps to Transforming Your Organization. Of key importance is that this process should be reviewed at each offsite as sort of a "sanity check."

This book was written to provide a way to move from that static, nonproductive state to one of continuous improvement and performance orientation, with an eye on results. The pathway that this book describes is a step-by-step process that can assist an organization in moving from one paradigm to another. That assistance begins with preparing for change by recognizing and accepting the need for it, articulating that need throughout the workforce, and beginning the process. That actual process must begin with a determination (assessment) of where the organization is currently. Having knowledge about that current state provides the baseline for the gap that will evolve as leadership envisions the organization's end state. Closing that gap then becomes the work of transition. That transition begins with the first offsite and the establishment of measurable objectives that define the way of the future.

Leadership now becomes a visionary driver that has engaged the organization to develop and deploy a roadmap that uses customers' input so that the goals of the organization are realized. This roadmap belongs to everyone in the organization and should be in everyone's possession. This roadmap can only be employed when it's deployed to the total workforce.

As transition occurs, everyone must know where they fit in the performance game; this is true empowerment. The workforce becomes involved in a culture that has as its main

**Figure 16-1.** Eight Steps to Transforming Your Organization

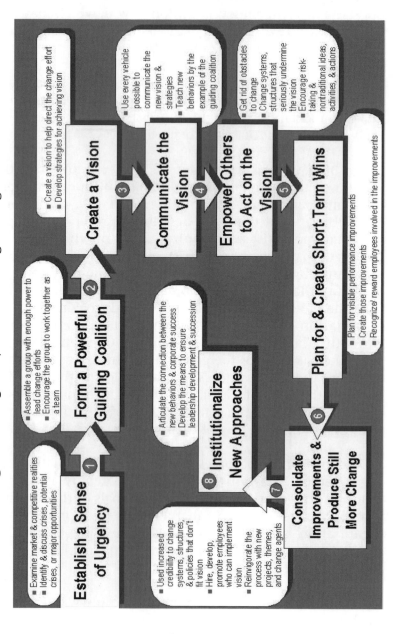

characteristics learning, innovation, and teamwork. All the organizational energy is pointed in the same direction. All the processes that the workforce is involved with are continually refined for effectiveness and efficiency. A strategy that is resourced and performance that is measured are the new way of doing business. The measurement system transforms the mountains of data generated by this new way of operating into information and eventually knowledge so that senior executive leadership has total visibility of the organizational scoreboard and can make strategic decisions rather than merely react to crises and put out fires.

# BIBLIOGRAPHY

Baldrige National Quality Award Program, United States Department of Commerce, Technology Administration, National Institute of Standards and Technology.

Blair House Papers, National Performance Review, President Bill Clinton, Vice President Al Gore (Washington, D.C.: The Government Printing Office, 1997).

Brown, Mark Graham. *Baldrige Award Winning Quality* (Portland, OR: Productivity Press, 2000).

Brown, Mark Graham. *Keeping Score* (New York: Quality Resources/AMACOM, 1996).

Brown, Mark Graham. *Winning Score* (Portland, OR: Productivity Press, 2000).

Camp, Robert C. *Benchmarking, The Search for Industry Best Practices that Lead to Superior Performance* (New York: ASQC Quality Press, 1989).

Champy, James. *Reengineering Management: The Mandate for New Leadership* (New York: Harper Business, 1995).

Covey, Stephen R. *The 7 Habits of Highly Effective People* (New York: Simon & Schuster, 1989).

Covey, Stephen R. *Principle-Centered Leadership* (New York: Simon & Schuster, 1990).

Dew, John R. *Quality-Centered Strategic Planning* (New York: Quality Resources, 1997).

Federal Human Resource Development Council. *Getting Results Through Learning* (Washington, D.C.: U.S. Government Printing Office, May 1997).

Gaebler, Ted. *Positive Outcomes: Raising the Bar on Government Reinvention* (Burke, VA: Chatelaine Press, 1999).

Galloway, Diane. *Mapping Work Processes* (Milwaukee: ASQ Quality Press, 1994).

Government Performance and Results Act, Public Law 103-62, 03 (Washington, D.C.: Government Printing Office, August 1993). www.asq.org.

Kaplan, Robert S., and David P Norton. *The Balanced Scorecard: Translating Strategy into Action* (Boston: Harvard Business School Press, 1996).

Kotter, John P. *Leading Change* (Boston, MA: Harvard Business School Press, 1996).

Nolan, Timothy, Leonard Goodstein, and J. William Pfeiffer. *Plan or Die!* (San Diego: Pfeiffer & Company, 1993).

Senge, Peter M. *The Dance of Change: The Challenges to Sustaining Momentum in Learning Organizations* (New York: Doubleday, 1999).

Senge, Peter M. *The Fifth Discipline: The Art and Practice of the Learning Organization* (New York: Doubleday, 1990).

Strebel, Paul. *Breakpoints: How Managers Exploit Radical Business Change* (Boston: Harvard Business School Press, 1992).

U.S. General Accounting Office. *Executive Guide: Effectively Implementing the Government Performance and Results Act* (GAO/GGO-96-118, June 1996).

U.S. General Accounting Office, Office of the Comptroller General. *Human Capital: A Self-Assessment Checklist for Agency Leaders* (Version 1, 2000, GAO/GGO-99-179).

U.S. General Accounting Office. *Management Reform: Using the Results Act and Quality Management to Improve Federal Performance* (GAO/T-GGD-99-151).

U.S. General Accounting Office. *Report to Congressional Requesters: Human Capital, Key Principles From Nine Private Sector Organizations* (2000).

# Appendix A

# THE SENIOR LEADER'S PERFORMANCE SURVEY

## INTRODUCTION TO THE SENIOR LEADER'S PERFORMANCE SURVEY

Congratulations! You are going to create a better management and leadership system to drive operational performance in your organization.

The survey you are about to complete has been designed to take a minimal amount of your busy time and, at the same time, maximize your knowledge about the seven business systems that drive your organization's performance. Those seven business systems are:

1. **Leadership**

2. **Strategic Planning**

3. **Customer Focus**

4. **Information and Analysis**

5. **Human Resource Focus**

6. **Process Management**

7. **Business Results.**

As you complete this survey, you will respond to statements about 'how' you conduct your operations within each of these systems. Your answers to these probing statements will be compared to a nationally recognized standard for excellence in organizations. To receive maximum benefit from this survey, you and your staff should answer each question carefully, objectively, and honestly. No one sees this survey but you. It's your tool to improve.

The answers available for each question are simple: 'yes,' 'no,' or 'not sure.' The checklist for each response is on the page preceding the guidelines.

At the conclusion of the survey, there is a method for calculating your overall score and for determining the strengths, opportunities for improvement, and major performance gaps of your overall organization management systems. We have also provided guidelines for areas that are deemed most *critical* to organization success and are first steps in the creation of a good organization system. Use this *critical* identification to help prioritize your strategies for improvement, for they represent major performance gaps if you answer 'no' to those.

You will notice on each matrix page there is a column heading titled "strategy." Use this space to record your thoughts on actions you need to take to confirm or clarify a 'yes' or 'not sure' answer, or to record steps you intend to take to rectify a 'no' answer. You might also want to enter your priority for addressing this issue in the "strategy" column.

That's all you need to get started. Good luck!

**TURN THE PAGE TO START YOUR SURVEY**

## TABLE OF CONTENTS

## GUIDELINES

Use the following guidelines to answer the questions that appear in the survey.

---

1. Answer "YES" if: (a) You have a system in place to achieve the requirement, <u>and</u>

(b) Your system is implemented throughout the organization, <u>and</u>

(c) Your system includes an improvement mechanism.

2. Answer "NO" if: (a) No system exists to meet the requirement, <u>or</u>

(b) System exists, but not implemented throughout the organization.

3. Answer "NOT SURE" if: (a) Not sure if system exists, or

(b) Not sure if system is fully implemented.

---

## For Business System 7—

1. Answer "**YES**" if: (a) You have a system to report your key measures of performance, <u>and</u>
   (b) Data is reported for all key measures, <u>and</u>
   (c) All trends are positive, <u>and</u>
   (d) Trends can be evaluated against benchmarks or comparisons.
2. Answer "**NO**" if: (a) If no system exists or data is not reported for all key measures, <u>or</u>
   (b) Trends show limited positive results, <u>or</u>
   (c) No evaluations can be made to compare competition or benchmarks.
3. Answer "**NOT SURE**" if: (a) Not sure if performance data exists, <u>or</u>
   (b) Not sure if system is fully implemented.

# BUSINESS SYSTEM 1: LEADERSHIP

> *The Leadership business system examines how organizational senior leaders address values and performance expectations, as well as a focus on customers and other stakeholders, empowerment, innovation, learning, and organizational directions. Also examined is how the organization addresses its responsibilities to the public and supports its key communities.*

**Business System 1:** How effectively do our leaders provide direction & performance expectations?

### 1.1 Organizational Leadership

a. Do senior leaders (1) personally and effectively set, communicate and deploy organizational values, performance expectations, and focus on creating and balancing value for customers and other stakeholders? (2) establish and reinforce an environment for empowerment and innovation, and encourage and support organizational and employee learning? (3) set directions and seek future opportunities for the organization?

b. Do senior leaders (1) review organizational performance and capabilities to assess organizational health, competitive performance, and progress relative to performance goals and changing organizational needs? What are the key performance measures regularly reviewed by the senior leaders? (2) translate organizational performance review findings into priorities for improvement and opportunities for innovation? (3) deploy throughout the organization, suppliers/ partners, and key customers recent performance review findings, priorities for improvement, and opportunities for innovation? (4) use organizational performance review findings and employee feedback to improve their leadership effectiveness and the effectiveness of management throughout the organization?

### 1.2 Public Responsibility and Citizenship

a. Does our organization (1) address the impacts on society of its products, services, and operations to include key practices, measures, and targets for regulatory and legal requirements and for risks associated with organization products, services, and operations? (2) anticipate public concerns with current and future products, services, and operations, and prepare for these concerns in proactive manner? (3) ensure ethical business practices in all stakeholder transactions and interactions?

b. Does our organization, senior leaders, and employees actively support and strengthen key communities? How does the organization identify key communities and determine areas of emphasis for organizational involvement and support?

| |
|---|
| 1. Answer "**YES**" if: (a) You have a system in place to achieve the requirement, <u>and</u> |
| (b) Your system is implemented throughout the organization, <u>and</u> |
| (c) Your system includes an improvement mechanism. |
| 2. Answer "**NO**" if: (a) No system exists to meet the requirement, <u>or</u> |
| (b) System exists, but not implemented throughout the organization. |
| 3. Answer "**NOT SURE**" if: (a) Not sure if system exists, or |
| (b) Not sure if system is fully implemented. |

**\*\*\*Now apply the same answer guidelines and respond to the criteria on the following page\*\*\***

**1.0 LEADERSHIP**

**CRITICAL TASK 1.1** *ORGANIZATIONAL LEADERSHIP*

| ITEM | DESCRIPTION | YES | NO | NOT SURE | STRATEGY |
|------|-------------|-----|-----|----------|----------|
| 1.1a(1) | Senior leaders set, communicate, & deploy organizational values, performance expectations, & a focus on customers, and learning & innovation. | | | | |
| 1.1a(2) | Senior leaders establish & reinforce an environment for empowerment and innovation, and encourage and support organizational & employee learning. | | | | |
| 1.1a(3) | Senior leaders set directions and seek future opportunities for the organization. | | | | |
| 1.1b(1) | Senior leaders review organizational performance and progress relative to performance goals. | | | | |
| 1.1b(2) | Senior leaders translate findings into priorities for improvement. | | | | |
| 1.1b(3) | Senior leaders deploy recent performance review findings and priorities for improvement. | | | | |
| 1.1b(4) | Senior leaders use performance review findings and employee feedback to improve their leadership effectiveness. | | | | |
| *TOTAL ITEM 1.1* | | | | | |

**CRITICAL TASK 1.2** *PUBLIC RESPONSIBILITY AND CITIZENSHIP*

| ITEM | DESCRIPTION | YES | NO | NOT SURE | STRATEGY |
|------|-------------|-----|-----|----------|----------|
| 1.2a(1) | Leaders address impacts on society of its products, services, and operations to include key practices, measures, and targets for regulatory and legal requirements and risks associated with organizational products, services, and operations. | | | | |
| 1.2a(2) | We are proactive in anticipating public concerns with current and future products, services, and operations. | | | | |
| 1.2a(3) | Leaders ensure ethical business practices in all stakeholder transactions. | | | | |
| 1.2b | Leaders and employees actively support and strengthen key communities. | | | | |
| *TOTAL ITEM 1.2* | | | | | |

COMMENTS

# BUSINESS SYSTEM 2: STRATEGIC PLANNING

> *The Strategic Planning business system examines the organization's strategy development process, including how the organization develops strategic objectives, action plans, and related human resource plans. Also examined are how plans are deployed and how performance is tracked.*

**Business System 2:** How do we develop and implement long-range plans?

## 2.1 Strategy Development

a. Does our organization (1) have a strategic planning process with identifiable key steps and key participants? (2) take the following into account in the process: customers and market needs/expectations, competitive environment and capabilities, financial and societal risks, human resource capabilities and needs, operational capabilities/needs and resource availability, and supplier and/or partner capabilities/needs?

b. Does our organization have key strategic objectives and a timetable for accomplishing them?

## 2.2 Strategy Deployment

a.(1) How do we develop action plans that address key strategic objectives? (2) What are our key human resource requirements and plans? (3) How do we allocate resources to ensure accomplishment of action plans? (4) What are our key performance measures and/or indicators for tracking progress relative to our action plans? (5) How do we communicate and deploy our strategic objectives, action plans, and performance measures?

b. Does our organization (1) develop two-to-five year projections for key performance measures? (2) compare projected performance with competitors, key benchmarks, and past performance?

1. Answer "**YES**" if: (a) You have a system in place to achieve the requirement, <u>and</u>
(b) Your system is implemented throughout the organization, <u>and</u>
(c) Your system includes an improvement mechanism.

2. Answer "**NO**" if: (a) No system exists to meet the requirement, <u>or</u>
(b) System exists, but not implemented throughout the organization.

3. Answer "**NOT SURE**" if: (a) Not sure if system exists, or
(b) Not sure if system is fully implemented.

**\*\*\*Now apply the same answer guidelines and respond to the criteria on the following page\*\*\***

## 2.0 STRATEGIC PLANNING

### CRITICAL TASK 2.1 *STRATEGY DEVELOPMENT*

| ITEM | DESCRIPTION | YES | NO | NOT SURE | STRATEGY |
|------|-------------|-----|-----|----------|----------|
| 2.1a(1) | Our organization has a strategic planning process. | | | | |
| 2.1a(2) | Customer needs, competitive environment, HR capabilities, supplier and partner needs, resource availability, and financial and societal risks are addressed by our strategy. | | | | |
| 2.1b | Our organization has identified key strategic objectives and has a timetable for accomplishing them. | | | | |
| *TOTAL ITEM 2.1* | | | | | |

### CRITICAL TASK 2.2 *STRATEGY DEPLOYMENT*

| ITEM | DESCRIPTION | YES | NO | NOT SURE | STRATEGY |
|------|-------------|-----|-----|----------|----------|
| 2.2a(1) | Our organization develops action plans that address key strategic objectives. | | | | |
| 2.2a(2) | Our organization has identified key human resource requirements based on strategic objectives and action plans. | | | | |
| 2.2a(3) | There is a process to allocate resources to ensure accomplishment of action plans. | | | | |
| 2.2a(4) | Strategy includes key performance measures for tracking progress relative to action plans. | | | | |
| 2.2a(5) | Our organization communicates and deploys strategic objectives, action plans, and performance measures. | | | | |
| 2.2b(1) | Our organization has two-to-five year projections for key performance measures with targets/goals. | | | | |
| 2.2b(2) | We compare projected performance with competitors, key benchmarks, and past performance. | | | | |
| *TOTAL ITEM 2.2* | | | | | |

COMMENTS

# BUSINESS SYSTEM 3: CUSTOMER FOCUS

> *The Customer Focus business system examines how the organization determines requirements, expectations, and preferences of customers and markets. Also examined is how the organization builds relationships with customers and determines their satisfaction.*

Business System 3: How do we determine customer preferences and satisfaction?

### 3.1 Customer and Market Knowledge

a. Does our organization (1) determine or target customers, customer groups, and/or market segments? (2) listen and learn to determine key requirements? (3) project key product/service features for the future and determine relative value to customers? (4) keep listening and learning methods current with business needs and directions?

### 3.2 Customer Satisfaction and Relationships

a. Does our organization (1) provide easy access for customers to seek information and assistance, to conduct business, and to voice complaints? (2) determine key customer contact requirements and deploy these requirements to all employees in the response chain? (3) have a complaint management process to ensure there is a prompt and effective resolution of complaints? (4) build relationships with customers? (5) keep our approaches to customer access current with business needs and directions?

b. Does our organization (1) have processes, measurement methods, and data to determine customer satisfaction and dissatisfaction? (2) follow up with customers to receive prompt and actionable feedback? (3) obtain and use information on customer satisfaction relative to competitors and/or benchmarks? (4) keep our approaches to satisfaction determination current with business needs and directions?

| |
|---|
| 1. Answer **"YES"** if: (a) You have a system in place to achieve the requirement, <u>and</u><br>(b) Your system is implemented throughout the organization, <u>and</u><br>(c) Your system includes an improvement mechanism.<br>2. Answer **"NO"** if: (a) No system exists to meet the requirement, <u>or</u><br>(b) System exists, but not implemented throughout the organization.<br>3. Answer **"NOT SURE"** if: (a) Not sure if system exists, or<br>(b) Not sure if system is fully implemented. |

\*\*\*Now apply the same answer guidelines and respond to the criteria on the following page\*\*\*

## 3.0 CUSTOMER FOCUS

### CRITICAL TASK 3.1 *CUSTOMER AND MARKET KNOWLEDGE*

| ITEM | DESCRIPTION | YES | NO | NOT SURE | STRATEGY |
|------|-------------|-----|----|----------|----------|
| 3.1a(1) | We have a process to determine and select customers and market segments. | | | | |
| 3.1a(2) | We have a process to listen and learn from our customers to determine their key requirements. | | | | |
| 3.1a(3) | We project our future key product & service features and determine their relative value to our customers. | | | | |
| 3.1a(4) | We have a process to keep our listening & learning methods current. | | | | |
| TOTAL ITEM 3.1 | | | | | |

### CRITICAL TASK 3.2 *CUSTOMER SATISFACTION & RELATIONSHIPS*

| ITEM | DESCRIPTION | YES | NO | NOT SURE | STRATEGY |
|------|-------------|-----|----|----------|----------|
| 3.2a(1) | A contact system is in place for customers to conduct business, seek assistance, and voice complaints. | | | | |
| 3.2a(2) | We have a process to determine key customer contact requirements. | | | | |
| 3.2a(3) | We have a complaint management process to ensure complaints are resolved promptly. | | | | |
| 3.2a(4) | We build relationships with customers for repeat business. | | | | |
| 3.2a(5) | We keep our methods for customers to access us current with our business needs. | | | | |
| 3.2b(1) | We have measures to capture customer satisfaction or dissatisfaction. | | | | |
| 3.2b(2) | We follow up with customers on products, services, and recent transactions to receive prompt and actionable feedback. | | | | |
| 3.2b(3) | We have objective and reliable information on customer satisfaction relative to competitors. | | | | |
| 3.2b(4) | We keep our methods for customer satisfaction determination current with our business needs. | | | | |
| TOTAL ITEM 3.2 | | | | | |
| COMMENTS | | | | | |

# BUSINESS SYSTEM 4: INFORMATION AND ANALYSIS

> *The Information and Analysis business system examines the organization's performance measurement system and how it analyzes performance data and information.*

**Business System 4:** How do we use information and analysis of data to manage performance?

### 4.1 Measurement of Organizational Performance

a. Does our organization (1) address the major components of an effective performance measurement system (like selections of measures of performance, reliability, financial)? (2) keep our performance measurement system current with business needs and directions?

### 4.2 Analysis of Organizational Performance

a. Do we (1) perform analyses to support the organization's performance review and to ensure we address the overall health of the organization? (2) ensure that the results of the organizational-level analysis are linked to work group and functional-level operations to enable effective support for decision making? (3) ensure that the analysis supports daily operations throughout the organization?

1. Answer "**YES**" if: (a) You have a system in place to achieve the requirement, <u>and</u>
    (b) Your system is implemented throughout the organization, <u>and</u>
    (c) Your system includes an improvement mechanism.

2. Answer "**NO**" if: (a) No system exists to meet the requirement, <u>or</u>
    (b) System exists, but not implemented throughout the organization.

3. Answer "**NOT SURE**" if: (a) Not sure if system exists, or
    (b) Not sure if system is fully implemented.

**\*\*\*Now apply the same answer guidelines and respond to the criteria on the following page\*\*\***

**4.0 INFORMATION AND ANALYSIS**

**CRITICAL TASK  4.1** *MEASUREMENT OF ORGANIZATIONAL PERFORMANCE*

| ITEM | DESCRIPTION | YES | NO | NOT SURE | STRATEGY |
|------|-------------|-----|-----|----------|----------|
| 4.1a(1) | We use financial and non-financial information and data relating to key organization processes and action plans. | | | | |
| 4.1a(2) | Information and data is kept current with changing business needs and strategies. | | | | |
| TOTAL ITEM 4.1 | | | | | |

**CRITICAL TASK  4.2** *ANALYSIS OF ORGANIZATIONAL PERFORMANCE*

| ITEM | DESCRIPTION | YES | NO | NOT SURE | STRATEGY |
|------|-------------|-----|-----|----------|----------|
| 4.2a(1) | We have a process to conduct a performance review analysis and to ensure it addresses the overall health of our organization. | | | | |
| 4.2a(2) | We ensure that results of the analysis are linked to work group and functional-level operations to enable effective support for decision making | | | | |
| 4.2a(3) | We evaluate this analysis to ensure it supports daily operations throughout the organization. | | | | |
| TOTAL ITEM 4.2 | | | | | |

COMMENTS

# BUSINESS SYSTEM 5: HUMAN RESOURCE FOCUS

> *The Human Resource Focus business system examines how the organization enables employees to develop and utilize their full potential, aligned with the organization's objectives. Also examined are the organization's efforts to build and maintain a work environment and an employee support climate conducive to performance excellence, full participation, and personal and organizational growth.*

**Business System 5:** How do we manage and develop our people conducive to performance excellence?

### 5.1 Work Systems

a. Does our organization (1) design, organize, and manage work and jobs to promote cooperation and collaboration, individual initiative, innovation, and flexibility, and to keep current with business needs? (2) encourage and motivate employees to develop and utilize their full potential? (3) use an employee performance management system that supports high performance? (4) use compensation, recognition, and related reward/incentive practices to reinforce high performance? (5) ensure effective communication, cooperation, and knowledge/skill sharing across work units, functions, and locations? (6) identify characteristics and skills needed by potential employees?

### 5.2 Employee Education, Training, and Development

a. Does our organization (1) have an education and training approach that balances organizational and employee needs? (2) have a process to design education and training to keep current with business and individual needs? (3) use employee and their supervisor/manager input for designing education and training needs? (4) deliver & evaluate education and training? (5) address key developmental and training needs, including diversity training, management/leadership development, new employee orientation, and safety? (6) address performance excellence in education and training programs? (7) reinforce knowledge and skills on the job?

### 5.3 Employee Well-being and Satisfaction

a. Does our organization establish appropriate measures and targets that provide for and maintain a safe and healthy work environment?

b. Does our organization (1) enhance employee work climate via services, benefits, and policies? (2) consider and support the needs of a diverse work force?

c. Does our organization (1) determine key factors that affect employee well-being, satisfaction, and motivation? (2) have assessment methods and measures to determine employee well-being, satisfaction, and motivation? (3) relate assessment findings to key business results to identify work environment and employee support climate improvement priorities?

1. Answer "**YES**" if: (a) You have a system in place to achieve the requirement, <u>and</u>
(b) Your system is implemented throughout the organization, <u>and</u>
(c) Your system includes an improvement mechanism.

2. Answer "**NO**" if: (a) No system exists to meet the requirement, <u>or</u>
(b) System exists, but not implemented throughout the organization.

3. Answer "**NOT SURE**" if: (a) Not sure if system exists, or
(b) Not sure if system is fully implemented.

**\*\*\*Now apply the same answer guidelines and respond to the criteria on the following page\*\*\***

## 5.0 HUMAN RESOURCE FOCUS

### CRITICAL TASK 5.1 *WORK SYSTEMS*

| ITEM | DESCRIPTION | YES | NO | NOT SURE | STRATEGY |
|------|-------------|-----|-----|----------|----------|
| 5.1a(1) | We design, organize, and manage work and jobs to promote cooperation and collaboration, individual initiative, innovation, and flexibility, and to keep current with our business needs. | | | | |
| 5.1a(2) | Managers & supervisors encourage and motivate employees to develop and utilize their full potential. | | | | |
| 5.1a(3) | We have an employee performance management system that supports high performance. | | | | |
| 5.1a(4) | Compensation, recognition, and related reward/incentive practices reinforce high performance. | | | | |
| 5.1a(5) | We ensure effective communication, cooperation, and knowledge/skill sharing across all work units. | | | | |
| 5.1a(6) | There is a process in place that identifies skills needed by potential employees. | | | | |
| *TOTAL ITEM 5.1* | | | | | |

### CRITICAL TASK 5.2 *EMPLOYEE EDUCATION, TRAINING, AND DEVELOPMENT*

| ITEM | DESCRIPTION | YES | NO | NOT SURE | STRATEGY |
|------|-------------|-----|-----|----------|----------|
| 5.2a(1) | Our education & training approach balances organizational and employee needs. | | | | |
| 5.2a(2) | Our education and training program design is kept current with our business and individual needs. | | | | |
| 5.2a(3) | The organization seeks input from employees and their managers in education and training design. | | | | |
| 5.2a(4) | We have a mechanism to deliver and evaluate education and training. | | | | |
| 5.2a(5) | A process is in place to address key developmental and training needs. | | | | |
| 5.2a(6) | We address performance excellence in our training and education programs. | | | | |
| 5.2a(7) | We have a process to reinforce knowledge and skills on the job. | | | | |
| *TOTAL ITEM 5.2* | | | | | |

## 5.0  HUMAN RESOURCE DEVELOPMENT & MANAGEMENT *(cont.)*

### CRITICAL TASK  5.3 *EMPLOYEE WELL-BEING AND SATISFACTION*

| ITEM | DESCRIPTION | YES | NO | NOT SURE | STRATEGY |
|------|-------------|-----|-----|----------|----------|
| 5.3a | There is a process in place to improve workplace health, safety, and ergonomic factors. | | | | |
| 5.3b(1) | The well-being, satisfaction, and motivation of employees via services, benefits, and actions are supported. | | | | |
| 5.3b(2) | Our organization's work climate considers and supports the needs of a diverse work force. | | | | |
| 5.3c(1) | Formal and informal methods to determine key factors that affect employee well-being, satisfaction, motivation are in use. | | | | |
| 5.3c(2) | We have a set of key measures to determine employee well-being, satisfaction, and motivation. | | | | |
| 5.3c(3) | Our organization relates assessment findings to key business results to identify work environment and employee support climate improvement activities. | | | | |
| *TOTAL ITEM 5.3* | | | | | |

COMMENTS

# BUSINESS SYSTEM 6: PROCESS MANAGEMENT

> *The Process Management business system examines the key aspects of the organization's process management, including customer-focused design, product and service delivery, support, and supplier and partnering processes involving all work units.*

**Business System 6:** How do we manage our organization's key and support processes?

### 6.1 Product and Service Processes

a. Does our organization (1) have design processes for products/services and their related production/delivery? (2) incorporate changing customer requirements into product/service designs? (3) incorporate new technology into products/services? (4) have design processes that address design quality and cycle time, cost control, productivity, and other efficiency/effectiveness factors? (5) ensure that production/delivery process design accommodates all key operational performance requirements? (6) coordinate and test design and production/delivery processes to ensure capability for trouble-free and timely introduction and products/services?

b. Does our organization (1) identify key production/delivery processes and key performance requirements? (2) ensure day-to-day operation of key production/delivery processes are meeting key performance requirements? (3) use key performance measures and/or indicators for the control and improvement of these processes? (4) improve production/delivery processes to achieve better process performance and improvements to products/services? (5) share improvements with other organizational units?

## 6.2 Support Processes

a. Has our organization (1) identified all key support processes? (2) determined key support process requirements? (3) effectively designed these processes to meet all key requirements? (4) determined if day-to-day operations of key support processes meet key performance requirements? (5) developed a method for improving support processes to achieve better performance and to keep them current with business needs?

## 6.3 Supplier and Partnering Processes

a. Does our organization (1) know what key products/services it purchases from suppliers and/or partners? (2) incorporate performance requirements into supplier and/or partner process management? (3) ensure performance requirements are met? (4) minimize overall costs associated with inspections, tests, and process and/or performance audits? (5) provide business assistance and/or incentives to suppliers and/or partners to help them improve their overall performance? (6) improve our supplier and/or partner processes to keep current with business needs?

| | | |
|---|---|---|
| 1. Answer "YES" if: | (a) | You have a system in place to achieve the requirement, <u>and</u> |
| | (b) | Your system is implemented throughout the organization, <u>and</u> |
| | (c) | Your system includes an improvement mechanism. |
| 2. Answer "NO" if: | (a) | No system exists to meet the requirement, <u>or</u> |
| | (b) | System exists, but not implemented throughout the organization. |
| 3. Answer "NOT SURE" if: | (a) | Not sure if system exists, or |
| | (b) | Not sure if system is fully implemented. |

**\*\*\*Now apply the same answer guidelines and respond to the criteria on the following page\*\*\***

## 6.0 PROCESS MANAGEMENT

### CRITICAL TASK 6.1 *PRODUCT AND SERVICE PROCESSES*

| ITEM | DESCRIPTION | YES | NO | NOT SURE | STRATEGY |
|------|-------------|-----|-----|----------|----------|
| 6.1a(1) | We have design processes for products/services and their related production/ delivery processes. | | | | |
| 6.1a(2) | Production/delivery processes are designed to meet customer, quality and operational performance requirements. | | | | |
| 6.1a(3) | We incorporate new technology into products/ services and into production/delivery systems and processes. | | | | |
| 6.1a(4) | Design processes are evaluated and improved to achieve better performance, including improvements to products & services, reduced cycle time, and transfer of learning to other work groups within the organization. | | | | |
| 6.1a(5) | We ensure production/ delivery process design accommodates all key operational performance require- ments. | | | | |
| 6.1a(6) | We coordinate and test design production/delivery processes to ensure capability for trouble-free and timely introduction of products/ services. | | | | |
| 6.1b(1) | Key processes and their principal requirements are defined. | | | | |
| 6.1b(2) | There is a mechanism to ensure that day-to-day operation of key processes meet key performance requirements. | | | | |
| 6.1b(3) | Key performance measures used for control and improvement of production/delivery processes are defined. | | | | |
| 6.1b(4) | We improve our production/delivery processes to achieve better performance. | | | | |
| 6.1b(5) | We share improvements with other organizational units. | | | | |
| *TOTAL ITEM 6.1* | | | | | |

COMMENTS (Item 6.0 Continues on Next Page)

## 6.0 PROCESS MANAGEMENT (cont.)

### CRITICAL TASK 6.2 *SUPPORT PROCESSES*

| ITEM | DESCRIPTION | YES | NO | NOT SURE | STRATEGY |
|------|-------------|-----|----|----|----------|
| 6.2a(1) | Key support processes are defined. | | | | |
| 6.2a(2) | We determine key support process requirements and incorporate input from our customers. | | | | |
| 6.2a(3) | We have identified all key require-ments for our support processes. | | | | |
| 6.2a(4) | We meet our performance require-ments in our day-to-day operation of key support processes. | | | | |
| 6.2a(5) | Our support processes are evaluated and improved to achieve better perform-ance. | | | | |
| TOTAL ITEM 6.2 | | | | | |

### CRITICAL TASK 6.3 *SUPPLIER AND PARTNERING PROCESSES*

| ITEM | DESCRIPTION | YES | NO | NOT SURE | STRATEGY |
|------|-------------|-----|----|----|----------|
| 6.3a(1) | Key products/services we purchase from suppliers and partners are identified. | | | | |
| 6.3a(2) | We incorporate performance requirements into supplier and/or partner process management. | | | | |
| 6.3a(3) | We ensure that our supplier and/or partner performance requirements are met | | | | |
| 6.3a(4) | We minimize overall costs associated with inspections, tests, and audits. | | | | |
| 6.3a(5) | We provide business assistance and incentives to suppliers and/or partners to help them improve their performance. | | | | |
| 6.3a(6) | Better performance is achieved through evaluation and improvement of supplier and partnering processes. | | | | |
| TOTAL ITEM 6.3 | | | | | |

COMMENTS

# BUSINESS SYSTEM 7: BUSINESS RESULTS

*The Business Results system examines the organization's performance and improvement in key business areas—customer satisfaction, product and service performance, financial and marketplace performance, human resource results, supplier and partner results, and operational performance. Also examined are performance levels relative to competitors.*

**Business System 7:** How is our organization performing and improving?

## 7.1 Customer Focused Results

a. Does our organization have relevant data and information that establish the organization's performance as viewed by the customer? Does this data and information include: (1) current levels and trends in key measures and/or indicators of customer satisfaction, dissatisfaction, and satisfaction relative to competitors? (2) current levels and trends in key measures and/or indicators of customer loyalty, positive referral, customer-perceived value, and/or customer relationship building? (3) current levels and trends in key measures and/or indicators op product and service performance?

## 7.2 Financial and Market Results

a. Does our organization have data that show current levels and trends in key measures and/or indicators of (1) financial performance, including aggregate measures of financial return and/or economic value? (2) marketplace performance, including market share/position, business growth, and new markets entered?

## 7.3 Human Resource Results

a. Does our organization have data that show current levels and trends in key measures and/or indicators relating to (1) employee well-being, satisfaction, dissatisfaction, and development? (2) work system performance and effectiveness?

## 7.4 Supplier and Partner Results

a. Does our organization have data that show current levels and trends in key measures and/or indicators of supplier and partner performance including organizational performance and/or cost improvements resulting from supplier and partner performance and performance management?

## 7.5 Organizational Effectiveness Results

a. Does our organization have data that show current levels and trends in key measures and/or indicators of (1) key design, production, delivery, and support process performance that include productivity, cycle time, and other appropriate measures of effectiveness and efficiency? (2) regulatory/legal compliance, citizenship, and accomplishment of organizational strategy?

1. Answer "**YES**" if: (a) You have a system to report your key measures of performance, <u>and</u>

(b) Data is reported for all key measures, <u>and</u>

(c) All trends are positive, <u>and</u>

(d) Trends can be evaluated against benchmarks or comparisons.

2. Answer "**NO**" if: (a) If no system exists or data is not reported for all key measures, <u>or</u>

(b) Trends show limited positive results, <u>or</u>

(c) No evaluations can be made to compare competition or benchmarks.

3. Answer "**NOT SURE**" if: (a) Not sure if performance data exists, <u>or</u>

(b) Not sure if system is fully implemented.

✷✷✷**Now apply the same answer guidelines and respond to the criteria on the following page**✷✷✷

## 7.0 BUSINESS RESULTS

### CRITICAL TASK 7.1 *CUSTOMER FOCUSED RESULTS*

| ITEM | DESCRIPTION | YES | NO | NOT SURE | STRATEGY |
|------|-------------|-----|-----|----------|----------|
| 7.1 | Summaries of current levels and trends in key measures and indicators of customer satisfaction and dissatisfaction, including competitors' data are maintained. | | | | |
| *TOTAL ITEM 7.1* | | | | | |

### CRITICAL TASK 7.2 *FINANCIAL AND MARKET RESULTS*

| ITEM | DESCRIPTION | YES | NO | NOT SURE | STRATEGY |
|------|-------------|-----|-----|----------|----------|
| 7.2a(1) | Summarized financial performance with comparative data is maintained. | | | | |
| 7.2a(2) | Quantitative measures of marketplace performance, market share, business growth and new markets are maintained. | | | | |
| *TOTAL ITEM 7.2* | | | | | |

### CRITICAL TASK 7.3 *HUMAN RESOURCE RESULTS*

| ITEM | DESCRIPTION | YES | NO | NOT SURE | STRATEGY |
|------|-------------|-----|-----|----------|----------|
| 7.3 | Appropriate indicators of all employee groups' satisfaction, well-being, development, work system performance, and effectiveness are maintained. | | | | |
| *TOTAL ITEM 7.3* | | | | | |

### CRITICAL TASK 7.4 *SUPPLIER AND PARTNER RESULTS*

| ITEM | DESCRIPTION | YES | NO | NOT SURE | STRATEGY |
|------|-------------|-----|-----|----------|----------|
| 7.4 | Current levels and trends in key measures and indicators of supplier and partner performance including comparative data are maintained. | | | | |
| *TOTAL ITEM 7.4* | | | | | |

### CRITICAL TASK 7.5 *ORGANIZATIONAL EFFECTIVENESS RESULTS*

| ITEM | DESCRIPTION | YES | NO | NOT SURE | STRATEGY |
|------|-------------|-----|-----|----------|----------|
| 7.5 | Specific results derived from product and service quality and performance, key process performance, productivity, cycle time, and other results supporting the organization's strategy and action plans, including comparative data are maintained. | | | | |
| *TOTAL ITEM 7.5* | | | | | |

COMMENTS

## CALCULATING YOUR SURVEY SCORE

### Directions:

1. Review your survey!

2. On a separate, clean copy of this survey, tally all your "YES," "NO," and "NOT SURE" responses checked for each item by all of the organizational senior leaders (e.g., 1.1, 1.2, etc.).

3. If the number of tallies for "YES" responses in an item is <u>greater than</u> the number of tallies for the sum of the "NO" <u>and</u> "NOT SURE" responses, consider the item as having an overall "YES" response. Conversely, if the sum of the number of tallies for both the "NO" <u>and</u> "NOT SURE" responses is <u>greater than or equal to</u> the number of tallies for the "YES" responses, consider the item as having an overall "NO" response.

4. Enter the number of overall "YES's" in the appropriate block (b) on the table below.

5. Multiply the number overall "YES" responses for each item in column b by the "WEIGHT FACTOR" in column c to get the "TOTAL" in column d for each item.

6. Calculate the "TOTAL POINTS SCORE," rounding to the nearest whole number, and enter the number in the table below.

9. Compare the "TOTAL POINTS SCORE" to the scoring table, next page, to determine your overall organizational performance status.

| ITEM | YES's | WEIGHT FACTOR | TOTAL | ITEM | YES's | WEIGHT FACTOR | TOTAL |
|---|---|---|---|---|---|---|---|
| a. | b. | c. | d. | a. | b. | c. | d. |
| 1.1* | | × 17.8 = | | 7.1* | | × 115 = | |
| 1.2* | | × 10 = | | 7.2 | | × 57.5 = | |
| 2.1* | | × 13.3 = | | 7.3 | | × 80 = | |
| 2.2 | | × 6.4 = | | 7.4 | | × 25 = | |
| 3.1* | | × 10 = | | 7.5 | | × 115 = | |
| 3.2 | | × 5 = | | | | | |
| 4.1* | | × 20 = | | | | | |
| 4.2 | | × 15 = | | | | | |
| 5.1* | | × 5.8 = | | | | | |
| 5.2 | | × 3.5 = | | | | | |
| 5.3 | | × 4.1 = | | | | | |
| 6.1* | | × 5 = | | | | | |
| 6.2* | | × 3 = | | | | | |
| 6.3 | | × 2.5 = | | | | | |
| Sub TOTAL | | | | Sub TOTAL | | | |
| | | | | TOTAL POINTS SCORE | | | |

*Critical Tasks. Considered as "major performance gaps" if overall response is counted as a "NO." All other items are considered as "opportunities for improvement" if response is counted as a "NO."

## NOW PLEASE TURN THE PAGE TO SEE WHERE YOUR ORGANIZATION CURRENTLY STANDS.

# Leader's Performance Survey Scoring Guidelines

| SCORE | OVERALL ORGANIZATIONAL BUSINESS SYSTEMS STATUS |
|---|---|
| 0 points | • No systematic approach evident; anecdotal information<br>• No results or poor results in all areas |
| 100<br>to<br>200 pts. | • Beginning of a systematic approach to the basic purposes of the Item<br>• Major gaps exist in deployment that would inhibit progress in achieving the basic purposes of the Item<br>• Early stages of a transition from reacting to problems to a general improvement orientation<br>• Results not reported for many to most areas of importance to the organization's key business requirements |
| 300<br>to<br>400 pts. | • An effective, systematic approach, responsive to the basic purposes of the Item<br>• Approach is deployed, although some areas or work units are in early stages of deployment<br>• Beginning of a systematic approach to evaluation and improvement of basic Item processes<br>• Results reported for many areas of importance to the organization's key business requirements and reflect improvements *and/or* good performance levels in many areas of importance to the organization's key business requirements |
| 500<br>to<br>600 pts. | • An effective, systematic approach, responsive to the overall purposes of the Item<br>• Approach is well-deployed, although deployment may vary in some areas or work units<br>• A fact-based, systematic evaluation and improvement process is in place for basic Item processes<br>• Approach is aligned with basic organizational needs identified in the other Business Systems<br>• Business results address most key customer, market, and process requirements and reflect improvement trends *and/or* good performance levels in most areas of importance to the organization's key business requirements<br>• Business results show no pattern of adverse trends or poor performance levels in areas of importance to the organization's key business requirements<br>• Some trends *and/or* current performance levels—evaluated against relevant comparisons *and/or* benchmarks—show areas of strength *and/or* good to very good relative performance levels |

*continues*

| SCORE | OVERALL ORGANIZATIONAL BUSINESS SYSTEMS STATUS |
|---|---|
| 700 to 800 pts. | • An effective, systematic approach, responsive to the multiple requirements of the item<br>• Approach is well-deployed, with no significant gaps<br>• A fact-based, systematic evaluation and improvement process and organizational learning/sharing are key management tools; clear evidence of refinement and improved integration as a result of organizational-level analysis and sharing<br>• Approach is well-integrated with organizational need identified in the other Business Systems<br>• Business results address most key customer, market, process, and action plan requirements and show current performance is good to excellent in areas of importance to the organization's key business requirements<br>• Business results indicate most improvement trends *and/or* current performance levels are sustained<br>• Many to most trends *and/or* current performance levels—evaluated against relevant comparisons *and/or* benchmarks—show areas of leadership and very good relative performance levels |
| 900 to 1000 pts. | • An effective, systematic approach, fully responsive to all the requirements of the Item<br>• Approach is fully deployed without significant weaknesses or gaps in any areas or work units<br>• A very strong, fact-based, systematic evaluation and improvement process and extensive organizational learning/sharing are key management tools; strong refinement and integration, backed by excellent organizational-level analysis and sharing<br>• Approach is fully integrated with organizational need identified in the other Criteria Categories<br>• Current performance is excellent in most areas of importance to the organization's key business requirements<br>• Excellent improvement trends *and/or* sustained excellent performance levels in most areas<br>• Evidence of industry and benchmark leadership demonstrated in many areas<br>• Business results fully address key customer, market, process, and action plan requirements |

## WHAT TO DO NEXT TO IMPROVE YOUR ORGANIZATION'S PERFORMANCE

1. Do a "reality check." Does the survey score reflect what's really happening in your business?
2. Analyze your "NO" and "NOT SURE" answers to determine actions necessary to produce a "YES."
3. Prioritize the items you must address first. Suggestion: Focus on <u>critical tasks</u> first, then proceed to issues less critical for your organization. Fixing a critical task can often serve to improve a host of other performance shortfalls down range.
4. Conduct a Gap Analysis. Understanding where your organization differs most from "the best in class" can help you decide where to focus the most improvement effort.
5. Prioritize and select 5-10 "high-leverage" improvement projects. How does all of this fit with your overall direction and strategy? How much can you really afford to expend on improvement efforts?
6. Consider convening a two or three-day strategic planning workshop with your staff and a qualified strategic planning facilitator to help—
   • define your organizational boundaries (installation, garrison, directorate, division, etc.);
   • determine who your customers and other stakeholders are;
   • develop your mission statement, vision statement, values, goals, strategies, measurable long- & short-term objectives, key processes, and key success factors;
   • build a Balanced Scorecard that translates your organization's strategy into a systematic review of a few key performance measures so that leaders can make informed decisions.

# Appendix B

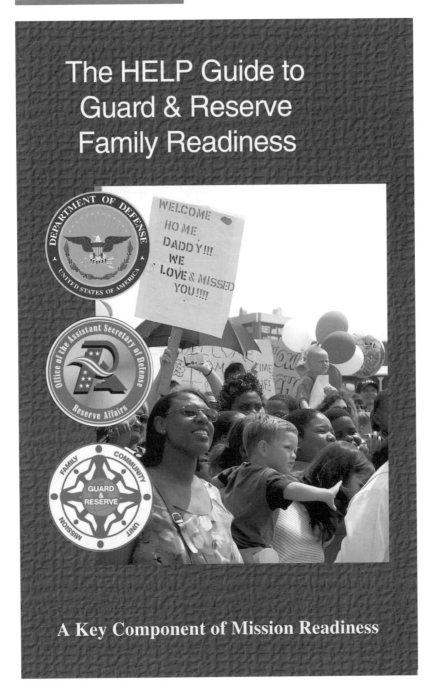

The HELP Guide to
Guard & Reserve
Family Readiness

A Key Component of Mission Readiness

## Family Readiness Paradigm

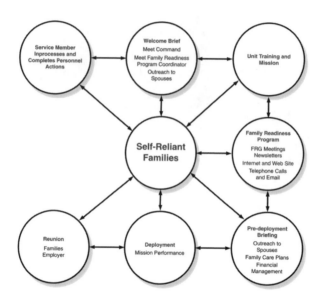

**Victory in battle requires planning and preparation. The families of those who are willing to fight for their country deserve no less effort.**

"The National Guard and Reserves are a vital part of America's national defense"

"[They] display values that are central to our nation: character, courage and sacrifice, [and demonstrate] the highest form of citizenship."

"And while you may not be full-time soldiers, you are full-time patriots"

*President George W. Bush*

# Mission • Family

# Family Readiness – A Key Component of the Total Force:

It is no longer rhetoric. Defense officials recognize the vital role that families play in supporting military readiness, and they are enhancing programs, forming partnerships, and resourcing programs to directly support family readiness. The stakes are high. Reservists are a critical part and a full partner of the Total Force. Frequent deployments and high OPTEMPO are a reality for some Guard and Reserve Service Members and families. Nearly 1.28 million reservists serve in the Army National Guard, the Army Reserve, the Naval Reserve, the Marine Corps Reserve, the Coast Guard Reserve, the Air Force Reserve, and the Air National Guard. Guard and Reserve members deploy as units and individually serve with service members in the Balkans – Bosnia and Kosovo, and in Southwest Asia. Ongoing missions for Guard and Reserve members include: humanitarian and support services; training throughout the nation and other countries; enhancement of regional security; and reinforcing democratic values around the world.

With over 50 percent of the force married, family separation is common and the need for self-reliant families is crucial. Defense leaders are committed to helping families and enhancing family readiness. Commanders and service members do not want families just to survive deployments and separations, but want family members to know how to access and utilize military quality of life services and support. Family readiness and self-reliant families are linked with the goal of having families function successfully within the military support network and to seek assistance during the challenges of separation.

In the Guard and Reserve, distance and isolation from military installations make it more difficult for commanders and Family Readiness Group Program Managers to reach the family members needing information, support, and access to resources. Reserve families are geographically dispersed in communities across the nation, and service members can be assigned to units one or more states away. Commanders and leaders have discovered that many Reservists do not share information with their families. When these Reservists are deployed or separated by duty requirements, their families are unable to easily secure the services and support they need.

This booklet is designed to provide Reservists, family members and those responsible for their support a clear understanding of the importance of family readiness, the challenges family members face during deployments, and how some elements of the Total Force have responded to those challenges through innovative programs. It is not intended to be a complete answer to the family readiness needs of the Total Force, but rather an introduction to those needs and an overview of how those needs are being met. For commanders and others responsible for family readiness and support, this booklet is a vision of how some have promoted family readiness and a mandate to examine their own programs with the goal of applying the best practices of others in combination with their own new initiatives.

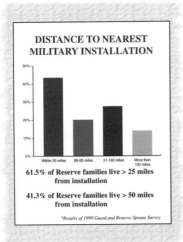

**DISTANCE TO NEAREST MILITARY INSTALLATION**

**61.5% of Reserve families live > 25 miles from installation**

**41.3% of Reserve families live > 50 miles from installation**

*Results of 1999 Guard and Reserve Spouse Survey*

# Community • Unit

## The Challenge – Impact of family readiness on morale, effectiveness, and retention – the spouses' perspective

Research and history have proven that the quality of life experienced by Reserve component members and their families directly impacts on unit readiness, mission accomplishment and the retention of experienced and skilled Reservists. While active duty families often have easy access to established family readiness programs and robust resources at their local military installation, spouses of Reservists are not so fortunate. Necessary resources and service providers are often located far away, and many spouses may not know how or where to get needed information and services.

In September 1999, a 34-question survey was sent to all spouses of Guard and Reserve members who were deployed under the three separate Presidential Reserve Callups (PRCs) in Southwest Asia, Bosnia, and Kosovo. The survey results revealed less than 36% felt they were well prepared and that they needed timely and accurate information. When family members have the information they need, they feel more supported during times of separation and deployment. Both Active and Reserve components have long understood the critical role of the family in the reenlistment decision. That understanding has been validated by a post-Gulf War RAND Study, which clearly demonstrated that experienced Reservists whose families experienced mobilization-related problems were less likely to reenlist. The link between family readiness and mission readiness is clear. Spouses want information on mobilization preparation, benefits and entitlements, military support services, and a point of contact from their sponsor's military unit or Family Readiness Program office. When they do not get the information and support they need, retention, morale, and readiness suffer.

DoD is accepting the challenge by proactively enhancing family readiness programs and outreach to Guard and Reserve families. DoD initiatives endorsing the integrated Total Force Concept and family readiness emphasis are increasingly prevalent. A striking example is the effort to improve the availability of health care. DoD is seeking ways to maintain uninterrupted health and dental care for National Guard and Reserve personnel. The expanded TRICARE Dental Program took effect February, 2001. DoD listens to the spouses' perspective and is committed to quality of life issues for Guard and Reserve members and their families.

**SPOUSE PRE-DEPLOYMENT PREPAREDNESS BAR CHART**

| | Very Well Prepared | Well Prepared | Neither | Unprepared | Very Unprepared |
|---|---|---|---|---|---|
| % | 7.4% | 28.0% | 29.2% | 22.7% | 12.7% |

*Results of 1999 Guard and Reserve Spouse Survey

# Mission • Family

## The DoD Response – A Strategic Plan

In September 1999, the National Guard & Reserve Family Readiness Strategic Planning conference developed a vision and a Strategic Plan for family readiness programs. The themes, goals and strategies of the plan are:

- Support mission readiness through Reserve component family readiness

- Develop family readiness programs and services that improve quality of life

- Provide Guard & Reserve members equitable and accessible benefits and entitlements

- Standardize family readiness programs

- Utilize technology

- Work together (joint) to share ideas

- Develop a Total Force approach for access to family readiness programs across services

## Ongoing Initiatives:

- A "Guide to Reserve Family Benefits" was developed and is downloadable from the Internet at http://www.defenselink.mil/ra/. This useful reference has been downloaded from the Web Site over 200,000 times. The booklet provides general information on how to access benefits and reach service providers.

- Recently held forums in 2000: DoD Military Family forum, DoD Senior Enlisted Advisors Forum, DoD Quality of Life Summit, DoD Quality of Life Technology Symposium, and the DoD Family Readiness Conference.

- Partnerships have been formed to share ideas and resources. The Department of Defense Office of Family Policy and Reserve Affairs formed a partnership to improve family readiness.

- A Reserve Affairs Executive Support Committee (ESC) consisting of representatives of each Services' Family Program Office was established and meets regularly to address family readiness issues, share ideas, and forge a joint approach to Family Readiness.

- In September 1999, a 34-question survey was sent to all spouses of Guard and Reserve members who were deployed under the three separate Presidential Reserve Callups (PRCs) in Southwest Asia, Bosnia, and Kosovo.

- In August 2000, a survey was sent to 75,000 Reserve component members and 43,000 spouses with questions on a wide range of programs, policies, and issues affecting their quality of life. The results will allow OSD and the Reserve component leaders to better understand and address family readiness issues.

# Community • Unit

# Family Readiness Programs

Family Readiness Programs are the commander's tool for developing strong, self-reliant families that can withstand the rigors of deployments and support continued participation in the Reserves. While Family Readiness Programs are the commander's tool, it is a team effort that requires the active involvement of unit support staff, Family Readiness Program staff and volunteers, the Family Readiness Group (also referred to as Family Support Group), and, last but certainly not least, service members and their family members. Family Readiness Programs vary from unit to unit; however, most are built on a six step process that involves the following activities: (1) **inprocessing**, (2) **welcome briefing**, (3) **training and unit mission**, (4) **predeployment**, (5) **deployment**, and (6) **reunion**.

The classic process begins when the service member signs into a unit (*inprocessing*). The service member will complete a personnel form that includes questions on where they live, immediate family members and next of kin, home of record address, and other vital information. Accurate information gives the commander and the Family Readiness Team the data they need to communicate with and support families. To improve unit cohesion, retention, and family readiness, many units conduct a "*Welcome Briefing*" for new service members and family members. This briefing allows Reservists and their spouses to meet unit leaders and the Family Readiness Program Coordinators, learn the unit's mission, discuss entitlements and benefits, obtain key contact information, and learn about valuable resources. Commanders who personally conduct the Welcome Briefing demonstrate their commitment to families. Unfortunately for Guard and Reserve members due to the distance they live from the unit, family members are often not able to attend this briefing. This places more responsibility on the members to be proactive and communicate with their spouses. It also means leaders at all levels must ensure that members serve as effective communication links for their spouses.

Family readiness is not the product of a one-time effort. Throughout *training and unit mission* activities, the Family Readiness Team must continually work to maintain the flow of information and provide support

services. Commanders use Family Readiness Group meetings, newsletters, phone calls, e-mail, and even the Internet to disseminate information. The Family Readiness Group (FRG) plays a significant role in linking the commander, service member, and family member in the unit. The FRG is an organization of officers, enlisted service members, civilians, and family members that uses staff and volunteers to provide social and emotional support, outreach services, and information to family members. The FRG gives moral support to family members, service members, civilians, and military units during periods of normal military life and military deployments and crisis.

As deployments near, the need for family readiness oriented activities increases. Effective commanders use the *predeployment* briefing as a means of demonstrating the unit's commitment to support families during the sponsor's absence. Commands also increase their outreach to spouses and work with unit members to review family care plans and financial issues to ensure that deployability is maintained.

Family support activities hit full stride during *deployments* as the Family Readiness Program staff assists families to meet their informational and service needs. After deployment, the command uses *reunion* activities to ease the return of Reservists not only to their families but also to their employers. Units can capitalize on technology to link members, family members, commanders, and Family Readiness Program staff. E-mail, video teleconferencing (VTC), Internet sites, Family Readiness Group meetings, and command information newsletters all contribute to maintaining the flow of information and reducing the stress of family separation.

Ultimately, the goal of Family Readiness Programs is the development and sustainment of self-reliant families that are prepared for and capable of surviving the stress of deployment. Successful Family Readiness Programs are the product of four key factors: command emphasis; effective staff support; dynamic Family Readiness Program leadership; and proactive, communicating members and spouses.

# Mission • Family

# Appendix C

**US Army Corps
of Engineers**
Huntington District

# Strategic
Business Plan

January 2001

# Strategic Business Plan

## U. S. Army Corps of Engineers' Huntington District

## (January 2001)

### Introduction

Like that of its predecessors, the focus of the current version of the Huntington District's Strategic Business Plan, a working document that's continually updated and otherwise improved, is one of organizational performance in a changing and increasingly competitive environment. Its problem-solving approach in making use of this focus is based on the Department of the Army's adaptation of the private sector's Malcolm Baldrige Criteria for evaluating and improving organizational performance. This approach above all calls for a systematic planning process involving the identification and alignment of key customers, markets, products, processes, and resources, and for monitoring the continuing process of alignment and realignment for purposes of continuous process improvement and, ultimately, performance improvement.

The plan's significance and power in application to the work of the District are pointed up in the three terms of its designation—"strategic," "business," and "plan."

• *It's a plan* in the sense that it identifies where we are and where we want to go and maps out an effective and efficient means for getting there.

• *It's a business plan* because the performance with which it's centrally concerned has to do with those actions and activities that align with factors of efficiency and effectiveness that, apart from profit, are of defining importance to the business concerns of the private sector. These factors include productivity and return on invested resources, for example.

• *It's a strategic business plan*, finally, because the activities and operations for which it plans are conceived, monitored, and improved from a corporate or "holistic" perspective—that of the "big picture." Within this strategic perspective, the chief concerns are with the why's of what the organization does and doesn't do rather than the what's and how's.

The Huntington District has reached a point in its continuing development as a planning organization where valid, reliable measures of organizational performance have become of central importance to improved performance. Together with the ground and framework provided by the District's vision for the future, its mission, and its strategies and initiatives for effectively carrying out its mission, these measures of performance better ensure that the right things are measured for the right reasons and the right ends. The following paragraphs provide an account of why and what current initiatives are either called for or already underway, and how these interrelated activities and underlying concerns are effectively aligned with one another. In this way, our documented plan provides a snapshot of where we believe we are at present in our committed effort to get from here to there in a spirit of dedicated service to the nation—the motive and motif underlying our organization's powerful motto, *Essayons,* Let Us Try.

## District Vision, Strategy, Mission, and Principles

**Vision Statement**. The U. S. Army Corps of Engineers is committed to becoming the world's premier engineering organization, deploying a workforce of highly trained and dedicated soldiers and civilians providing a full spectrum of engineering support anywhere, anyplace. The Corps is and, in realizing its vision, will remain

- a vital part of the U. S. Army

- the engineer team of choice, responding to our nation's needs in times of peace and war

- a values-based organization—respected, responsive, and reliable.

**Master Strategy**. As a key component of the U. S. Army Corps of Engineers, the Huntington District is a quality-driven service organization—efficient, people oriented, customer focused, and committed to excellence.

**Mission Statement**. The Huntington District's mission is to support the nation's security and well being, militarily, economically, and environmentally.

- We develop and manage projects and programs that provide for inland navigation, flood-damage reduction, environmental protection and restoration, recreation, water supply, and other public benefits.

- We help protect and maintain the region's waterways and wetlands.

- We support emergency preparedness, disaster relief, and recovery work.

- We provide a wide range of engineering and technical support for other customers.

**Guiding Principles**. In adhering to the following guiding principles, we support the creation of an organizational culture that continuously

1. empowers people to execute missions efficiently, effectively, and safely

2. encourages open and honest communication

3. stresses individual and organizational accountability and timeliness

4. meets our customers' needs

5. strives for excellence

6. encourages learning to maintain our competitive edge

7. fosters teamwork and celebrates team accomplishments

2

8.  encourages and rewards innovations and improvements

9.  supports "coaching" and mentoring as leadership methods

10. attracts and retains a diversified, high-quality workforce

11. embraces the Corps' values of professionalism, integrity, quality, and *esprit de Corps.*

## Key Success Factors (KSFs)

The following are those key factors (expressed in imperative form) currently driving the Huntington District's business processes.

*KSF 1*—Invest in people.

*KSF 2*—Meet or exceed customer expectations.

*KSF 3*—Meet emerging regional and national needs.

*KSF 4*—Improve partner and supplier performance.

*KSF 5*—Ensure organizational effectiveness.

## KSF Strategies and Initiatives

The following strategies have been developed to address the key success factor with which each strategy is associated. Similarly, the initiatives have been developed to carry out the strategy with which each initiative is associated. Presented in narrative form, these same KSF strategies and initiatives are appended to the present document in tabular form for those who may find it useful for purposes of detailed review, discussion, and decision making.

- *KSF 1—Invest in People.*

*Strategy 1*—Recruit and retain highly qualified and diverse work force.

*Initiative 1*—Develop a 2- to 5-year forecast model profiling the District work force. (Civilian Personnel Advisory Center [CPAC], by 01 Jun 01)
*Initiative 2*—Maintain and update work-force profile model annually. (CPAC, by 01 Jun 02)
*Initiative 3*—Execute Strategic Human Resource Initiative. (CPAC) Phase 1: Fill five needed positions (by 15 Jan 01). Phase 2: Obtain QC approval of plan (by 15 Jan 01). Phase 3: Fill additional needed positions (by 01 Jun 01).
*Initiative 4*—Develop marketing plan that highlights benefits of working in District. (CPAC, by 01 Feb 01)

*Strategy 2*—Align recognition and reward practices to support strategic-performance objectives.

*Initiative 1*—Review and approve District bonus award. (Quality Committee [QC], by 17 Nov 00)
*Initiative 2*—Review and evaluate District bonus award annually to ensure continuing alignment with Strategic Business Plan. (QC, by 17 Nov 00)
*Initiative 3*—Align individual performance objectives with organizational strategic objectives. (QC, by 01 Dec 00)

3

*Initiative 4*—Review and evaluate individual-awards system annually for fairness at all levels. (Internal Review Office [IR], beginning 01 Jan 01)

*Strategy 3*—Provide education and training to support customer requirements and achieve strategic performance objectives.

*Initiative 1*—Design system to ensure that training provided supports strategic objectives and individual needs. (Quality Committee [QC], by 01 Jul 01) Phase 1: Conduct and analyze an assessment of current training needs to identify baseline training requirements for the work force. (Training Action Team, by 01 Apr 02) Phase 2: Design a core training curriculum based on findings deriving from the needs assessment. (QC, by 01 Jul 02)
*Initiative 2*—Create and communicate developmental opportunities for growth and advancement. (QC/Equal Opportunity Office [EO], by 15 Nov 02)
*Initiative 3*—Promote leadership training. (District Training Coordinator, by 01 Jan 01)

*Strategy 4*—Support employee well being, satisfaction, and motivation.

*Initiative 1*—Conduct annual employee-satisfaction survey and provide feedback to work force within 120 days from completion date of survey. (Customer Service Center [CS], annually)
*Initiative 2*—Simplify and refine employee-satisfaction survey. (CS, by 01 Sep 01)
*Initiative 3*—Identify and implement actionable items annually, and begin with FY 99 employee-satisfaction survey. (CS, by 01 Jan 01)
*Initiative 4*—Establish and develop formal union/management partnership between AFGE local 3729 and District Office. (Centralized Personnel Advisory Center [CPAC], by 01 Aug 01) Phase 1: Establish partnership committee. (CPAC and AFGE, by 01 Nov 00) Phase 2: Conduct one-time partnership training for committee members. (CPAC, by 01 Mar 01) Phase 3: Negotiate partnership agreement. (CPAC, by 01 Aug 01)

*Strategy 5*—Develop and implement a comprehensive and effective internal District communication program.

*Initiative 1*—Develop a District Communication Plan and present plan to Quality Committee (QC) for approval. (Quality Management Board [QMB], by 30 Jun 01)
*Initiative 2*—Deploy Communication Plan. (PA/QMB, by 31 Dec 01)
*Initiative 3*—Review and modify Communication Plan. (QMB, by 30 Jun 02)

*Strategy 6*—Achieve "five-star" recognition for safety through participation in the Seven Castles Program.

*Initiative 1*—Achieve 100 percent Seven Castles "readiness" status. (District team, by 01 Jun 01)
*Initiative 2*—Notify Division (LRD) that the District is ready for "five-star" recognition. (Safety Office [SO], 31 Sep 01)

- **KSF 2—*Meet or exceed customer expectations.***

*Strategy 1*—Identify the customer.

*Initiative 1*—Design and document process for identifying customers and developing customer list by business segment and product line. (Customer Service Center [CS]/Outreach Team, by 31 Mar 01)
*Initiative 2*—Update customer list prior to next strategic-planning off-site meeting. (CS, by 31 Jul 01)
*Initiative 3*—Maintain and publish customer list annually. (CS, by 31 Sep 01)

*Strategy 2*—Identify customer requirements.

*Initiative 1*—Identify actionable items from Division (LRD) and District (LRH) listening-session output. (Customer Service Center [CS], Quality Committee [QC], Planning Branch [PD], by 01 Nov 00)
*Initiative 2*—Use District's Customer Service Education Plan to deploy listening-and-learning strategies throughout business processes. (CS, by 30 Sep 01)

4

*Initiative 3*—Deploy customer-requirement and customer-requirement-analysis processes. (CS, by 31 Dec 01) Phase 1: Develop process to analyze customer requirements (CS, by 01 Jul 01). Phase 2: Deploy customer-requirement-analysis process (CS, by 31Dec 01). Phase 3: Evaluate process and results (CS, by 01 Jul 02). Phase 4: Deploy process improvements (CS, by 31 Dec 02).

*Initiative 4*—Develop and deploy process for ensuring mutual agreement regarding customer requirements. (CS, by 01 Jan 02)

*Strategy 3*—Satisfy the customer.

*Initiative 1*—Develop and deploy a customer-satisfaction measurement system applicable to all business segments and product lines of goods and services. Phase 1: Develop system (Customer Service Center [CS], by 01 Apr 01). Phase 2: Deploy system (CS, by 01 Jun 01).

*Initiative 2*—Develop and deploy process for customer feedback analysis to include both present and former customers. Phase 1: Develop system (CS, by 01 Oct 01). Phase 2: Deploy system (CS, by 01 Mar 02).

*Initiative 3*—Fully integrate customer feedback and analysis to improve work processes and strategic planning. (CS, by 01 Aug 02)

*Strategy 4*—Align District customer outreach and customer-service programs with Regional Business Center.

*Initiative 1*—Establish and maintain dialogue with Regional Management Board (RMB) to determine lead District for common customers. (Customer Service Center [CS], by 01 Mar 01)

*Initiative 2*—Identify District responsibility regarding support role. (CS, by 01 Jun 01).

- **KSF 3—*Meet emerging regional and national needs.***

*Strategy 1*—Develop plan for 5-year prioritized civil workload.

*Initiative 1*—Establish and implement a process to identify new civil-works needs. (Planning Branch [PD], by 01 Mar 01)

*Initiative 2*—Establish and implement a process to identify and develop new opportunities. (Planning Branch [PD]/Programs and Project Management Division [PM], by 01 Jul 01)

*Initiative 3*—Develop long-term prioritized District workload plan, review it quarterly, and communicate status to work force. (PM, by 01 Jul 02)

*Strategy 2*—Develop plan for 5-year prioritized RFWO workload (Reimbursable Work for Others).

*Initiative 1*—Finalize and deploy customer-outreach plan. (Customer Service Center [CS]/Quality Committee [QC], by 01 Jul 01)

*Initiative 2*—Develop long-term prioritized workload plan relative to operating-budget cycle, and communicate to work force quarterly. (CS/Programs and Project Management Division [PM], by 01 Jul 02)

*Strategy 3*—Build and enhance relationships with governmental and non-governmental leaders.

*Initiative 1*—Develop an approach for building and enhancing relationships with governmental and non-governmental leaders. (Customer Service Center [CS], by 01 Mar 02)

*Initiative 2*—Approve and deploy the approach. (Quality Committee [QC], by 01 Jul 02)

- **KSF 4—*Improve partner and supplier performance.***

*Strategy 1*—Establish partnering as a business process.

*Initiative 1*—Establish criteria for identifying partners who need formal partnership agreements. (Contracting Division [CT], by 01 Mar 01)

*Initiative 2*—Establish criteria for formal partnership agreements. (CT, by 01 Mar 01)
*Initiative 3*—Identify education required and types of partner to be educated. (CT, by 01 Mar 01)
*Initiative 4*—Educate selected partners within 30 days of contract award or entering into partnership. (Requesting organization, as needed.)
*Initiative 5*—Establish formal partnership agreement with US Fish and Wildlife Service (USFWS), Elkins Office. (Planning Branch [PD], by 15 Nov 00)

*Strategy 2*—Develop a quality-assurance system that ensures that performance requirements are met.

*Initiative 1*—Improve implementation and use of past performance-rating system for Federal contractors. (Contracting Division [CT], by 30 Sep 01)
*Initiative 2*— Phase 1: Annually review contractor ratings to better ensure accuracy and timeliness. (CT, by 30 Sep 01)
*Initiative 3*—Improve process used to select and evaluate contract type and contract suppliers. Phase 1: Develop criteria for choosing each contracting option (CT, by 06 Apr 01). Phase 2: Develop acquisition plan according to criteria (CT, by 07 Sep 01). Phase 3: Check the acquisition plan versus the acquisition goals (CT, by 14 Sep 01). Phase 4: QC approves acquisition plan. (CT, by 28 Sep 01).

• *KSF 5—Ensure organizational effectiveness.*

*Strategy 1*—Identify and improve key processes.

*Initiative 1*—Finish Action Team C assignment regarding the identification of key business processes. (Action Team C, by 15 Jan 01)
*Initiative 2*—Assign "ownership" of each key process. (Quality Management Board [QMB], by 01 Apr 01)
*Initiative 3*—Flowchart each process. (process owners, by 01 Aug 01)
*Initiative 4*—Review key processes annually. (QMB/process owners, 01 Aug 02)

*Strategy 2*—Maintain an efficient, effective quality-management system, addressing key customer requirements.

*Initiative 1*—Register engineering-construction process with the ISO 9000 International Standard. (Engineering-Construction Division [EC], by 01 Apr 02)
*Initiative 2*—Investigate registering PMBP with the ISO 9000 International Standard. (Quality Management Board [QMB], by 01 Jul 01)

*Strategy 3*—Fully implement project-management business process.

*Initiative 1*—Annually assess District (LRH) scores on Corporate Focus, Project Management, and Team Building scorecard. (Programs and Project Management Division [PM], by 31 Jan 01)
*Initiative 2*—Develop action plans to address opportunities for improvement. (PM, by 01 Apr 01)

*Strategy 4*—Improve teamwork among technical, G&A (General and Administrative), and field elements.

*Initiative 1*—Develop rotational-assignment and/or cross-training plans to improve organizational effectiveness. (Centralized Personnel Advisory Center [CPAC], by 01 Jan 01)
*Initiative 2*—Schedule team-building and team-training sessions. (District Training Coordinator, by 01 Jun 01)
*Initiative 3*—Establish and deploy an employee-feedback process for identifying problems. (Quality Management Board [QMB], by 01 Dec 00)

*Strategy 5*—Ensure that information technologies (IT) and other technologies are appropriate for key business processes.

*Initiative 1*—Analyze key business processes to identify where IT can improve effectiveness and efficiency. (process owners, by 01 Apr 02)

6

*Initiative 2*—Monitor cost of IT to ensure affordability. (Information Management Office [IM], by 01 May 01)

*Initiative 3*—Continue to employ IM Steering Committee to improve District's IT Strategic Plan. (IM, by 30 Jul 00)

*Initiative 4*—Use IT resources appropriately to support Regional Business Center initiatives. (Quality Committee [QC], by 01 Nov 00)

*Strategy 6*—Track District performance relative to that of market-segment leader.

*Initiative 1*—Identify market leaders in each of our District's market segments. (Customer Service Center [CS], by 01 Mar 01)

*Initiative 2*—Identify competitive criteria for each market leader. (CS, by 01 Oct 01)

*Initiative 3*—Evaluate market-segment performance. (CS, by 01 Jan 02)

*Initiative 4*—Recommend adjustments to improve our market-segment performance to Quality Committee (QC) for approval. (CS, by 01 Apr 02)

*Strategy 7*—Benefit customers by minimizing cost of doing business.

*Initiative 1*—Meet or exceed targets assigned by Regional Management Board (RMB) for Total Labor Multiplier (TLM) and G&A (General and Administrative) rates and AE (Architect-Engineer) targets. (District team, by 30 Sep 00)

*Strategy 8*—Improve systems for financial management and analysis.

*Initiative 1*—Deploy Corporate Automated Information System (P2) to enable us to identify resources available for customers. (Programs and Project Management Division [PM], by 28 Feb 02)

*Initiative 2*—Deploy the District's Performance Measurement System by mission area. (Customer Service Center [CS], by 15 Apr 01)

*Initiative 3*—Assist Corps Headquarters (HQUSACE) in obtaining an unqualified audit under the Chief Financial Officers (CFO) Act.

Phase 1: Complete CIP-expense (Construction in Progress) audit report. (Internal Review Office [IR], by 30 Sep 00) Phase 2: Complete top three new and critically important CFO items (IR, by 01 Apr 01)

*Strategy 9*—Develop annual review process to continuously improve G&A (General and Administrative) efficiencies.

*Initiative 1*—Identify common tasks performed by G&A organizations. (Deputy District Engineer [DD], by 01 Jun 01)

*Initiative 2*—Identify lead organizations to flowchart process and recommend process improvements. (DD), by 01 Jul 01)

*Initiative 3*—Establish baseline measurements. (DD), by 01 Aug 01)

*Initiative 4*—Implement improvements. (DD), by 01 Oct 01)

*Initiative 5*—Evaluate and revise processes for improvement. (DD), by 01 Apr 02)

*Strategy 10*—Develop a District automated information system (AIS) for measuring District performance and displaying performance data.

*Initiative 1*—Identify corporate-level measures and associated performance indicators for all areas. (Quality Committee [QC], by 01 Dec 00)

*Initiative 2*—Establish, charter, and resource data-collection team. (Quality Management Board [QMB], by 01 Jan 01)

*Initiative 3*—Identify AIS alternatives. (Information Management Office [IM], by 01 Feb 01)

*Initiative 4*—Approve District AIS. (QC, by 01 Mar 01)

*Initiative 5*—Implement AIS. (IM, by 01 Oct 01)

**Strategic Business Plan**

**U. S. Army Corps of Engineers' Huntington District**

**(January 2001)**

# Appendix—KSF Strategies and Initiatives

The foregoing narrative account of the Huntington District's key success factors (KSFs) is here supplemented by the following tabular account for those who may find it useful for purposes of detailed review, discussion, and decision making. The substantive content is identical, but changes in format call for a heavy reliance on acronyms and abbreviations without accompanying spellouts.

8

| KSF 1-Invest in people. | | |
|---|---|---|
| **Strategy 1:** Recruit and retain a highly qualified, diverse work force. | **Initiative 1:** Develop and maintain 2- to 5-year workforce-profile forecast model (**CPAC**). | 31 Dec 00 |
| | **Initiative 2:** Execute Strategic Human Resource Initiative (**CPAC**). | |
| | Ph. 1: Hire 5 people. | 15 Nov 00 |
| | Ph. 2: Obtain QC approval of plan. | 01 Feb 01 |
| | Ph. 3: Hire "x" people. | 01 Jun 01 |
| | **Initiative 3:** Develop marketing plan that highlights benefits of working in LRH (**CPAC**). | 01 Feb 01 |
| **Strategy 2:** Align recognition and reward practices to support strategic-performance objectives. | **Initiative 1:** Execute LRH bonus award (**QC**). | 17 Nov 00 |
| | **Initiative 2:** Review LRH bonus award annually and align with strategic plan (**QC**). | 17 Nov 00 |
| | **Initiative 3:** Align individual performance objectives with organizational strategic objectives (**QC**). | 01 Dec 00 |
| | **Initiative 4:** Review individual awards system for fairness at all levels annually (**IR**). | 01 Jan 01 |
| **Strategy 3:** Provide education and training to support customer requirements and achieve strategic performance objectives. | **Initiative 1:** Design system to ensure provided training supports strategic objectives and individual needs. (**QC**) | 01 Jul 01 |
| | Ph. 1: Conduct and analyze training needs assessment to determine baseline training requirements for the workforce (**Training Action Team**). | 01 Apr 01 |
| | Ph. 2: Design a core curriculum of training based on the needs of assessment (**QC**). | 01 Jul 01 |
| | **Initiative 2:** Create and communicate developmental opportunities for growth and advancement (**QC/EEO**). | 15 Nov 00 |
| | **Initiative 3:** Promote leadership training (**Carol Chaffin**). | 01 Jan 01 |
| **Strategy 4:** Support employee well being, satisfaction, and motivation. | **Initiative 1:** Conduct annual employee-satisfaction survey and provide feedback to work force within 120 days from completion date of survey (**CS**). | Annually |
| | **Initiative 2:** Simplify and refine employee-satisfaction survey (**CS**). | 01 Sep 01 |
| | **Initiative 3:** Identify and implement actionable items annually, and begin with FY 99 employee-satisfaction survey (**CS**). | 01 Jan 01 |
| | **Initiative 4:** Establish and develop union/management partnership (AFGE Local 3729 and District Office) (**CPAC**). | 01 Aug 01 |
| | Ph. 1: Establish partnership committee (**CPAC & AFGE**). | 01 Nov 00 |
| | Ph. 2: Conduct one-time partnership training to committee members (**CPAC**). | 01 Mar 01 |
| | Ph. 3: Negotiate partnership agreement (**CPAC & AFGE**). | 01 Aug 01 |
| **Strategy 5:** Develop and implement a comprehensive and effective internal District communication program. | **Initiative 1:** Develop a District Communication Plan. Present communication plan for approval to Quality Committee (**PA/Action Team**). | 15 Oct 00 |
| | **Initiative 2:** Deploy communication plan (**PA/Action Team**). | 01 Nov 00 |
| | **Initiative 3:** Review and modify communication plan (**PA/Action Team**). | 01 Oct 01 |
| **Strategy 6:** Achieve 5-Star Recognition for Safety through the Seven Castles Program. | **Initiative 1:** Attain 100 percent Seven Castle readiness (**District Team**). | 01 Jun 01 |
| | **Initiative 2:** Notify LRD that the District is ready for 5-Star Recognition (**SO**). | 31 Sep 01 |
| KSF 2-Meet or exceed customer expectations. | | |
| **Strategy 1:** Identify the customer. | **Initiative 1:** Design and document process to identify customers and develop customer list by business segment and product line (**QMB/Action Team**). | 31 Mar 01 |
| | **Initiative 2:** Update and maintain customer list prior to next strategic-planning offsite, and publish annually (**CS**). | 31 Dec 01 |
| **Strategy 2:** Identify customer requirements. | **Initiative 1:** Identify actionable items from LRD and LRH listening-session output (**CS/PD/QC**). | 01 Nov 00 |
| | **Initiative 2:** Use Customer Service Education Plan to deploy listening and learning strategies throughout business processes (**CS**). | 30 Sep 01 |
| | **Initiative 3:** Deploy customer-requirement process and customer-requirement-analysis process (**CS**). | 31 Dec 01 |
| | Ph. 1: Develop process to analyze customer requirements (**CS**). | 01 Jul 01 |
| | Ph. 2: Deploy customer requirement analysis process (**CS**). | 31 Dec 01 |
| | Ph. 3: Evaluate process and results (**CS**). | 01 Jul 02 |
| | Ph. 4: Deploy process improvements (**CS**). | 31 Dec 02 |
| | **Initiative 4:** Develop and deploy process for ensuring mutual agreement regarding customer requirements (**CS**). | 01 Jan 02 |
| **Strategy 3:** Satisfy the Customer. | **Initiative 1:** Develop and deploy a customer-satisfaction measurement system applicable to all business segments and product lines. (**CS**) | |
| | Ph. 1: Develop system (**CS**). | 01 Apr 01 |
| | Ph. 2: Deploy system (**CS**). | 01 Jun 01 |
| | **Initiative 2:** Develop and deploy process for customer feedback analysis to include both present and former customers. | |
| | Ph. 1: Develop system (**CS**). | 01 Oct 01 |
| | Ph. 2: Deploy system (**CS**). | 01 Mar 02 |
| | **Initiative 3:** Fully integrate customer feedback and analysis to improve work process and strategic planning (**CS**). | 01 Aug 02 |

| Strategy 4: Align LRH customer outreach and customer-service programs with Regional Business Center (RBC). | Initiative 1: Establish and maintain dialogue with Regional Management Board (RMB) to determine lead District for common customers (CS). | 01 Mar 01 |
| | Initiative 2: Identify district responsibility regarding support role (CS). | 01 Jun 01 |

**KSF 3-Meet emerging regional and national needs.**

| Strategy 1: Develop plan for 5-year, prioritized civil workload. | Initiative 1: Establish and implement a process to identify new civil works needs (PD). | 01 Mar 01 |
| | Initiative 2: Establish and implement a process to identify and develop new opportunities (PD/PM). | 01 Jul 01 |
| | Initiative 3: Develop long-term, prioritized District workload plan, review quarterly, and communicate status to work force (PM). | 01 Jul 02 |
| Strategy 2: Develop plan for 5-year, prioritized RWFO workload. | Initiative 1: Finalize and deploy customer-outreach plan (CS/QC). | 01 Mar 01 |
| | Initiative 2: Develop long-term prioritized workload plan relative to operating budget cycle, and communicate to work force quarterly (CS/PM). | 01 Jul 02 |
| Strategy 3: Build and enhance relationships with governmental and non-governmental leaders. | Initiative 1: Develop an approach for building and enhancing relationships with governmental and non-governmental leaders (CS). | 01 Mar 02 |
| | Initiative 2: Approve and deploy the approach (QC). | 01 Jul 02 |

**KSF 4-Improve partner and supplier performance.**

| Strategy 1: Establish partnering as a business process. | Initiative 1: Establish criteria for identifying partners who need formal partnership agreements (CT). | 01 Jan 01 |
| | Initiative 2: Establish criteria for formal partnership agreements (CT). | 01 Jan 01 |
| | Initiative 3: Identify education required and types of partners to educate (CT). | 01 Jan 01 |
| | Initiative 4: Educate selected partners within 30 days of contract award or entering into partnership. (Requesting organization). | As needed |
| | Initiative 5: Establish formal partnership agreement with USFWS (Elkins office)(PD). | 15 Nov 00 |
| Strategy 2: Develop a quality-assurance system that ensures performance-require-ments are met. | Initiative 1: Improve implementation and use of past performance-rating system for Federal contractors. (CT) | |
| | Ph. 1: Annually review contractor ratings to ensure accuracy and timeliness (CT). | 30 Sep 01 |
| | Initiative 2: Improve process used to select and evaluate contract type and contract suppliers. | |
| | Ph. 1: Develop criteria for choosing each contracting option (CT). | 06 Apr 01 |
| | Ph. 2: Develop the Acquisition Plan according to criteria (CT). | 07 Sep 01 |
| | Ph. 3: Check the Acquisition Plan versus the acquisition goals (CT). | 14 Sep 01 |
| | Ph. 4: QC approves Acquisition Plan (QC). | 28 Sep 01 |

**KSF 5- Ensure organizational effectiveness.**

| Strategy 1: Identify and improve key processes. | Initiative 1: Finish Action Team C assignment identify key processes. (Action Team C) | 15 Jan 01 |
| | Initiative 2: Assign ownership of each key process (QMB). | 01 Feb 01 |
| | Initiative 3: Flowchart each process. (Process Owners) | 01 Apr 01 |
| | Initiative 4: Review key processes annually. (QMB/Process Owners) | 01 Aug 02 |
| Strategy 2: Maintain an efficient, effective quality-management system addressing key customer requirements. | Initiative 1: Register Engineering-Construction process with the ISO 9000 International Standard (EC). | 01 Apr 02 |
| | Initiative 2: Investigate registering PMBP with the ISO 9000 International Standard (QMB). | **01 Jul 01** |
| Strategy 3: Fully implement project management business process. | Initiative 1: Annually assess LRH scores on Corporate Focus, Project Management, and Team Building scorecards (PM). | 31 Oct 00 |
| | Initiative 2: Develop action plans to address opportunities for improvement (PM). | 01 Jan 01 |
| Strategy 4: Improve teamwork among technical, administrative support and field elements. | Initiative 1: Develop rotational-assignment and/or cross-training plans to improve organizational effectiveness (CPAC). | 01 Jan 01 |
| | Initiative 2: Schedule team-building and team-training sessions (Carol Chaffin). | **01 Jun 01** |
| | Initiative 3: Establish and deploy an employee feedback-process for identifying problems. | **01 Dec 00** |
| Strategy 5: Ensure IT* and other technologies are appropriate for key business processes. | Initiative 1: Analyze key business processes to determine where advanced technologies can improve effectiveness and efficiency. (Process Owners) | 01 Apr 02 |
| | Initiative 2: Monitor cost of technology to ensure affordability (IM). | 01 May 01 |
| | Initiative 3: Continue to employ IMSC to improve LRH's IT Strategic Plan (IM). | 30 Jul 00 |
| | Initiative 4: Appropriately use IT resources to support Regional Business Center initiatives (QC). | 01 Nov 00 |
| Strategy 6: Track LRH performance relative to that of market-segment leader. | Initiative 1: Identify market leaders in each market segment (CS). | 01 Jul 01 |
| | Initiative 2: Determine competitive criteria for each market leader (CS). | 01 Oct 01 |
| | Initiative 3: Evaluate market-segment performance. | 01 Jan 02 |
| | Initiative 4: Recommend adjustments to improve our market segment performance to QC for approval (CS). | 01 Apr 02 |

| Strategy 7: Benefit customers by minimizing cost of doing business. | Initiative 1: | Meet or exceed RMB assigned targets for TLM and G&A rates and AE targets. | 30 Sep 00 |
|---|---|---|---|
| Strategy 8: Improve systems for financial management and analysis. | Initiative 1:<br>Initiative 2:<br>Initiative 3:<br>Ph. 1:<br>Ph. 2: | Deploy P2 to enable us to identify resources available for customers (PM).<br>Deploy the performance measurement system by mission area (CS).<br>Assist HQUSACE in obtaining an unqualified audit under TLE CFO Act.<br>Complete CIP expense audit report (IR).<br>Complete 3 items (IR). | ?<br>15 Apr 01<br><br>30 Sep 00<br>01 Apr 01 |
| Strategy 9: Develop annual review process to continuously improve G&A efficiencies. | Initiative 1:<br>Initiative 2:<br><br>Initiative 3:<br>Initiative 4:<br>Initiative 5: | Identify common tasks performed by Support Organizations (DD).<br>Identify lead organizations to flowchart process and recommend process improvements (DD).<br>Establish baseline measurements (DD).<br>Implement improvements (DD).<br>Evaluate and revise processes (DD). | 01 Jun 00<br>01 Jul 00<br><br>01 Aug 00<br>01 Oct 00<br>01 Apr 01 |
| Strategy 10: Develop a corporate automated information system (AIS) for measuring and displaying District performance. | Initiative 1:<br>Initiative 2:<br>Initiative 3:<br>Initiative 4:<br>Initiative 5: | Identify corporate level measures with indicators for all program areas (QC).<br>Establish, charter, and resource data collection team (QMB).<br>Identify AIS alternatives (IM).<br>Approve corporate AIS (QC).<br>Implement AIS (IM). | 01 Dec 00<br>01 Jan 01<br>01 Feb 01<br>01 Mar 01<br>01 Oct 01 |

# INDEX